AF290904

THINKING THE PLANT

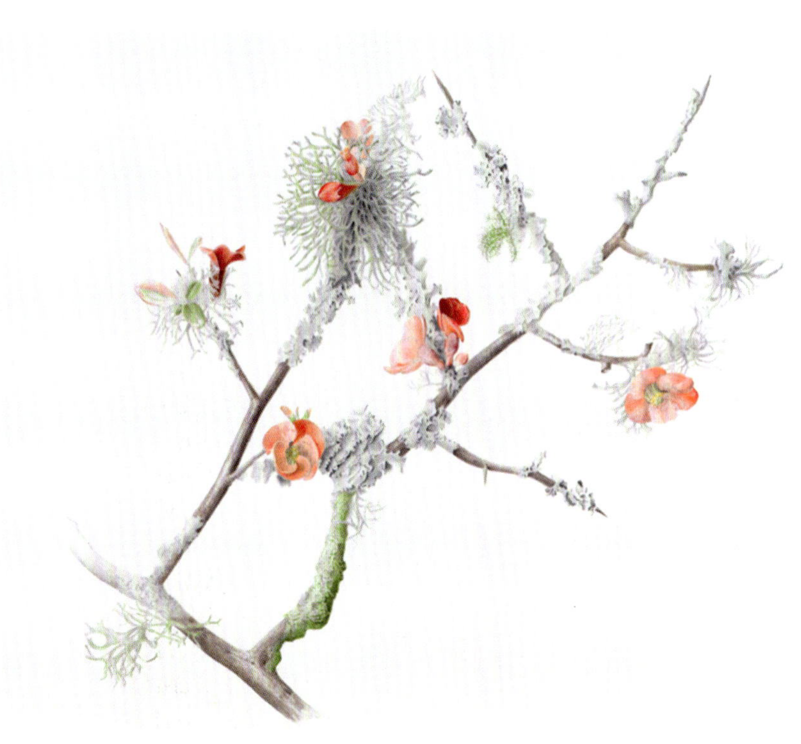

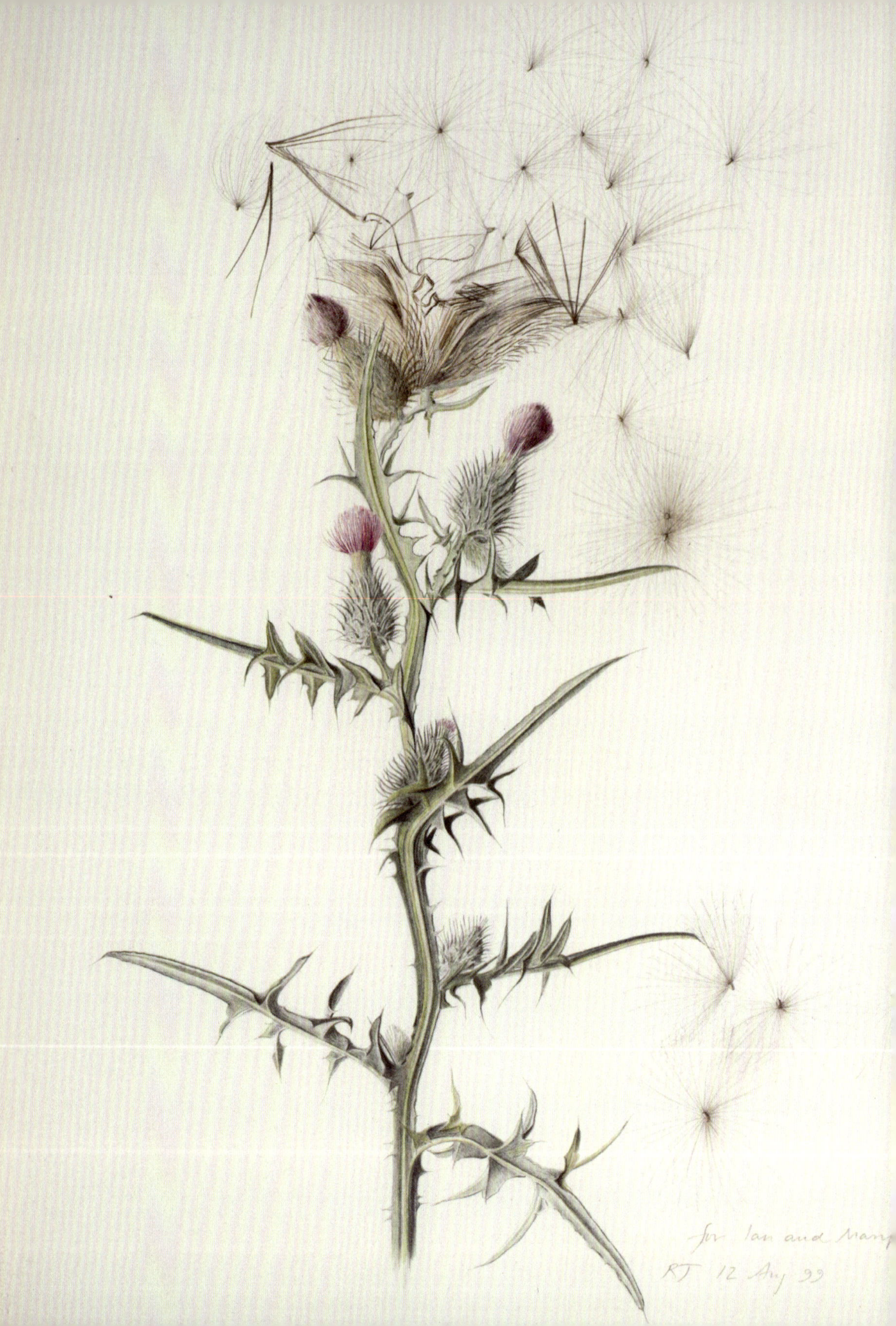
for Ian and Mary
RT 12 Aug 99

THINKING THE PLANT

THE WATERCOLOUR DRAWINGS OF

Rebecca John

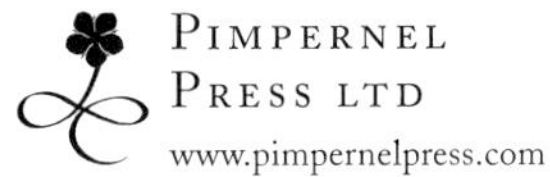

Pimpernel Press Ltd
www.pimpernelpress.com

Pimpernel Press Limited
www.pimpernelpress.com

Thinking the Plant
© Pimpernel Press Limited 2020
Text © Rebecca John 2020
All illustrations © Rebecca John
except for those identified otherwise on page 167

Rebecca John has asserted her right to be identified
as the author of this work in accordance with the
Copyright, Designs and Patents Act 1988 (UK).

Design by Becky Clarke Design

A catalogue record for this book is available from
the British Library.

ISBN 978-1-910258-31-6

Typeset in Bembo
Printed and bound in China
by C&C Offset Printing Company Limited

9 8 7 6 5 4 3 2 1

HALF-TITLE PAGE *Japonica branch with lichens,*
April 2007
FRONTISPIECE *Exploding thistle I,* August 1999

CONTENTS

AUTHOR'S NOTE

I began writing to find out what could explain my unexpected new identity, at mid-life, of botanical artist. I was not a gardener, nor a botanist, and until then I did not know how to paint.

This accounts for the form of the book, which falls naturally into two distinct parts. The first concerns people and places, with a few plants pushing up through the narrative. The second is firmly rooted in nature, crowded with plants and sparsely populated.

I am aware that events of the past can acquire exaggerated importance when writing about them retrospectively. I hope to have avoided this trap by drawing on contemporary diaries, notebooks and letters.

The watercolour drawings I have selected represent about half the number of works completed over a period of twenty years. There are other works that I would have included but for various reasons this was not possible.

All works are watercolour over pencil on paper, unless otherwise stated. Dimensions are given in the List of Illustrations at the back of the book.

I

Early morning, June 2005. I am seated at a table with a jar of water, a muslin cloth, some paintbrushes and a box of watercolours. In front of me a sheet of white paper and a dock leaf. Red, yellow, violet, ochre. I have mapped its veins and wavy edges in pencil and begun to paint. I add patches of colour in short strokes of the brush, being careful not to use too much water, so that I can define the upward and downward sweep of its surface, showing light and shadow. Colours must not be allowed to bleed, light must appear to be falling over the surface from one direction. Soon I am travelling over the leaf, encountering dimples and folds, peaks and hollows, speckled areas, bare areas. Thin lines dip and swerve disjointedly over the surface before disappearing in a curl at a jagged edge. In a few days I will have abandoned the painting and I will not want to look at it again for a long time.

How did I get here? How is it that I am able to conjure shape and colour from empty white space, without fear? How is it that I am loving the sensation of looking down on a mountainous landscape from a great height, high enough to be flying?

Recalling my earliest encounters with plants I find that each memory is inseparable from place, each tellingly vivid with the colour of a gemstone. These memories begin my account of how I came to be painting that leaf as if, to recall Ruskin's words, I was painting the world.

★ ★ ★

Cornwall, age four or five. Sea pinks blowing in a hot summer breeze high on a cliff. Pink against blue; cheerful, open air. Now the mysterious underwater world of the rock pool: dark crevices laced with green seaweed, red sea anemones, limpets. I would crouch over these miniature sea-gardens watching for the flash of a silver shrimp; plunge my hand in to watch the sea anemones clamp shut.

In the Devon lanes now, hunting for violets. I'd reach for their leaves and turn them over to find the purple flowers hiding below. Treasure.

Age nine or ten. I'm painting a yellow rose in powder paints for a local art competition in East Sheen, south-west London. I get lost in a sea of yellow petals. Wave upon wave heaped with thick powder paint. I am conscious of creating a place I've not been to before. The painting won first prize, and was stored at home in a cupboard under the stairs for safekeeping, never to be seen again.

Holidaying in spring 1960 on the northern tip of Mallorca, and needing to escape family bickering, I went for a walk down to the sea. All was blue and fresh spring green. My self-appointed task was to collect one specimen of every wild flower I passed. The grand total was seventy. It was a revelation.

Age fifteen, and by now keeping a diary. School holidays were spent at Needlehole, a two-up two-down stone cottage without plumbing or electricity, remotely situated in Cotswold country. It was early May 1963. I wrote that with my sister Caroline we picked three hundred daffodils at the farm and after quarrelling with my mother I went to cool off in the woods: 'I found my paradise there. I picked a bunch of bluebells and primroses and some strange leaves from a tree I'd never seen before.'

And so the association of unthreatening plants with quarrelling family was established.

NEEDLEHOLE

So named because it was thought to be sited at a threading point for the movement of sheep and cattle between different landowners, Needlehole and the surrounding countryside was where I first became intensely aware of nature in its wild state. My mother had discovered the cottage while staying with friends nearby. She'd been out walking her dog and had followed a path through a wood, emerging the other side to find the cottage abandoned and filled with bales of straw. Having traced its owner – a retired army colonel named Bertie Bingley – she decided it would be ideal for school holidays and a place where my father could wind down after long hours working in Whitehall.

A mile-long track with gates led to the cottage, accessible only by Land Rover. It stood at the edge of fields facing an expanse of grass and a dense wood. There was no local village and the nearest neighbour could only be reached on foot through the wood. We'd think nothing of picking our way home through the trees at night with a torch and storm lantern. With my brother and sister, I would try to get lost in the wood, or we would deliberately set out walking so that it would be dark by the time we were still some distance from home. I felt intense excitement as the light faded and I imagined we were about to begin an adventure 'out in the world'. Laurie Lee came to visit – he lived not far away in Slad village – and I remember walking by a thicket of dog roses as he talked about the pre-history of the Cotswolds, and trying to picture the hills under seawater. I read his poetry, sentimental maybe, but to my young mind vivid with imagery of wild flowers and weather effects. I became acutely conscious of the seasons: in winter we could be cut off by deep snow, and on hot summer nights we would sleep out under the stars, laying our sleeping bags along a hedge so as to protect us from the dew. Other nights we'd snuggle down among the prickly straw bales in the Dutch barn or sleep on the floor of an old animal shed roofed with corrugated iron.

One cold December night in London when I was lying awake in my attic bedroom unable to sleep, a vision of a summer's day at Needlehole suddenly flooded the dark room with sunlight. It was so vivid that I sat up to write it down:

> I was stretched out on some hay under the corrugated iron roof. At my feet grew a large, tall stinging nettle patch silhouetted black against the blue sky, and the sun shone brilliantly behind the jagged edges of the leaves.

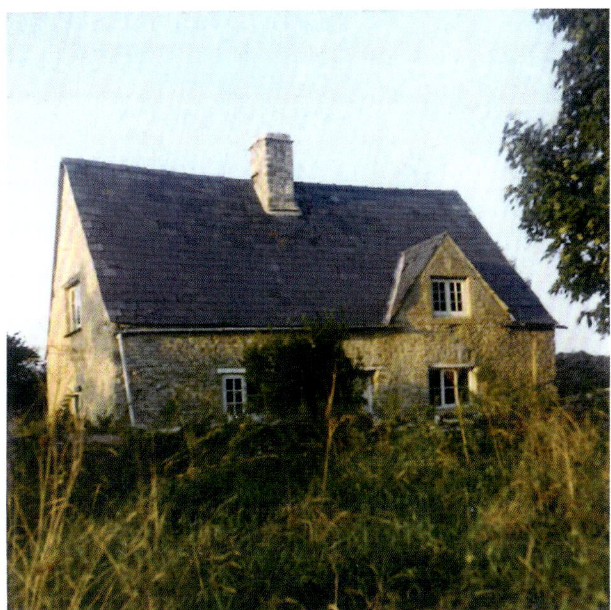

Needlehole, Gloucestershire

The nettles stood up quite rigidly and everything was dead, and silent. Some tall slim grasses grew behind the nettles. They also stretched to the sky, black and brown. The sun's rays mingled and darted through the tall stems. A bee hummed loudly and a cloud of flies jiggled above me. The hay pricked me. I got up and sank into the burning hot straw in the Dutch barn. A cuckoo called from the old tree down by the gate. I was in utter, helpless bliss.

So, paradise in a wood, heaven in a pile of straw. 'Royal Gloucestershire' was still a world away in the 1960s; this old stone cottage, roughly furnished and lit with candles and paraffin lamps, was a place where nothing was expected of you except a willingness to put up with discomfort. Calor gas for cooking and paraffin for heating would sometimes run out and if the water supply ran low, or dried up altogether, we learnt to save water in jugs and bowls. In the garden a few bulbs were planted here and there; otherwise it was just a matter of cutting the grass and scything nettles.

My father's promotion to First Sea Lord in 1960 meant that he had to be contactable by telephone when away from Whitehall. Needlehole was a long way from the nearest telegraph link; fifteen telegraph poles had to be erected over fields before a telephone could be installed, an operation which was financed by the Admiralty. The sight of the black telephone sitting on the windowsill seemed an intrusion from the modern world; it was as if an alien had taken up residence in the cottage, but it proved useful. Certain

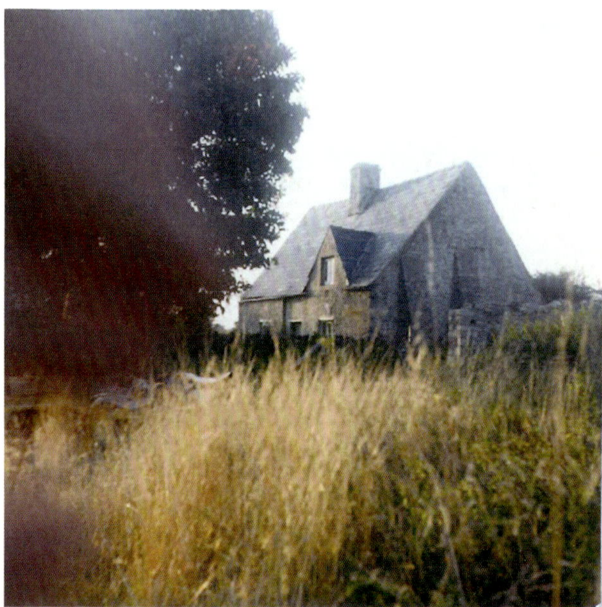

Needlehole

individuals would make free use of it, and woe betide anyone who stayed without replacing the firewood or tins of food. This would infuriate my father. He left a note:

> To all Interlopers, Trespassers, Lay-abouts and others who trade on charitable human nature. This cottage is not yours. Nor is the firewood! In other words, give in order to receive . . . better still . . . stay away!

Some weeks later a reply was left on the table:

> To all Warlords, Sealords, Landlords – and others who trade on Servile Human Nature – The cottage belongs to Colonel B., the telephone to the G.P.O., the firewood to Mr E. – You belong to the Navy, the Navy belongs to us – so (Chorus) You belong to me, I belong to you. I can't give you anything but LOVE (Baby) . . . Goodbye, Goodbye, Goodbye.

There was no mistaking who had left the note: white-haired Irish Ben, who had once been a classics scholar but had chucked convention, lived in a caravan and was now living freely in the vicinity, distributing his news-sheet, *The Rooster*, on his bicycle; a wild-wooder who could 'pace the woods at night with the stealthiness of a cat'.[1]

---

1 Quoted from Annette Macarthur-Onslow, *Round House*, Collins, 1975.

During our stays at Needlehole – no one ever stayed there very long – life revolved around the weather, the farming season, when we'd join in with the grain harvest, and all the usual jobs such as cleaning the lamps and collecting firewood for the great fires that my father would make in the cottage. He would emerge from the wood hauling bundles of dead branches with a rope, then chop and saw until the sweat ran down his face.

We were taught to drive on a Land Rover by Colonel Bingley and I was still only fifteen when he put me on a tractor, showed me how to change gear and sent me off to harrow a field. It was simple enough, steering round and round the field, though I had to stop every now and then to disentangle great clods of earth and grass from the harrow spikes.

More often it was the opening times of the Green Dragon pub near Cowley Manor that defined the day. While the grown-ups drank, we children explored the river, or we'd row out on the lake, before being driven home over the fields for a late lunch – a roast perhaps, or a hearty soup which my mother had left to warm on a paraffin stove. Games of racing demon might follow – hotly competitive and often ending in argument. At bedtime, long after my father had retired to his 'bunk' in the living room (he'd fall asleep instantly whatever the racket going on around him), we'd clean our teeth in the kitchen, where there was a single cold water tap over a stone sink. We'd take a candle up the narrow winding stairs to where we slept on camp beds in a room that was always gloomy, and where nothing was ever touched; cobwebs in the raftered ceiling flickered pale gold in the candlelight. Grey glinting with gold. I liked that.

We had twelve years at Needlehole; no rent was ever charged, and since little had been done to improve the cottage, conditions had deteriorated by the time we left for good in 1971. We'd got used to mice, but rats had moved into the icy cold sunken outhouse at the back of the kitchen where wood was stored. My sister Caroline was due to arrive for a short stay, and found a note from our mother telling her to keep all edibles in the safe.

> There's a wren also living in the cottage who is especially curious and lively in the early morning – she gets in and out through the bottom of outside door, or through broken glass in sit room but this is apt to make room cold. 2 more mice have been seen so you won't be lonely . . . Have a lovely time. Wren just tried to fly out of broken window *so don't forget* to leave it open when you leave otherwise she might DIE.

Not long after we left Needlehole we heard that it had been renovated with all mod cons and electricity installed. One day when I was in the area I drove up the long track to take a look. I stared in disbelief: an extra wing had been built on where a ruined stone outhouse once stood and I saw how the 'old quarter' of the new house was once our cottage.

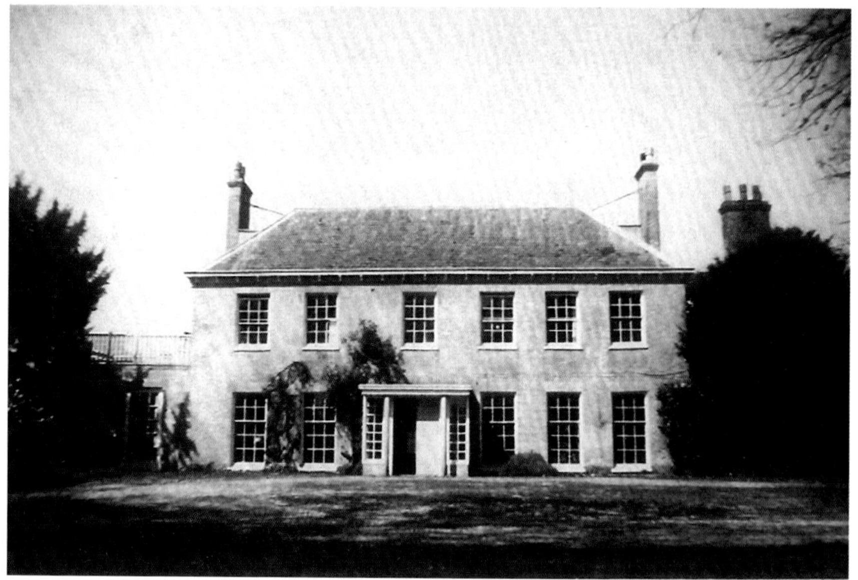

Fryern Court, Hampshire

FRYERN COURT AND BARNES

Two other 'still points' from this time are associated in my mind with growing things: the grounds of Fryern Court, home of my grandfather Augustus and step-grandmother Dorelia, and the London garden of my parents, Caspar and Mary.

Fryern Court stood on flat land between the Wiltshire Downs and the New Forest. The grounds were formally laid out into flower garden, kitchen garden, orchard, paddock, stable yard. A high scalloped brick wall divided flowers from vegetables; straight paths were edged with box and yew, serpentine paths fringed with laurel.

Two square fishponds thick with water lilies lay close by a lawn where two immense copper beech trees stood sentinel in front of the house. I remember the thrill of tangling with waist-high summer grass in the apple orchard, then walking the paths dividing the vegetable beds – up, down, up, down – and nervously skirting Augustus's 'old' wooden studio and into Love Lane before turning into a dense thicket of trees where an imaginary wolf lived, and hurrying through the low dark branches to a winding path homewards, terrified that some fabulous beast would leap out from the laurel bushes around the next bend. It was a relief to step out into the drive in front of the house, to see those friendly sash windows and Augustus's 'new' pink-washed studio, visible through some fruit trees.

A grapevine had filled the interior of an old greenhouse leaning against a wall. I had never seen anything so exotic. I'd walk round and round the flower garden, sit at the edge of the fishponds watching goldfish gliding below the water lilies.

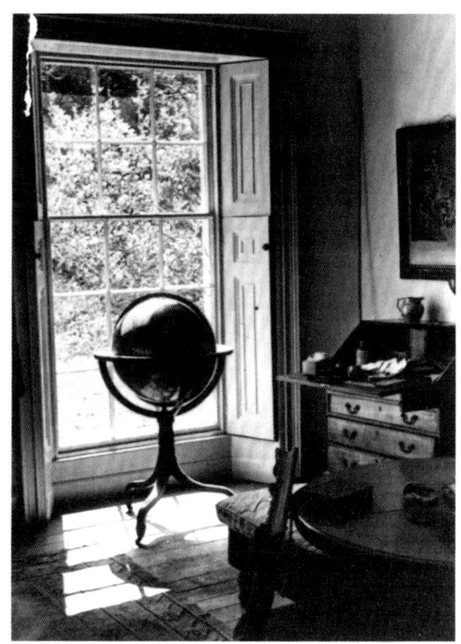

The wooden globe at Fryern Court

There was nothing bright and hard-edged at Fryern. The fraying geometry of the grounds seemed to blend seamlessly with the interior of the house: instead of paths, scuffed passages; instead of trees, oak furniture. Floors sloped and changed level from one end of the house to the other; the outdoor scents of apples, woodsmoke and lavender seemed always to hang in the air. A narrow flight of stairs led up from the kitchen to the rooms above, where a bogeyman lurked in a cupboard at the end of a dark passage. He frightened me more than the wolf. He had long arms that could shoot out of two holes in the door and grab me so I always took a running leap whenever I passed by.

Pictures were sparsely hung throughout the twenty-odd rooms. In one of the bedrooms were two works by Dora Carrington: *Amaryllis Flower* and *Spanish Lady*. They were painted on silver paper and seemed to me magical because they shone. An oil portrait by Augustus of Señora Gandarillas in a black lace mantilla hung in a corner behind a wind-up gramophone. Her pale skin emphasized her dark eyes which looked directly out at us. She fascinated me. In the opposite corner Gwen John's oil painting *Dorelia by Lamplight* hung above a desk. Painted in Toulouse in the winter of 1903–4, it has since become one of her most famous portraits, but at the time I was unaware that the sitter – dark hair drawn back, flushed cheeks, eyes cast down reading a book – was the same Dorelia I would see sitting at the desk writing letters, her pale face covered in fine lines, white hair entwined in a single plait around her head.

A bright little jewel of apples by Matthew Smith hung near an oil painting of flowers in a terracotta jar which I didn't think was very good. It looked to me as if it had been painted in a hurry – the background colour had been scribbled in around the feathery green leaves and red flowers, which were unidentifiable. I later learnt that it was Augustus's first flower painting, painted in Ischia in 1925. The paintings hung in a room that was permanently cold, and where a Steinway grand piano and an old wooden globe held greater fascination.

I am remembering Dorelia and Augustus now. They are in old age and inseparable in my memory from Fryern Court. Dorelia, a figure of extraordinary natural grace, is moving quietly across the room in one of her long handmade dresses – gathered at the waist, fitted bodice, long sleeves, no collar or cuffs. I hear her husky voice, her low giggle. I am watching her driving goats across the lawn to the stables, filling paraffin stoves in the house, knitting a sock with four needles, sitting at table pouring tea from a large teapot, her packet of Woodbines to hand. At the sound of the bell for lunch or tea, Augustus walks slowly across the grass from his studio to take his place at the long oak table where everyone gathers for meals. He is very deaf, and glares at us through horn-rimmed spectacles as he draws on his pipe to light it. I watch the flame leap on the match, notice his hands, the fingernails blackened with paint, watch the smoke curl around his white hair, his black beret. The smell of tobacco and the sound of his voice – low, sonorous – stay with me. I am aware of his fame, but know almost nothing about his life. If I am aware that he has lost his way as an artist it makes no difference to me. He and Dorelia live on in the indefinable beauty of Fryern Court, a fading kingdom that became for their grandchildren a lost Eden.

★ ★ ★

At home in south-west London, my parents' Victorian house backed on to a lawn bordered on two sides by flower beds and at the far end by lime trees. Crazy paving separated house from lawn. There were no curves, no meandering lines; everything grew between straight lines in a restricted space: a rectangle.

I had no interest in gardening, but it was here that I registered every shrub and flower planted by my parents and it was where I became aware of the differing needs of plants and of the microclimate of a garden. I became conscious of a warm, sunny side alive with colour, and a shady side dark with ivy and shrubs. The sunny side, backed by a wooden fence, seemed friendly, safe, held no mysteries; an apple tree grew here which bore sweet yellow-red apples every autumn. The shady side, backed by a high brick wall, seemed always to be a source of anxiety, where two apple trees fruited erratically with hard, sour green apples.

My father, who did much of the planting, saw it differently: 'My Meconopsis B is blooming. What a thrill! Peruvian daffodils on the other hand are still hibernating – I suppose they've missed the point that it's a bit further North for them up here. Acidantheras well on the move.' And a year later: 'Camellia bloomed for first time, but blossom weak in the stem and fell off early. Why? Himalayan Poppies look promising. Also Peruvian daffodil. Ethiopian Acidantheras now well established. So my little UNO Nature study flourishes in spite of veto.'

I do not know what veto he was referring to, but I remember that the Himalayan poppy, or *Meconopsis betonicifolia*, caused quite a stir amongst our neighbours when it flowered. It was reputed to be very difficult to grow successfully, and it was my father's gardening triumph. To me it was all a bit of a mystery: a *blue* poppy from the *Himalayas* blooming in a back garden in *Barnes*? And how come this wondrous thing was saddled with a most un-poppy-like name, *Meconopsis B?*

ITALY

I had decided to apply for art school and built up a portfolio of drawings for the one-year pre-diploma course which gave students the chance to find out what they wanted to specialize in. I joined life-drawing classes at a studio in Fulham and night classes at the London College of Printing, a tower block at Elephant and Castle. Left to my own devices I liked drawing objects, to look at outline and shape, see how an object would become 'something other' in a drawing. I never felt any compulsion to draw from the imagination.

I submitted my portfolio to the Central School of Art and Design and was accepted for interview. I was very nervous and things got off to a rocky start when a lecturer asked: 'What are all these ducks walking about?' as he waved his hand over a drawing of a nude girl lying on a patterned bedspread. I didn't like the way he did that. This man then asked: 'What do you think of war?' I didn't like that either; he'd taken me off guard and confused me, so I lowered my head and said something unoriginal about war being terrible. Was the man bored? Did he not like the way I sat there in my short skirt looking nervous? He was unimpressed and I was refused a place.

It had not been explained to me that, after the diploma courses were introduced in 1960, the Central, along with other London art schools, had gradually increased the intellectual content of their teaching and established courses in history of art, philosophy and literature ('liberal studies'). The aim was to raise the standard of education to a level comparable to that of the Royal College of Art. But observational drawing still lay at the core of art school teaching and I had been told that an aptitude for drawing was a safe bet for entry to Central. 'War' had never been discussed at home, my parents preferring to forget what they had lived through. In retrospect, I could have launched into a diatribe about the Russian submarine threat which had obsessed my father while he was head of the Navy. Such was his paranoia that in my last year at school I joined Russian classes in order to learn the enemy's language.

To fill the months before art school my father had planned for me to spend the spring and summer learning Italian at L'Università per Stranieri in Perugia. I went with a girlfriend from school, travelling on the overnight train to Florence. We were eighteen years old and beside ourselves with excitement. Waking at 5 a.m., I peered out in amazement at an Alpine landscape of fantastic mountain outlines and pine forests; now and again fields of buttercups and chalets. By mid-morning we were rattling through Lombardy – all green pastures and rows of dainty trees – and breakfasted in a *ristorante* packed with cigar-smoking Dutch and German *fraus*.

Arriving in the medieval city of Perugia I was overwhelmed by a sense of the past. Walking its steep streets and dark alleyways sent shivers down my spine. I became enthralled by its history, 'soaked in blood and boiling pots of water', I wrote to my parents. 'Perugians were renowned to be ruthless and barbaric, and lived a pretty bloodthirsty life up here tucked safely behind their walls. I'm surprised they didn't eat each other – always at war with neighbouring cities – even Assisi.'

We found a room in an apartment in the city walls overlooking a spectacular Umbrian landscape. The hills twinkled with lights at night and immediately below us church bells rang out daily. We soon made friends with other students and when we came home late our kindly landlady, Signora Minchiatti, would chide us with a pitying '*Che disgraziate!*'

I took everything in very seriously, and resolved to see more of Italy, so in between Italian language lessons and visits to Florence and Venice I went travelling with English friends, writing home ecstatic descriptions of everything I saw and felt, exaggerating my handwriting to make a point. We stayed in cheap *pensiones* and one night bedded down on a grassy hillock overlooking a landscape winking with thousands of glow-worms and fireflies. Bread and cheese, salami, a bottle of wine; a visit from the local peasant farmer; all seemed well with the world. We assured the farmer that we were very happy and snuggled down for a night under the stars. We thought we were in heaven, until the worrying sound of approaching engines grew louder and out of the dark six *carabinieri* suddenly appeared shining torches into our faces and demanding to see our passports. They couldn't understand why we hadn't gone into an *albergo*, so in our best Italian we explained we thought the countryside so beautiful we wanted to sleep out in it. They trooped off and at four in the morning, already bright with sunshine, the farmer reappeared to invite us for breakfast: stale bread, greasy salami, glass of vinegary wine. We knew it was he who had gone to the police but we never said a word.

During four months away from home I badly missed the piano and by chance found a religious school where an understanding priest offered me an hour's practice on their piano three times a week. 'Playing the piano changes my whole life, no one can imagine,' I told my father. 'The priest in charge is going to let me play the organ all to myself for a whole hour. Oh Paradise . . . I think maybe after all music is my soul. I feel so completely happy when I'm playing.'

The language course ended in July; with an Italian friend we travelled to the wild west coast of Sardinia where we stayed in a grass and bamboo hut on the beach, a short walk from Tharros, the deserted ruins of a Phoenician city. Women wore long gathered skirts to their ankles, which brought Dorelia into my dreams. We made friends with the locals, went fishing for lobster and at a *festa* in the mountainous area inland witnessed a terrifying horse race – 'beautiful horses mounted by very fierce-looking dark Sardinians, some carrying banners which they used to beat each other's horses with . . . viciousness was all part of the "fun" . . . one saw quite a lot of blood.' I later learned that the best jockeys racing in Siena's famous Palio are Sardinian.

In August heat I took the long night train to Lecce squashed up in an airless compartment full of friendly farm workers and spent three days exploring the heel of Italy – acres of old twisted olive trees and tobacco fields, baked red earth dotted with white stones, terraced slopes and houses painted every pastel shade. I was on my way to Corfu and made the night sea crossing from Otranto in a 'tiny, boiling boat, everything dripping with grease and sweat'. The boat was moving very slowly when at dawn I came out on deck and thought I'd walked into a dream: dark shapes shrouded in mist rose from a milk-white sea; not a breath of wind, not a ripple on the water, and where sea met sky, no horizon. The scene was so eerie that it took a few seconds to realize we were sailing past the rocky islets on the approach to Corfu.

Knowing I was to visit Corfu, my father made a special request: would I find the English cemetery where men killed in the 1946 Corfu Channel Incident had been buried after two British naval ships were blown up by mines laid by the Albanians against the Greeks. My father at the time was stationed off Corfu, captain of the aircraft carrier HMS *Ocean*. It was a pitch-black night when he was alerted of the disaster; immediately he went to help rescue many badly burnt men, an ordeal that had a profound effect on him. He wanted to know if the cemetery was well kept. 'When I went in a little bell rang and a lady came out of a house but she didn't stop me,' I told him. 'It was very peaceful and shady, with cypress trees everywhere.' Most of the men who died were stewards, cooks, stokers, and many bodies were never recovered. Ten of the dead were buried in the cemetery. I found the graves and assured him that it was a lovely cemetery and that, although the grass was very burnt, flowers were in bloom.

After spending a few days in Athens I crossed back to Italy and on the way home to Perugia I fell asleep on the train, ending up in Florence where I decided to re-visit the Ufizzi to take a long look at Rembrandt's self-portraits and glance again at the Botticellis. On the last leg of the journey I sat writing a letter home to avoid eye contact with 'an anaemic Italian' who had followed me in the train. 'I tricked him and things, but guess where he's landed himself. Bang opposite.'

It was 1966 and we English girls were unprepared for the effect we had on sex-starved Italian men. Italian girls did not walk out alone and in those days women could not enter a church with arms uncovered or wearing trousers. The problem was our skirts: they were one inch above the knee. (During my first days in Italy I kept my coat on to hide my skirt.) We were stared at everywhere we went and, being English, we were identified with the Beatles. On a visit to Assisi we nearly caused a riot when a huge crowd began following us, thinking we were pop stars. We learnt to ignore the hissing and shouts of *'Che bella!'* but we were driven mad when men followed us and called out *'Vieni qua, gira ti!'* (Come here, turn around!) or stopped their car dead in front of us when we were waiting to cross the street. We soon found ways to trick them, and if a man came too close a quick slap across the face would see him off.

It seems not much had changed since the late nineteenth century when it first became acceptable for English girls to travel unaccompanied to Florence to study art. My grandmother Ida, with skirts down to her ankles, attracted a lot of attention as she walked around Florence during her stay there in 1897. 'Something so funny happened today,' she wrote to her sister. 'I was sketching, and a curious-looking youth with a book under his arm appeared greatly interested in me. That is nothing uncommon; but I found he followed me everywhere. I wandered far and wide, often making a circle and coming back to where I started from, because I can't keep count of where I'm going when I sketch, and always the youth at my elbow. After about ¾ of an hour

I said "*Non siete stanco?*", which means you are not tired? He looked very shame-faced, and next time I looked he was gone. Poor youth.'

After four months in Italy I couldn't take any more. Young Italian men, I concluded, were 'very well groomed' but their talk bored me and I couldn't wait to return to leafy S.W. London. I had learnt enough Italian to speak and write, but apart from a brief visit one freezing New Year I did not return to Italy for almost forty years.

ART SCHOOL

Once home, I was told that Central School's newly organized fine jewellery department had space for more students – only eight had been accepted – and since it had not yet been given diploma status (only recently awarded to other departments) a pre-diploma course was not required. It was explained to me that the course entailed a great deal of design work, and therefore a lot of drawing. That was fine by me and the head of department was willing to give me a place. A tall, pale-faced man with a goatee beard, he seemed friendly enough at first but his mission to gain diploma status for the department made him tense and increasingly unpleasant to be around.

Central School of Arts and Crafts had been renamed Central School of Art and Design in 1966,[2] the year I joined the fine jewellery department. The art school had been established in 1896 by William Lethaby to encourage the 'industrial application of decorative art', as practised by the Arts and Crafts movement, and by the 1960s had well-established departments in graphic design, textile, ceramic, theatre and industrial design, as well as painting and sculpture. It had been built in Holborn, close to the diamond and jewellery trade in Hatton Garden and the light industry warehouses of Clerkenwell. With the new emphasis on design, the gold and silversmithing department was reorganized into a three-year course which concentrated on the teaching of metal techniques: materials such as beads, plastics, shells and feathers were forbidden. (Today it is the reverse: metals have given way to wood, natural fibres, acrylic – any material that can be adapted to wear as fashion accessories.)

I was very excited to be going to art school, but from day one I found Central a cold, unfriendly place – more like a factory, with long stone corridors and departments segregated over five floors. Apparently the building had been designed to create 'an empire of autonomous departmental kingdoms'.[3] Sculpture was situated in the basement, Painting on the fifth floor. Theatre Design was opposite Jewellery but we rarely set foot in each other's departments. The best way to meet other students was in the queue at the canteen.

We began by learning to solder on copper, to clean it in acid and to polish it on a terrifying electric polisher. We learnt to 'draw' wire and to pierce sheet metal with a

---

2 Merged with Saint Martin's to become Central Saint Martin's College of Art and Design in 1989, when art schools were renamed colleges, and this was eventually absorbed by the University of the Arts in 2004.
3 Nigel Llewellyn (ed.), *The London Art Schools: Reforming the Art World, 1960 to Now*, Tate Publishing, 2015.

saw; to drill, punch, chase and enamel. Tweezers and needle files were indispensable. We learnt to cast from wax by the centrifugal system, and were introduced to the uses of a lathe. I soon discovered that jewellery was the first cousin of sculpture.

Over three years we progressed from base copper to semi-precious silver, to precious gold. Gold was three or four times as expensive as silver: mistakes could not be allowed to happen and gold dust was not to be scattered on the floor. It took a strong nerve to work in gold.

It was all about working with metal – I never learnt to set a stone – but drawing was given equal importance, and was not restricted to design work. Life drawing was still compulsory and in a bid to widen my skills I learnt to etch with Norman Ackroyd, celebrated today for his masterly, atmospheric etchings of the Western Isles. I well remember the first line I etched: I drew the needle through the resin on to the zinc plate as if my life depended on it. I did not get very far with etching; lacking the imagination to loosen up with a needle, I felt safer with pencil in hand and began to look for ideas in nature. I would draw a natural object and abstract it down into a design which, if it was ever realized in 3D, would bear little resemblance to the finished piece. Jewellery is made to be worn and it was easy to run away with a design too heavy or awkward to wear. (Today's students are pushing the boundaries of what could reasonably called 'jewellery' by titling their designs 'head piece', 'neck piece', or 'body sculpture'.) Sometimes I'd rely on the memory of a detail of landscape, which required no drawing at all: I constructed a gold wire bracelet while recalling a walk through a wood. This created a dizzying sense of scale, now macro, now micro. I drew a piece of coral in minute detail so that after a while I began to imagine I was walking over its surface: it became a vast, alien landscape.

History of art and architecture lectures were compulsory across all departments, with end-of-term three-hour exams and a 10,000-word thesis in the final year. The department of liberal studies offered a choice of literature or philosophy – in my case twentieth-century American and nineteenth-century Russian literature. I was never good at discussion and during seminars I was happy for other students to do all the talking with our tutor, A. S. Byatt (at the time publishing her second novel). Many students resented having to attend these lectures and sitting exams; they felt strongly that they were at art school to learn techniques, not to sit through lectures that bored them and had nothing to do with learning how to weld steel or throw a pot. I never felt this way and was glad to be introduced to a wider appreciation of art – especially architecture; I made a study of Frank Lloyd Wright, fascinated by his love of the horizontal line and its affinity with landscape. But it was 1968. Student-led protests spread through a number of London art schools and within a couple of years history of art lectures and liberal studies were reappraised and broadened into 'cultural studies', with less emphasis on chronology and written exams.

My own problem concerned the behaviour of the head of department. Things had got so bad by the second year – his short temper and impatience were getting me down (and I was not alone) – that I made up my mind to leave. After all I was there only by default. I was taken aside by another lecturer and persuaded to complete the course.

To study the history of jewellery we were sent off to the British Museum and the V&A to draw examples through the ages. I began with a diagrammatic analysis of the construction of a Greek gold wreath. Paper-thin gold was used to create the leaves, usually ivy or myrtle, and arranged in zigzag or symmetrical patterns; or the leaves would be assembled more naturalistically in entangled or knotted layers. I drew pieces from the Anglo-Saxon, Byzantine, Renaissance, Baroque and Rococo periods, colouring the gold and gemstones with watercolour. By the time I reached the Victorian period I felt bold enough to draw a 'bodice ornament'; this had three detachable diamond-encrusted flowers set on springs so that they would tremble and sparkle in the new electric light – the 'trembler roses'. It was the size of a hand. Art Nouveau designs were based on linear patterns in nature, and were easier to draw. Sometimes I'd select odd pieces to draw that had no place in European social history: a wood and mother-of-pearl comb from Papua New Guinea doubled as a comb and hair ornament – I liked pieces that had a use – and on a piece of graph paper I worked out the linking system of a silver Indian bracelet, a mathematical exercise to discover the secret of its flexibility.

A gold wreath of two hinged branches of myrtle had caught my eye. I made a crude drawing of it, attracted by the naturalistic arrangement of the leaves. Berries and flowers were dotted amongst the leaves on thin gold wire 'stems'. I thought this was a decorative device, until decades later I collected a branch of myrtle to paint and saw that it was fruiting and flowering simultaneously. The white flowers, maroon berries, dark green leaves and cinnamon bark of the living plant did not trigger any memory of the pencil drawing I'd made in the British Museum. When I rediscovered the drawing in a file I was curious to find out if the wreath was still on display. I found it high up on a glass shelf and stood looking at it for a long time, enjoying the significance of the moment. In the intervening thirty years the wreath had been reattributed from Greek 600–400 BC to Etruscan 400–300 BC.

I left Central in summer 1969, third out of nine in the final year. Within two years the course was given diploma status and we were retrospectively awarded a Dip A.D. (Diploma in Art and Design). Almost all the jewellery I made at Central was sold, lost, broken or destroyed. Of the two pieces I kept, the silver chain-necklace was eventually stolen. That hurt. But the unfinished piece that I keep at the bottom of a wooden box means more to me than any of the pieces I finished at Central: cut from silver sheet, the outline of a tree is blowing in the wind; within its streaming branches a fiery opal. I take it from its box . . . hold it in the palm of my hand . . . hear the wind blowing . . . see a fire blazing . . .

COVENT GARDEN

During my last six months at Central, I had left home and moved into a two-room flat in Endell Street, Covent Garden − £5[4] a week, loo in the back yard. It was on the first floor of a badly neglected building dating back to 1720; the original panelling on the stairs had been painted red, the plastered walls were cracked and pitted, and there was a smell of old damp as you opened the front door. But the flat was bright and cosy, home to Georgina Barker, daughter of the writer Elizabeth Smart, a friend of my parents, and the poet George Barker. Georgina was several years older, beautiful, independent. She had trained as a ballet dancer and was now working in publishing. She wanted to move on, and I wanted to leave home. Never mind that there was no bathroom; the Oasis public baths[5] were at the end of the street. A bath cost 1*s*.6*d*.[6] with a towel thrown in. The baths were enormous and if you wanted more hot water you'd shout 'More hot water please!' and a lady attendant would turn on the giant brass tap with a spanner outside the cubicle. Best of all, you didn't have to clean the bath afterwards.

On my first night, at around 2 a.m., a roaring noise woke me up. The windows were rattling and I couldn't make out what on earth was happening until I realized lorries were thundering up the street delivering flowers, fruit and vegetables to Covent Garden Market on the Piazza. Towards dawn a new noise: the steady thud of sacks of peeled potatoes being unloaded for the fish and chip shop on the corner. During the day I'd hear the faint sounds of a harp from the harp shop next door and from the wood yard at the back the intermittent whine of a circular saw. None of this bothered me − it was all part of the excitement of living alone for the first time, in anonymity, in an area of London that seemed foreign to me. Once the Market had ceased trading in the early morning (business hours peaked around 3 a.m.) the streets emptied of people and traffic. There were almost no shops or restaurants - only Boulestin on the Piazza (long gone) and Rules in Maiden Lane. Ringed by theatres, crisscrossed by narrow streets and alleyways, the area was dominated by the rhythms of the Market and the Royal Opera House. Musicians from the Opera House would dash to a nearby pub during performance intervals; they were easy to spot drinking beer in black tie, and I soon learnt to recognize ballet dancers crossing James Street from the tube, feet pointing outwards, ramrod-straight backs, hair pulled into a bun.

The eighteenth-century buildings lining the gaslit streets around the Piazza were used by Market traders to store fruit and vegetables and conduct business. The smell of cabbage leaves and spilt fruit seemed always to hang in the air. Red earth from Devon swedes smeared the junction of James Street with Long Acre, where every morning the greengrocer Robert Bruce would set out a spectacular display of exotic fruit and vegetables outside Covent Garden tube; the station was barely used in those days and closed on Sundays.

---

4 The equivalent in 2020 would be approximately £80.
5 Today the Oasis Sports Centre and Swimming Pool.
6 Approximately £1.20 in 2020.

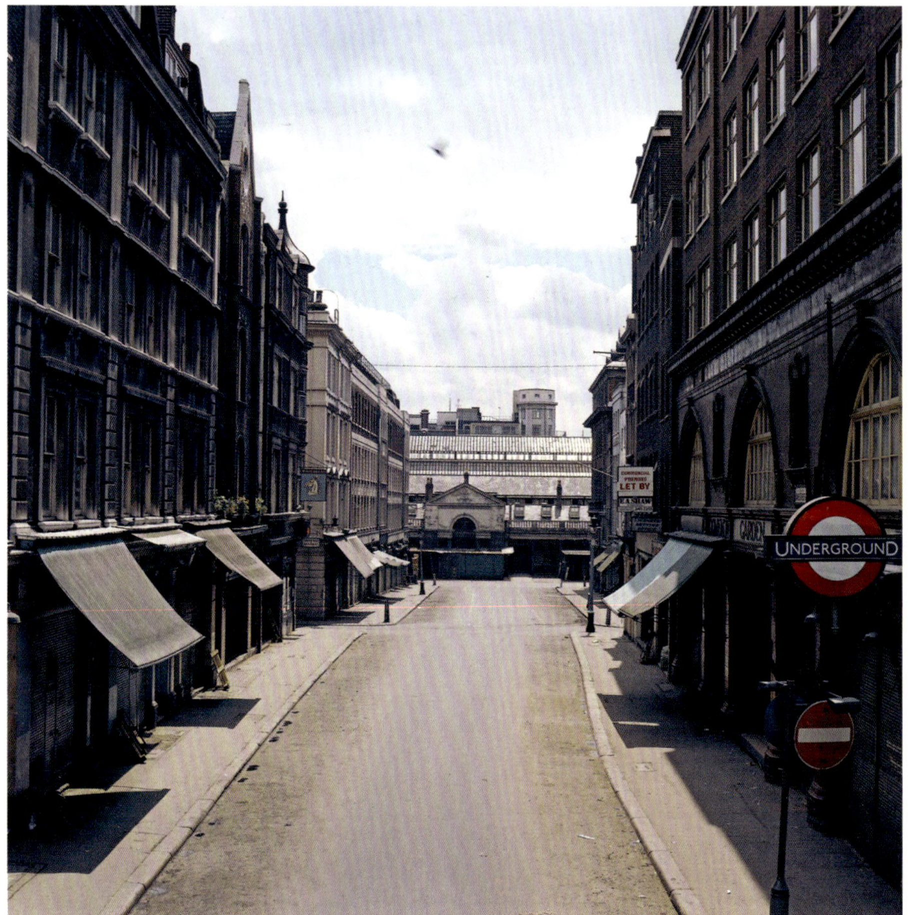

James Street, Covent Garden, early 1970s

My room took on the feel of a cell. Isolated from the noise and drama of family life, I sometimes felt strangely disorientated, a feeling that was intensified by the drabness of inner London, the blacks and greys of night and day, the absence of green. It was not long before I learnt that to be able to be alone was an essential part of life, a first step towards independence. Sometimes I'd go down to the Floral Hall at 4 or 5 a.m. and seek out one of the flower men willing to sell a single bunch of flowers. It was a scene of constant activity, brightly lit and quivering with flowers and flitting sparrows; but if you weren't in there on wholesale business you were usually ignored. It was a famous dropping-in point for all-night revellers and performers from the Opera House and nearby theatres.

After the Market moved to Nine Elms in 1974 the area became a ghost town. The friendly cafés and many of the pubs that had stayed open all night for the Market traders began to close. The plan to demolish the area to make way for a highway and conference hall was fought tooth and nail by Covent Garden's residents and workers. Meetings were held, leaflets were printed in a Neal Street basement, we marched in the streets and went fly-posting – and won the battle when the Secretary of State for the Environment, Geoffrey Rippon, listed over 250 buildings as of historic interest. At a stroke he made demolition illegal.

At first a number of art galleries sprang up and for a few short years the area became the 'happening place'. I was newly married to John Sharkey, ex-gallery manager at the ICA in Dover Street, who was, at the time, writing a book about Celtic mythology. In the empty top floor of the building where I was living he held a series of artists' talks and poetry readings, and in a local gallery he organized week-long performance art events. Among the participating artists was Susan Hiller, then at the beginning of her extraordinary career which culminated with a retrospective at Tate Britain in 2011. I was sceptical about her belief in the paranormal, but admired her meticulous approach to her work, her pioneering spirit, and we became friends, although were very different: she was strongly motivated, I was not; she was articulate, I could barely finish a sentence; and I was never a feminist. Her exhibitions soon took her around the world and we lost touch, but we were reunited when John Sharkey died in 2014. A few weeks before her own death in January 2019 she asked to see my latest paintings. She gave me a sound ticking-off for failing to exhibit the work.

The art galleries did not survive long; soon property developers moved in, and over the next decades I witnessed the transformation of Covent Garden. It was quickly colonized by businesses and became unrecognizable as scaffolding went up and plate glass shop fronts began to appear. I remember the shock of seeing snakeskin boots for sale where once sacks of vegetables had been stored. Gone was the Dickensian atmosphere of dark deserted streets. The majority of residents lived in Peabody tenements which are surrounded today by beauty and perfume shops, fashion stores and restaurants (eighty are listed for tourists today). Long-time residents feared that the Piazza, once the beating heart of the Market, would become an overspill from Leicester Square; and the three old Market ladies who every evening would take their seat in the Cross Keys pub predicted that Long Acre would become a new 'King's Road', impossible to imagine when I knew it only as home to Harvey's auction house, Bertram Rota's rare books and Edward Stanford's map shop.

FINDING WORK

The sculptor Lynn Chadwick was a family friend and after leaving Central I went to work briefly with him at Lypiatt Park, his vast manor house in Gloucestershire. Dating mainly from the eighteenth century, the house stood in grounds that dropped steeply away into a wide valley. A lovely dovecote, granary and chapel survived from the fourteenth century; the stable block was converted into the studio.

Early in his career, he had lived in Pinswell, a cottage without water or electricity (a walk from Needlehole through woods and fields). There he had made some rings, and now wanted to revive the idea. I had seen photographs of jewellery made by sculptor-artists such as Georges Braque and Jean Arp, and the Surrealists had titled their pieces as if they were works of art, thereby giving 'gold brooch set with pearls' an exciting new identity. Since then many contemporary artists – Conrad Shawcross and Cornelia Parker to name two – have at some point made work to be worn as 'body pieces'. Jewellery made by artists usually consists of brooches, pendants or rings, pieces that don't require flexible linkage systems or hinges. I was familiar with Lynn Chadwick's early work and was intrigued by his series of iron and glass sculptures from 1952, among which were a number of maquettes for his famous work *Inner Eye*. One of these was displayed at Lypiatt: inside an iron armature, pincers gripped a chunk of rough cut glass. These pincers would revolve when pushed, which set the glass 'eye' glinting at the centre of its cage. The pincers might be seen as the sculptor's version of the claw setting designed by jewellers to allow more light on to a diamond to intensify its sparkle.

Lynn set up a workbench in a room overlooking a huge cedar of Lebanon, and a view down the long valley. He began by giving me some rough drawings of a design for a ring which I decided to model in wax. A series of unique rings were made in this way and cast in 18-carat gold; papal in size and weight, the flat gold surface would shine brilliantly whenever it caught the light.

I loved thinking 'sculpturally': I thought of volume, space, shape; of correct positioning and the importance of siting sculpture. It was liberating to be made to think on a large scale, but when I was given the opportunity to learn to weld, I had not the faintest idea of what to make. I managed only to weld a bunch of iron rods to a base, and ran out of ideas immediately. It seemed to me a pointless exercise, but it helped me to realize that I was not destined to 'think in metal'.

I began to feel inhibited working with an established artist and seemed unable to develop my own ideas. I needed to regain independence so I returned to my flat in Covent Garden, where I had already set up a jewellery bench in the kitchen. I worked on a number of commissions – mainly rings – but when a friend asked me to make a tiepin (not so different in principle from the gold hair ornaments I had made at Central) I could not get started. I dreamt instead that I was building a pylon.

★ ★ ★

I had always been happier working in 2D with pencil and paper than in 3D with soldering torch and metal, and was forever being told that I could draw. 'So what?' I would say to myself. What is there to celebrate about that, given that within family circles it was considered extremely unwise to think of becoming an artist 'after Augustus'. His son Edwin and daughter Vivien both trained at art school and were at their best painting in watercolour, a medium barely used by their father. His sister Gwen did not pose a threat in those days. Even so, to me the idea was risible.

When I entered art school, Augustus had only been dead five years; he was still famous in Britain and had not yet been overshadowed by the sudden explosion of interest in the life and work of Gwen during the 1980s. There was still much to sort out after his death, and at home a steady flow of his work came and went. I began looking at the work, puzzling over his wildly differing styles. Certain traits would be discussed – how in an oil portrait the eyes would often be shooting us a sideways glance from a three-quarter profile, and how in his later portraits he would over-emphasize the curves of a mouth and elongate the face.

I would look at his drawings, in folders from his studio and in reproduction in books, and gaze at his female figures – so many flowing pencil lines. I would wonder how it was that he could switch from rapid pen-and-ink studies to the minutely executed shading of a face. I had read in one of his obituaries that he could draw 'like a god'. I decided there would be no point whatsoever in pursuing a career in drawing. And drawing what?

My father's only advice to me as a young girl was to beg me not to marry an artist. He himself had joined the Navy at the age of thirteen in order to seek 'a more orderly existence' away from his father's unpredictable moods and itinerant lifestyle, and although he later joined in parties with my mother's artist friends, he viewed artists as on the whole self-centred, unreliable and 'impossible to live with'. When he was First Sea Lord from 1960–63 we had lived with the trappings of high office, but my mother never felt at ease with naval formality; she thrived in a 'happy-go-lucky existence', a phrase my father liked to use to describe his own upbringing. 'Uncertainty is the life-blood of Mary,' he once said, and in his view the same could be said of artists in general. Marriage was in any case not something he regarded as a priority or a necessity for his children. He encouraged independence and said to us, 'I will support you in anything you choose to do as long as it makes you happy.'

I knew now that I did not want to work as a jeweller, nor become an artist. My solution was to combine the two and make scaled-down drawings of plant details that, framed in silver, could be worn as brooches. I decided to revive the idea that a brooch could be functional – I'd admired the Anglo-Saxon 'disc brooches' which were designed to hold cloth together – and paid a silversmith to make the frames with brooch attachment. I drew 2-inch-wide circles on a piece of paper and crisscrossed them with stems or leaves, or simply filled the 'globe' with a flower, using pencil and watercolour. I began to fill these circles – these worlds – with diagrammatic mappings, geometric patterns, an object, a word. I was working on the same scale, I was later to discover, as the roundels (or medallions) of certain Western illuminated manuscripts. It is astonishing to see how much can be depicted within a circle measuring anything from an inch to a massive 3 inches.

In 1970 I exhibited eight picture brooches at the Arnolfini Gallery in Bristol – my second show there – but sales weren't enough to live on, so I got a job as a picture researcher, attracted by what I'd heard about the work from Georgina Barker.

★ ★ ★

My first assignment was to help an author find a few missing illustrations for a book about the hare in mythology, which included a hunt for a hieroglyph of a hare on an Egyptian mummy in the British Museum. My fee for the job was £5, which exactly matched my rent for one week. After a few months on a children's encyclopaedia, typing letters from an office in Old Compton Street, something altogether different: from 1971–73 I was the picture 'researcher' on *Time Out*. It was a period in which the magazine was in debt and undergoing endless editorial and management crises. The offices were in a rundown building at the midst of swirling traffic in King's Cross, 'the armpit of London', and it was here that I learnt about the pressures of working to a weekly deadline. The entire magazine was put together by hand, with scalpel, ruler and cow gum. Eleventh-hour panics became part of life – section editors would fall down the twisting stairs in the rush to deliver late copy to the typesetter – and I soon got used to sending out *Time Out*'s motorbike messenger to collect last-minute photographs and commissioning illustrators to deliver work 'by tomorrow'. There was no 'research' involved at all. Every Friday I'd foot it to the film distributors on Wardour Street to collect publicity stills from newly released films. At some point an enormous and very noisy Xerox machine was installed in my office, the latest technology that everyone was learning to use, and which I had to keep topped up with soot-black powdered ink.

It was an exciting time; everyone knew in advance what was happening on the London arts scene. Fringe theatre groups were making a mockery of traditional theatre and performance artists were beginning to attract small audiences in venues unknown to the general public. I would come away from these events wondering what I *had* seen. I loved most of all seeing foreign films that were being shown in London for the first time; I still remember walking home on a dark night over Waterloo Bridge after seeing a black-and-white Japanese film on the South Bank and the sensation that I was no longer walking in a familiar place.

One morning I got to my office and found a placard of photographs lying on the desk. It was made up of images cut from past issues of the magazine that portrayed women as 'sex objects' and had been paraded by a group of Women's Liberationists during a *Time Out* media conference at the Roundhouse. The conference was broken up, and the next day somebody had left the placard on my desk. Heated discussions followed and it was decided that henceforth I was to censor all photographs portraying women as 'subordinates' or 'sex objects'.

Time Out was expanding and so too was the number of black-and-white photographs I was handling each week. It soon became impossible to keep up with the filing and it was hard for *Time Out*'s photographers, too, as they had to cover an assignment at short notice, develop their photographs in their own darkrooms and deliver them at the last minute. One photographer who covered rock groups in dark interiors and was always in a hurry made an art form of the blurred image. I would look at these photographs as 'atmosphere', look for abstract qualities, pick out certain pleasing rhythms, see how the distribution of shapes near and far made a good or bad composition. I was always looking for that 'something other' in a bad photograph. It was time to leave.

EDWARD NORGATE'S TREATISE

I was still experimenting with ideas, in a desultory kind of way, so when in 1974 the National Portrait Gallery mounted an exhibition of the work of the seventeenth-century English portrait miniaturist Samuel Cooper, I was immediately inspired. I had no interest in learning miniature painting technique, but I was curious to find out how the portrait miniaturists of the period were able to paint in such exquisite detail on so small a scale. What were the tools of the trade? How were the frames constructed?

I made an appointment with Mr Murrell, conservator of portrait miniatures at the V&A. He had written an essay about Cooper's technique in which he described the miniaturists of the period as painting in a 'strictly observed procedure'. I was intrigued by this, and his descriptions of the colour pigments used by Cooper made me dizzy with excitement. Mr Murrell advised me to read *Miniatura, or the Art of Limning* by Edward Norgate, *c*.1650.[7]

This little book revealed a universe. The names of the pigments alone alluded to geology and chemistry, to the animal, vegetable and mineral. I became enthralled and wrote the names of the pigments over and over again like a mantra, in order to familiarize their names, ignorant as I was of their root meanings; nor was I certain of their colour. How would I distinguish 'ultramarine' from 'cobalt', 'red lake' from 'crimson'? What shade of green was 'verditer'? The mystery deepened . . . ultra-marine and ver-di-ter: beautiful names, meaning 'from beyond the sea' and 'green earth'.

Norgate opens his treatise with a list of the 'Severall Colours commonly used in Limning' (seventeenth-century spelling reads today like a child's misspelling), describing their qualities variously as 'friendly', 'fair', 'hurtfull', and suggesting their best uses: '*Umber* is a coarse, greazy and foule colour yet very usefull for shadowes, haire, perspective and almost any thing.' His advice on brushes, called 'pencills' in the seventeenth century, is just as relevant today: 'Your next care must bee to provide your selfe with good pencills well chosen, cleane and sharp pointed, not dividing into two parts as many times they doe, nor stufft with stragling haires, which later you may take away with a sharp penknife, or by passing the Pencill through the flame of a Candell. The best are of a reasonable length full round and sharpe, and not too longe, nor too slender, which are troublesome to work with.' Great care has to be taken over the preparation of the 'Table' (today's 'support'), this being vellum pasted on to card, and the correct direction of light, 'the greatest importance of all'.

The painting of the face is to begin with 'the Lines'. At the second sitting 'you are to goe over the face, very curiously', before blending in shadow and colouring: 'Over and about the eyes, you will perceave a dellicate faint rednes, and underneath the Eyes inclining to a blewish and purple colour (above the powere of a pen to describe).' Next, the painting of the ground, when the picture will appear 'strangely changed'.

---

7 Edward Norgate was employed at the courts of James I and Charles I as musician, limner (painter), herald, connoisseur and secretary. He wrote two versions of his treatise on miniature painting (1627–8 and 1648–9), the second version published by Clarendon Press in 1919. It was republished in a new edition for the Paul Mellon Centre for Studies in British Art, Yale University Press, extensively edited and annotated by Jeffrey M. Muller and Jim Murrell, in 1997.

Pausing to spare a thought for his reader – 'To particularize every thing would be thought a plot upon your patience' – he hastens on with instructions to 'sweeten' the ground colour so that it does not 'rest hard upon the face with an edge' and then to 'go over your haire heightening and deepening it as you shall see cause, and making out the extremities of the loose, and scattered haires to fly and play over the ground which will give a grace to your worke'.

His advice on painting the sitter's clothes and jewels concerns the correct use of liquid silver to create the 'lustre of pearles', the 'brightness of diamonds' and the mix of colours for rubies, emeralds and sapphires. Finally, in '*Landscape, or shape of Land*', which a miniaturist might want to paint as background in a larger scale work (the cabinet miniatures), he cautions that 'Trees require great Judgement' and sweetly adds that 'the leaves must bee flowing, and falling one over another, some spreading forward, others lost in shadowes'.

Norgate's treatise overwhelmed me. I could not tell if I was feeling confident or fearful, but I resolved to bear in mind certain of his instructions to help develop my ideas, but not to paint 'in miniature', which held no attraction for me. It was interesting to learn that miniatures from this period were sometimes worn as adornment, usually in an oval frame, and that the smallest were set into finger rings.

So, how to begin again? I already had a box of Winsor & Newton watercolour pans; the only material required for my purpose was vellum.

I wasn't at all sure about vellum. I knew it was not widely available, and that it was expensive. I associated it principally with the work of monks, although I now knew that the English portrait miniaturists Nicholas Hilliard and Samuel Cooper had painted on it, leaving no part of its surface visible. It would be years before I discovered the exquisite stippled still lifes of Giovanna Garzoni (the seventeenth-century Italian female artist) and the great eighteenth-century French botanical 'velins'. Calfskin was highly sensitive to water and would cockle at the stroke of a wet brush. This added to its mystique, and did not do much for my confidence.

Winsor & Newton in those years was in Rathbone Place off Oxford Street, where it had been established in 1832. I stood at the counter and asked to see some vellum. It was fearfully expensive. I could afford only a single sheet measuring 5 × 7 inches (13 × 18 cm). It was for me the equivalent of making the leap from silver to gold in my jewellery-making days. From paper to vellum . . . I walked home as if laden with gold; I may even have walked down Wardour Street, past Blundell's, where I would go to buy small amounts of gold when a student at Central.

From silver to gold . . . I sat in front of the sheet of vellum. I held my pencil over the skin. Those 7 inches became a void. Nothing happened. The void grew and grew until I sat paralysed in front of it. Nothing on earth could enable me to enter that expensive void, to mark it, to make the wrong mark. Then the thought: if I daren't draw on it, how on earth will I be able to paint on it? After all, I'd had no training in watercolour technique. I lost my nerve. I put the sheet into a brown envelope and wrote in green ink: 'In here there's vellum.' I tucked it inside the lid of my jewellery box, and there it remained for twenty-four years.

My beautiful idea to become a painter-jeweller came to an abrupt end. In truth I had begun to feel restless seated in my flat thinking only of small-scale images. I had been distracted, too, when for the first time I saw the work of Hiroshige and Utamaro, and the sixteenth-century Iranian manuscript *A King's Book of Kings*, newly published in book form. I stared for hours at the Japanese prints – pale, asymmetrical, faultless in execution – and at the brilliantly coloured, complex miniatures illustrating Iran's national epic. I could not fathom how these pictures were made. They seemed miraculous, and they unsettled me. My drawings seemed reduced to insignificant nothings.

★ ★ ★

I wanted to get out into the world, move among people, so I decided to concentrate on picture research and looked for work in book publishing.

Picture research occupied a low rung in publishing, but by the 1970s improvements in colour printing had created a boom in illustrated books. This meant that publishers were increasingly reliant on researchers to source illustrations and deal with the thankless tasks of clearing copyright and negotiating reproduction fees which were becoming increasingly complex. There was no shortage of work. Initially the job entailed hours of polite letter writing and travel in search of specific illustrations, always to a deadline. In those days a written request to reproduce a painting from a museum in America, say, could take up to three months to process; in today's digital world a request can be processed within days.

I was given access to London's libraries and museums, photographers' collections and press agencies. I would spend hours in these places – in the labyrinthine basement of Camera Press, where thousands of old black and white press photos were stored floor to ceiling in cardboard boxes; or at the secretive Mansell Collection, tucked away in a leafy corner in Bayswater; or at the notoriously slow Radio Times Hulton Picture Library, a vast collection of historical prints and photographs, since digitized and absorbed into Getty Images. In time I learnt to use the cataloguing systems of the London Library and the British Library, which was to prove invaluable when I later began my own research.

CHINA

A two-year assignment to coordinate 450 illustrations for *The Cambridge Encyclopedia of China* (published in 1982) gave me the opportunity to meet some of the country's leading sinologists. It was exciting to be given first-hand insights into Chinese landscape painting in the British Museum's Chinese art department, and on one occasion I travelled to Cambridge to meet Dr Joseph Needham, the renowned author of the multi-volume *Science and Civilisation in China*. For some reason we easily began a discussion about ink, which in China had been made from various soots – pine soot, kitchen soot, lampblack, soot made from dust – then mixed with animal glue to form small sticks or blocks, unrecognizable as ink until liquidized by rubbing on a smooth stone with a little water.

I read every entry in the encyclopedia, learnt the all-important sequence of dynasties, and by the end of the job had glimpsed China through thousands of still photographs and transparencies. This made me long all the more to see the living China. In 1981 I signed up to a group trip, attracted by the opportunity to visit Szechuan (Sichuan) province, which bordered Tibet in the far west and had only recently opened up to foreign visitors.

We began our itinerary in Canton and travelled anticlockwise around the country, but it was not until day twelve of our three-week tour that I began to feel I was penetrating China. We had arrived in Szechuan and were to visit the seventh-century T'ang dynasty Giant Buddha of Leshan, carved out of a vertical cliff face at the confluence of three rivers. Leaving Szechuan's capital Chengdu, we were driven for a hundred miles along roads lined all the way with eucalyptus trees through an exquisite man-made landscape of tea plantations and fields of broad beans, wheat, hemp. Thatched farmhouses sheltered among bamboo groves; now and again a water buffalo and lone farmer at work with a wooden plough. Most impressive to me were the young mulberry trees which had been planted along the edges of the thin paths dividing the rice paddies. This method not only helped to stabilize the soil; the trees were being planted to replace the thousands that had been destroyed during the Cultural Revolution when the silk industry had been condemned as 'Capitalist Road'. It seemed to me that not an inch of land was left to waste.

To reach Buddha we had to take a boat across the spiralling grey waters of a wide river and climb thousands of steps up the cliff and slowly make our way through

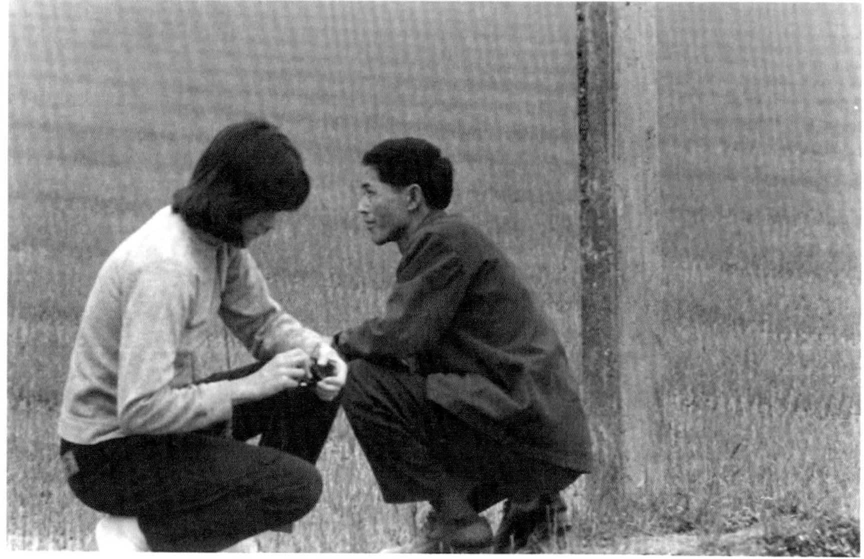

In Szechuan with our guide

bamboo groves towards a T'ang temple. A group of us crossed the courtyard and made the acquaintance of a monk-scribe, who invited us into a dark room. After the usual pleasantries he sat down, picked up a brush and, holding it vertically, dipped it in black ink and began a poem about the three rivers. We watched as he carefully timed each stroke, controlling the brush with his wrist so as to balance the thick and thin strokes – the 'flesh and bones' of Chinese calligraphy. His concentration only broke at the moment of completion: with a flourish and a smile the scribe handed the poem to the Chinese-speaking member of our band. We applauded as is customary in China, and reluctantly left him to continue our walk, drifting down now through tall bamboo groves before crossing a bridge and working our way upwards before arriving at Buddha's giant head. His nose was blackened, ferns grew out of his lap; some two hundred feet below a man was sitting on Buddha's big toe. It dwarfed him.

Until that day I'd not felt I'd touched ground in China; our group had travelled at speed by train, bus and aeroplane between cities, marvelling at the sights, eating exquisitely prepared dishes and snatching conversations with the Chinese whenever possible. They would cross the street to practise their English – some were concerned that they were speaking with an American accent – and on one occasion in Yangzhou a group of students waved and beckoned me to join in a game of shuttlecock, but we were incapacitated by laughter. Later in Canton I had a chance to talk to our guide, Huang Tsan-hui. He was alert as a bird and told me what had happened to him during the Cultural Revolution. He'd had to learn to plough with a water buffalo, cut down trees in the countryside and transplant rice. He didn't resent having to learn these skills and was now engaged to a girl working in a tractor factory. His was a very different attitude from that of the young intellectual we'd met in Suzhou, a city graced with ancient walled gardens and canals. He had conducted us around the Garden of the Master of Fishing Nets and the Lingering Garden (which swarmed with Chinese tourists), but he was still smarting from his ten years in the countryside and was now studying to 'gain knowledge'.

We gave away Western literature and were greeted with smiles and laughter almost everywhere, but although I felt at ease with the Chinese it was impossible to forget the dark side of life in China. It was alarming to see the giant hoardings of a smiling couple holding a young child with the command: 'YOU'D BETTER HAVE ONE CHILD ONLY', a policy that had been introduced in 1979 (and continued until 2015). In Beijing a few of us were called to a meeting with a dissident, a sculptor who had been inspired by Brancusi after seeing photographs of his work in a book. He told us that he had been forbidden to exhibit his Western-influenced work and when, back home in England, I heard that he had run into serious trouble with the authorities, I felt the guilt of having met him and left him to his fate, safe in the knowledge that I'd soon be leaving China.

At home my shelves had begun to fill with books on China and Chinese art. I still feel that shiver of excitement each time I reread Kuo Hsi's *An Essay on Chinese Landscape Painting* – a twelfth-century treatise on correct handling of the brush and use of different inks to suggest distance and seasonal atmosphere; to hint at the hidden forces of nature. The book *Flowers in Art from East and West*[8] became one of my most treasured possessions. Concerned only with work in pencil, ink or watercolour, the authors set out to analyse the principal motives behind floral representation in (broadly) three main geographical areas: Europe (scientific curiosity); India and Persia (pleasure); China and Japan (aesthetics and philosophy).

Distinguishing the key periods of floral painting in these areas, and beginning with naturalism in Sung China and its 'rebirth' in Europe, the authors take the reader on a marvellous illustrated journey through early herbals and manuscript illustration, the work of European 'artists of discovery', the decorative miniatures of India and Persia, and floral painting in the Far East. Two chapters on Chinese and Japanese ink painting and woodblock prints held particular fascination for me – I loved the affinity of brushwork with calligraphy, which brought a plant to life in ways that European concern with 'accuracy' could not – and I resolved to find a way into the world of botanical art.

But life at home had become very unsettled. My marriage was ending and I was having to adjust to becoming a single parent. In addition, a traumatic event in the family was already putting new demands on me, both physical and emotional.

MY FATHER'S TRAUMA

Towards the end of 1977 my father had been diagnosed with arterial sclerosis (the hardening of the arteries) and in January and February the following year he suffered a double leg amputation. Everyone was in shock – family, friends, naval colleagues. My father had never smoked (the first question doctors asked him); he was tall, fit, had never suffered anything more serious than a broken ankle (and that was in 1924, in a tackle against the captain of the English rugby team). Now he was reduced to a dwarf-like figure as he struggled to learn to walk on false legs. I would watch him lurch up and down the enormous gym at the naval hospital in Plymouth, sweating with the effort. But, at seventy-six, age was against him and after a year he gave up the fight. My mother had rallied; until now she had been living in Wales – they had gradually gone their separate ways – but with her help he left his Devon cottage, which was too small for a wheelchair, and together they moved back to Mousehole, the Cornish fishing village where we had lived in the early 1950s, when he was away at sea as captain of the aircraft carrier HMS *Vengeance*.

Whenever work and motherhood allowed, I would make the six-hour drive to Cornwall to relieve my mother. There were moments of crisis, as when he'd fall out of his wheelchair – it wasn't easy, physically or psychologically, to pick my father up

---

8 By Paul Hulton and Lawrence Smith, published to accompany the British Museum's 1979 exhibition.

off the floor, and I once returned home to find him sitting in the flower bed calling for help. I was devastated, but we both laughed as I disentangled him from the roses. The worst moment came when I was driving him to London. He was on the front seat slumping forward so I drew up on the hard shoulder to transfer him on to the back seat where he could lie down. During the manoeuvre from car seat to wheelchair he slipped on to the hard shoulder. There was only one thing for it: I convinced myself that I was strong as a crane and hoisted him up off the tarmac on to the back seat, an operation that practically killed me. We drove on.

My parents weren't short of friends in the village, some of whom they'd known in the 1950s. Trevelyan Richards, a fine man who drowned in the 1981 Penlee lifeboat disaster, would bring fresh fish and crab to the house. And there were days when everything seemed as it always had been: the usual moods and family quarrelling, a lot of drinking and spontaneous partying. But there were times when I felt overwhelmed with sadness at his fate and I needed to find an escape. I'd go down to the rocks below the harbour and stand over the rock pools that had captivated me as a child. They seemed smaller now, less colourful.

★ ★ ★

One day, while looking after my father, I sat down and drew an anemone in a jug. Just one fully opened pink anemone, in faint coloured pencil, in a black jug. I felt as if I'd entered a strange place, and yet the conduit to this place was a familiar flower in an everyday jug. The feeling of strangeness was the act of drawing, and the image I made was a stranger to the real thing.

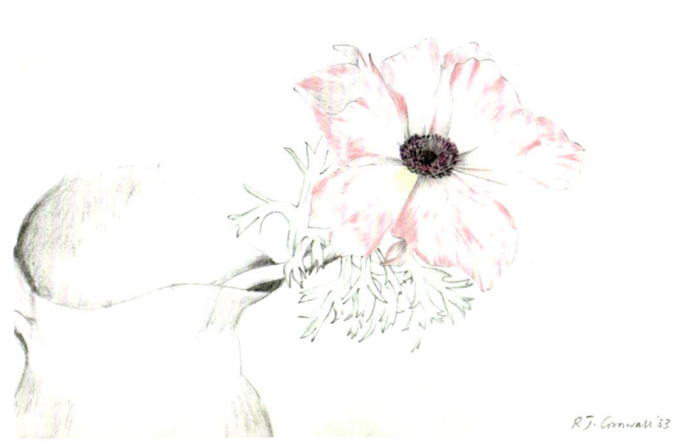

Anemone (coloured pencil), 1983

And so, partly to escape the sadness surrounding my father's fate, and partly owing to a friend, Pat Kavanagh, who, in her no-nonsense way, said, 'I think you should draw, Rebecca,' I started to make tentative pencil studies of flowering plants.

It occurred to me that I'd never seen the flower of a chestnut tree close up; the distant 'candle' became unrecognizable in a drawing. That excited me. I was excited too by certain flowers I'd never seen before: *Ranunculus, Alstroemeria,* and *Gloriosa superba* 'Rothschildiana' were for sale for the first time at a Covent Garden flower stall and seemed to me wonderfully exotic. I drew them in a kind of awe – it was as if I was visiting a foreign country – and up in the Welsh hills I began to make studies of the wild flowers growing in the lush summer months.

A box of seventy-two coloured pencils was all I needed. I was concerned mainly with shape and placement, having no understanding at this stage of weight or depth.

GWEN JOHN

In the month that my father had his first leg operation his brother Edwin died. The two brothers did not get on. My father, in hospital at the time, barely reacted to the news, but Edwin's death was to have huge consequences for the work and reputation of my great-aunt Gwen John.

Five years previously Edwin had left his Paris studio in the rue de Vaugirard and moved into a farmhouse on the edge of the Berwyn Mountains in Wales, close to where my parents had bought a derelict cottage. Everyone hoped that the beauty of the landscape and ever-changing light would inspire him to continue painting. He had trained at the Academy Schools and after he befriended his aunt Gwen in Paris in the 1930s she encouraged him to concentrate on painting. He admired the great eighteenth-century English watercolourists, with special reverence for the work of John Cotman, and learnt to apply colour in flat washes which required controlled handling of the brush. He would set up colourful still lifes of flowers and fruit in his Paris studio. and on his travels painted landscape in France, Spain and England. Fearful of exhibiting lest he be linked with his father's name, he never sold his work, and after moving to Wales he became preoccupied with maintenance problems (having rescued the farmhouse from dereliction) and caring for the vast quantity of drawings and paintings left to him by Gwen on her death in September 1939. In the intervening forty-odd years he guarded her work as if he owned her. This rattled certain members of the family, especially Augustus, who had been Gwen's first champion – and as I grew up I became very aware of the hold my eccentric uncle Edwin had over the name of Gwen John.

Edwin was alone in his farmhouse when he died unexpectedly. Like Gwen, he had stopped painting and become reclusive. He lost interest in food and spent long hours writing letters in his beautiful handwriting. He had an idiosyncratic way with language – he liked to write in mock pomposity – and disliked modernity to the point of phobia. 'Is the world beautiful?' he once wrote to me. 'I thought so once, long ago, but homo sapiens is fast transforming it into a desert of devastating vulgarity. I do not, of course, presume on your agreement with this view, so, if you please, rest easy and enjoy your promenade round this wrecked world of ours. Don't forget your transistor set for God's sake.' I picture him now, seated at the kitchen table in his farmhouse: check shirt, cigarette, a bowl of fruit, his favourite Quimper pottery . . . dimly lit rooms with views over breathtaking scenery. Here he could withdraw from the world and avoid people. 'Absence, rather than presence, makes the heart grow fonder, an illusion I was loth to destroy,' he wrote after declining my father's invitation to Christmas. He lived as an ascetic – he once wrote from Paris telling me of his Christmas lunch of tinned tomato soup 'with tap water added, a little pepper perhaps', and that he gave his two meat pies to a 'shivering beggar'. When, on a rare visit to London in the 1960s, he heard the Beatles song 'Nowhere Man', he claimed with some mirth to be that man.

Perhaps the only thing that united the brothers was a small repertoire of songs inherited from Augustus. Letters recalling forgotten lyrics and correct accentuation would be exchanged. My father's special song was the chilling ballad 'Lord Randal', which he would sing slightly off-key and with sudden crescendos at the end of a long Christmas lunch, when light was fading and candles were lit. Edwin's song was the sad story 'My Darling Clementine', which he sang so movingly that everyone fell silent and my mother would cry.

Did Edwin have any idea what would happen to Gwen's reputation and her art after he died? The art dealer Anthony d'Offay had persuaded him not to leave the bulk of Gwen's estate to the National Museum of Wales, which would have drastically reduced the number of works available to buy. Under d'Offay's care, her pictures began to appear on the market in carefully timed exhibitions, the first of which was planned for summer 1982. A week before the exhibition opening I had a vivid dream that all the pictures sold except the 'not very good ones' and that among the works was a drawing of trees, a subject I had never associated with her and could not recall seeing. The anticipation of Gwen's exhibition gave me butterflies. Something was about to change, although none of us were prepared for the overnight rise in the value of her work, and I felt very nervous walking to the Anthony d'Offay gallery for a preview. The pictures were lined along the floor, ready for hanging; there were her girls, her orphans in church, her tiny flower pieces and, lying at the midst of all this, a single painting of trees: *Clump of Trees* was loosely painted in a pale green wash against a mauve sky, but the trees I had seen in my dream were most un-Gwen like; they had been drawn in black ink with a scratchy pen.

The only time I'd seen her work in any quantity was in the Arts Council's 1968 retrospective, which was held in Edwin's lifetime. That year he wrote to tell me that he regarded Mary Taubman as 'the most reliable authority on Gwen John now living'. She too was an artist who had lived in France, had taught painting and spent years studying Gwen's work. Her quiet nature appealed to Edwin and she in turn respected his extreme sensitivity about Gwen's private life. Fearful of Edwin's aversion to anything he regarded as 'journalistic', she is noticeably discreet about Gwen's love for Rodin in her catalogue essay; the word 'affair' was to be avoided, so she wrote that Rodin 'became for her the object of a deep and characteristic devotion whose intensity was heightened by her solitary mode of life.'

The first books on her life and work began to appear and during the 1985 retrospective at the Barbican there was a great deal of press. Everyone was now writing about her affair with Rodin, something that had only ever been mentioned in a casual remark at home. If we were to follow Edwin's example, we had to respect her privacy. It was of no concern to us and besides it was all so long ago. But after Edwin's death the floodgates had opened, and even Mary Taubman, in her book of the same year, was able to write that Gwen had become 'enmeshed in a traumatic love affair' and was 'passionately in love'.

Until this time Gwen had always seemed to me a kind of family secret, shared only by a small handful of devoted collectors. I had grown up knowing only a few bare facts about her – that she lived alone in Paris, painted and never married. *Lived alone. Painted. Never married.* It was enough. I never expected I would know anything more about her. She simply existed in my mind as an admirable example of a woman who had defied convention at a time when marriage would have been expected of her. Wasn't it thought to be 'odd' for a woman to live alone? 'Ah, but she's an artist!' In a rare moment of openness Edwin, who had a habit of talking with eyes closed then with one eye open, once spoke to me of her tones, emphasizing the word *tones*. That was all. His sister Vivien was soon to find herself the last person alive to have met Gwen but not quite known her, and as interest in Gwen grew throughout the 1980s, Vivien was occasionally interviewed. She joked to me that she felt as though people wanted to strangle her in frustration . . . surely she knew her aunt! Surely she could describe her! It was as if people could not get enough of her. Biographers, art historians, feminists and journalists all had their say, and it was both fascinating and worrying to learn from them so much about the great-aunt I never knew; but I could not help thinking how dismayed Gwen would have been by the exposure, and how ironic it was for her that her reputation now stood so high. It was a mercy that my father had never shown any interest in Gwen – her art meant nothing to him, which was just as well given his brother's claim over her. My mother felt more warmly towards her and when I was feeling despondent about my stop-start attempts at drawing she referred me to Gwen, remarking that she was 'very good at drawing cats'. Cats! I loved cats, but if I were to choose a work to own it would be one of her early oil paintings of a girl reading by a window – or a watercolour of a street at twilight: her nocturnes.

CASPAR JOHN

While Gwen's star was rising, my father was living out his last years in Cornwall and had been persuaded to write his life story. He was given a publisher's contract but with the proviso that I would help him. What was I doing messing about with pictures? 'You seem hesitant!' I was told: 'Your father is far more important!' I had reason to hesitate. I knew little of naval history, and it was an enterprise he openly mocked, since he never thought of himself as an 'I Am'. Neither did he approve of dwelling on the past. 'Think ahead! Think ahead!' he used to say, and he never did talk about his past. As children, he only allowed us glimpses of his early life in the Navy when we wanted to know such things as how many countries in the world he'd been to, and the worst thing he'd ever seen. 'Seeing a man being beheaded in China' was the answer that gave the most satisfaction.

I worked with my father in the last year of his life and, as I recorded conversations with him, he began to tell his story. It was as if I was learning about a man who was not my father, since he had already reached the age of forty-four when I was born. By the time he died, aged eighty-one, I knew I had to complete the book, and there were people who had known him and insisted on it.

When people said to me, 'It must be extraordinarily difficult to write about one's father', I replied that yes, it was, and I would think of the numerous books that have been written about fathers. I thought too of a letter his mother, Ida, had written long ago in which she expressed a desire to help her sick father complete a painting: 'Strange audacity!' she wrote.

Since he had rarely talked about himself, it was a revelation to discover his pioneering exploits in open cockpit 'flying machines' in the 1920s. Born in 1903, the year of the Wright Brothers' first-ever powered flight, my father's career fell in step with the unfolding story of flight and he became passionate about 'the air', rebelling against 'warship mentality' and 'dyed-in-the-wool' naval thinking. During the late 1920s and 1930s, he pioneered aircraft-carrier landing and take-off – the most dangerous form of flying. Describing this period in his life, when naval pilots were flying at low altitude and always 'in weather', he told me something that has always stayed with me: 'Those men who pioneered deck landing had to *feel* their way back down on to the carrier. One had to have a very fine sense of balance and timing to make a good deck-lander, and like a pianist who suddenly discovers he can play the notes, or a jockey and his horse who can win the Grand National, the technique came to me, and I clung to it. I was confident that whatever I did was right and I felt master of my own destiny.' In 1930, with a loan from his father, he bought his own aeroplane, an Avro Avian. Using it instead of a car, he flew all over England and across to France, sometimes with members of his family, taking off and landing in a field, or on a beach. A founding father of the Fleet Air Arm, he rose to Admiral of the Fleet and was the only naval pilot ever to become First Sea Lord, the pinnacle of his profession.

I met and talked with many of his naval colleagues, all of whom offered anecdotes and vital information. I shall not forget the tall and handsome Vice Admiral in his late eighties who in 1922–3 was anchored off Constantinople during my father's first year at sea in the flagship of the Mediterranean Fleet, HMS *Iron Duke*. He and his wife invited me to stay so he could check I'd quoted his recollections to his satisfaction –

chief of which concerned the plight of White Russians flooding the city following the 1917 Revolution. At cocktail hour we drank gin and tonic. 'Have another!' he said. 'You can't fly on one wing!'

I interwove my father's life in the Royal Navy with his bohemian family background, and all this was set against the image I had of him in old age, confined to a wheelchair and, as he wryly put it, 'three feet closer to the ground'. It was hard to come to terms with his fate, and this made the telling of his story all the more urgent.

While his childhood and flying experiences at sea became for me the most interesting aspect of my father's life, there were those who only wanted to know one thing: what made my father decide at the age of thirteen to join the harshest discipline in the world, coming from a background 'like that' – an oblique reference to his father, Augustus. It was a question my father was asked throughout his life (and I am asked today). His answer was always the same: 'I joined the Navy to seek a more orderly existence, to get away from a disorderly home life.' This was his way of referring to an itinerant upbringing dominated by an artist father who was frequently absent, behaved unpredictably and showed little affection towards his sons. All the same, his upbringing enabled him to make a start in life 'completely lacking in class-consciousness' and he never forgot his father's advice to 'take people as he found them, wherever they come from, high or low'. He was not indiscriminate: through conversation and argument he could read an individual and discern character very quickly. But, in his later years, when my sister and I were in our teens, he became very uneasy in the presence of long-haired young men.

I worked for three years on his life story and after publication in July 1987 a stream of letters arrived thanking me for writing the book. These were very personal letters, and some of them moved me to tears – but I shall always be haunted by my error of switching the Caspian Sea with the Black Sea (overlooked by my editors and three admirals).

ELIZABETH DAVID

From naval flight to still life: my last job as a picture researcher was to find 150 photographs of still-life paintings and related subjects to illustrate three new editions of Elizabeth David's books. The original editions had been published between 1950 and 1955 and had been used by my mother, and at Fryern Court by Dorelia, who had learnt to cook in Paris and in Provence during the years before the First World War, when she had six growing boys to feed. French recipes were frequently talked about at home and I grew up thinking Elizabeth David was queen of cookery.

I knew Elizabeth David had always resisted colour photography in her books, but she did not object to paintings of food appearing among her recipes. She gave me long handwritten lists of specific works that she had seen, always with an eye on quality. If there was one thing she could not abide, it was the 'typical English chaos' of loose watercolour painting featuring a jug here, lemon there, flower here, scrap of pattern there. She revered Chardin – his still lifes seemed to belong among her recipes – told me that she would tolerate Bonnard, and when I showed her works that I had found for her approval, she would say, 'I think this perfectly charming' or a straight 'perfectly ghastly'.

I enjoyed the work so much that I wrote an article about the experience and asked Elizabeth to vet what I'd written. She sent a postcard from California to say she found it 'very good, and very comprehensive and informative', and went on to say: 'There are one or two other points you could make, such as the problems of dealing with publishers' art editors and their well-developed sabotage techniques – but perhaps you'd rather not . . . Good that you emphasise the poor quality of many of the transparencies.'

Bad colour reproduction from a poor colour transparency was one thing, but in previous jobs I'd also seen many good-quality photographs miniaturized to pointless rectangles yet always incurring a fee. I was disturbed too by deceptive caption writing and how a photograph of a person would be used indiscriminately above a caption that turned the photograph into a lie. I felt a growing desire to retreat into my own creative world, to be freed from deadlines and copyright laws, to be freed from handling other people's property.

Many of the still-life paintings Elizabeth had asked me to find were a revelation. Sebastian Stoskopff's painting of wine glasses in a basket astonished me – I had not heard of this seventeenth-century artist – and I still savour the first time I saw George Henry Hall's *Raspberries on a Cabbage Leaf.* I loved the simplicity of Henri Fantin-Latour's *White Cup and Saucer* (one of Elizabeth's favourite paintings) and Jean-Etienne Liotard's *Figs and Bread*, which, true to tradition in still-life painting, featured a knife. How was it possible to paint a knife, I wondered?

I looked into the transparencies of these paintings and saw tenderness. I saw beauty and gemstone colouring and, in the simpler still lifes, a certain pleasing tautness. I felt inspired to continue my pencil work, and slowly I built up a good number of drawings – about forty between 1988 and 1989 – of which twenty-five were sold or given away to friends. It was very strange to receive money. I first asked around £40, then with great daring I asked for £60, £75 even. I got bolder: for an agreed £120 I sold a drawing I thought quite ambitious, given the random arrangement of flowers.

I drew only flowers and leaves, tentatively working my way into a world free of words and people. It was a faint world, without shadow, two-dimensional and devoid of intellectual meaning.

AMARYLLIS FLEMING

I knew that I would eventually become frustrated with the limitations of pencil, that I would have to learn to use paint if I was to develop my ideas. I was still not ready to break into paint when I received a letter from the cellist Amaryllis Fleming, asking if I would consider working with her on her life story. I weighed up the risks – she was a relative, and she was alive – but I reasoned that I did not know her, and I could not resist the opportunity to work closely with a musician. Classical music had been central

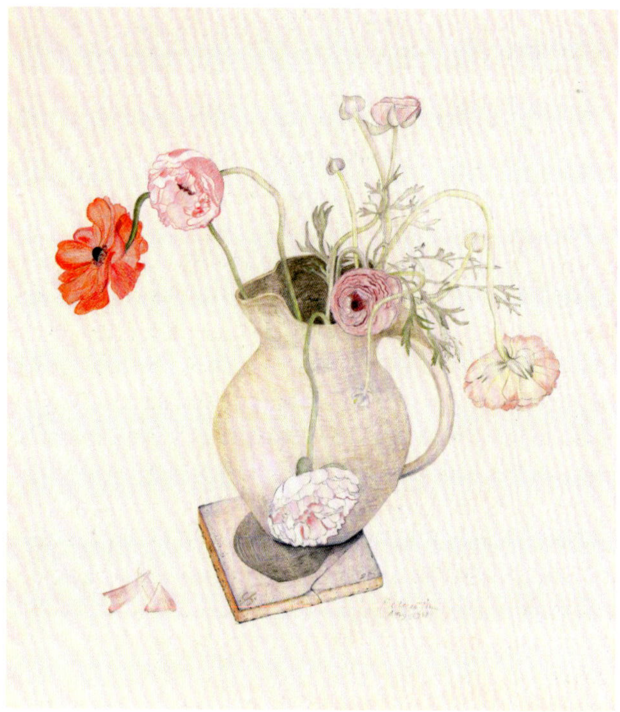

Ranunculus in a jug (coloured pencil), 1988

to my life both at home and at school but, having gained merit and distinction in the higher grades of the dreaded Associated Board examinations, I could never achieve the confidence to play in front of people, and I revered any musician who could.

I'd heard Amaryllis play on a few occasions: once when she joined the Amadeus Quartet in a concert at the Royal Academy during the 1966 Bonnard retrospective. She stepped on to the platform in a dark green evening dress that drew gasps from the audience. I was eighteen, and unfamiliar with Bonnard's paintings; to this day I have an image of a girl lying in a bath – all pinks, violets and yellows, and very strange to my eyes – fused with the exquisitely sad music of Schubert's string quintet.

Amaryllis – she learnt to live down her name – was the illegitimate daughter of Augustus and Eve Fleming, a wealthy society hostess (and mother of the writers Ian Fleming and Peter Fleming) who had been widowed in the First World War. She was therefore a half-aunt but she might as well have been living on the moon for all the contact we'd had. Nonetheless, I'd formed a strong image of her from accounts of her Titian-red hair and smoker's voice. I knew that she had made her name from among a tiny handful of solo female cellists in the 1950s and had performed at the Proms, but mystery surrounded the circumstances of her birth, and she had a lively story to tell.

She was not dissimilar from Elizabeth David: an independent woman of strong character who loved a cigarette and a strong drink, a beauty who enjoyed the company of men. They both had a sharp ear for language and a strong aesthetic sense. Neither had any children and both remained resolutely dedicated to their life's work, bringing fresh thinking to their respective fields.

I worked with Amaryllis from 1989 to 1992. She told me extraordinary stories about her solo career and her adventures on and off the platform; her concerns with technique and musicianship, her analysis of Bach's Cello Suites and her knowledge of bows. She was the first cellist to resurrect the five-string cello for which the sixth Suite had been written. She spoke openly about her love affair with her teacher Pierre Fournier, with whom she had fallen in love after hearing him play — and described her lessons with Pablo Casals and Guilhermina Suggia, the subject of Augustus's famous portrait *Madame Suggia*. (They did not get on and she did not admire Suggia's playing; this in turn threw new light on the portrait, not least Amaryllis's criticism of Madame Suggia's straight-fingered 'bow-hold'.) I attended cello master classes — always moving, always intense, but with sparkly moments as when the cellist William Pleeth instructed a pupil to 'Doodle around . . . talk sweet nothings to your favourite girl!' to help him through a difficult passage in Dvorak's concerto. I talked with musicians who had played with Amaryllis, some of whom clearly had reservations about her playing.

She told me a great deal about her very difficult relationship with her mother, who until her dying day denied that she was her mother, and of her fondness for her half-brothers Peter and Ian. Such was her disdain for the Bond stories that she was barely aware that she was the model for the cello-playing girl in *The Living Daylights*. She would have made mincemeat of the actress who'd had to pretend to play the cello in the film.

When, in the third year of our collaboration, progress slowed to a halt owing in part to her growing impatience and to my uneasiness about the unrelenting emphasis she gave to her unhappy relationship with her mother, I had gained valuable insight into the life of a solo musician: the solitary hours of practice and the stresses of travel between concerts, the loneliness of the dressing room and pre-concert nerves, the problems with conductors. But she never gave in to self-pity: her stories were laced with Fleming black humour (and her distinctly unmusical laugh), and she delighted in recalling the more racy moments in her career, as when William Walton instructed her to play a passage in his cello concerto 'more clitorisically'. She revealed her softer side when she talked about her concern for troubled fellow musicians and for her pupils — she was Professor of Cello at the Royal College of Music — and when she died she left bequests to the RCM — the concert hall has been named the Amaryllis Fleming Hall — and to the Buddhist cause in Tibet.

I had done a lot of background reading — mainly musicians' life stories, among which Artur Schnabel's *My Life and Music* made a lasting impression. 'He was Austrian, very correct, and kissed a lady's hand on greeting,' Amaryllis remembered. 'Once when I dropped my gloves he clicked his heels and picked them up for me in a proper, old-fashioned manner.' He suffered agonies during recording sessions and on the matter of tempo he confessed to having 'fast years' and 'slow years'. Today his name is barely mentioned without reference to the fact that he was the first to record all thirty-two Beethoven piano sonatas (in 1932–35), but he mentally recoiled at the thought of his recordings being played in the privacy of the home where, free of the strictures of the concert hall, the listener could walk about, read, sit playing cards perhaps, or *talk* – and, equally unthinkable, be *improperly dressed* while his records were playing. I sometimes think of Schnabel when driving down a motorway at night, engine humming, CD playing, wrong clothes.

★ ★ ★

I discovered Paul Klee's *Notebooks* for the first time. I was enchanted. He had been a violinist, playing in quartets and orchestras while at the same time developing his ideas as an artist. A photograph of Klee in a string quintet shows the musicians seated on art school 'donkeys' with their music propped on the easels. I copied out his entries concerning the relationship of music to painting and listed all the words that could be applied to both, though I still had no idea how to paint. I discovered Kandinsky's *Concerning the Spiritual in Art* (the title, translated from German, alludes to Kandinsky's theory that musical harmony should be central to painting), and Rilke's *Letters on Cézanne*:

> And that was Bohemia as I knew it, hilly like light music and suddenly flat again behind its apple trees, flat without much horizon and divided by ploughed fields and rows of trees like a folk song from refrain to refrain.

I thought that was beautiful.

Abstract art, which had meant nothing to me, began to make sense once I linked its 'birth' to the beginnings of jazz, albeit jazz with rhythm.

I read *Notes on the Science of Picture-Making* by Charles Holmes, Director of the National Portrait Gallery at the time of publication in 1909. His 'notes', arranged under headings such as 'The Value of Emotion' and 'Emphasis of Recession', were written in a style that has heavily dated, and I loved them all the more for that. A note headed 'Infinity and Vitality' stayed with me. I later came to think of 'infinity' as the blank paper and 'vitality' as the subject.

In 1992 I went to an exhibition called *The Embroiderer's Flowers* at the Museum of Garden History in Lambeth. I marvelled at the skill with which the shape of a flower could be moulded in tones of silk thread, and looked at each stitch as if it were a pencil stroke. A bedspread rippling with russet-coloured leaves caught my eye. Ottoline Morrell's name on the label swam in my head with Augustus's unflattering portrait of her and I had to wrestle for a few moments with the idea that she could embroider. She'd posed for him in a huge shapeless hat shooting us a sideways glance, jaw jutting forward, mouth open, something that had always puzzled me dreadfully until I decided that she was talking. But she stitched with muscle; her leaves seemed to rustle with life and appeared to be blowing across the bedspread in a gust of wind.

A NEW DIRECTION

There are moments in life when a thought, an idea, makes clear sense. I don't know when it was that I read an article by Anthony Huxley in the RHS magazine about plant hunting in the Himalayas, but for some reason I felt unusually excited. Surely, if I concentrated on drawing plants, I would be able to work anywhere in the world. I would need only a table and chair by a window, paper, pencils, brushes, paints. That way lay freedom!

During the research for Elizabeth David I had begun to look more closely at the way plants were portrayed in paint. 'Flowers in a Vase' had become predictable through repetition (Van Gogh's series of *Sunflowers* no exception), and the proliferation of limp-wristed flower paintings typical of today's birthday card industry seemed to me an insult to plants. I preferred Lucian Freud's unsentimental depictions of plants: buttercups in a sink, gorse by an old wall, black-and-white drawings of thorns and thistles.

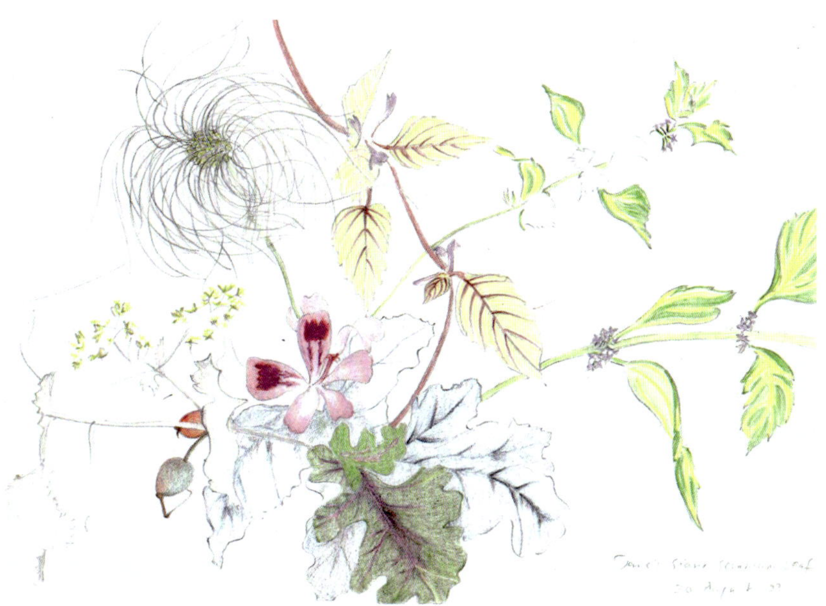

Ginger mint and oak-leaf geranium (coloured pencil), 1993

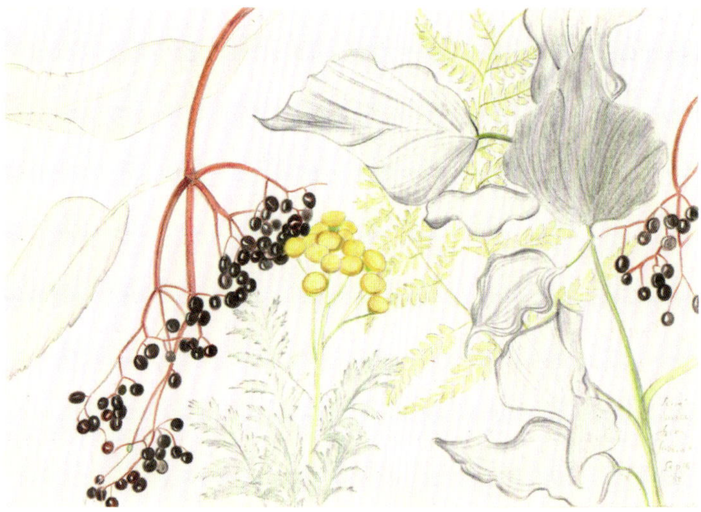

Elderberries (coloured pencil), 1993

In the scientific camp, botanical illustration concentrated on plant specimens, drawn and painted in great detail for the purposes of identification. This allowed little room for play and, although much of what I saw lacked life, I admired the devotion of plant illustrators, their loyalty to their subject.

The work of the great eighteenth-century botanical artist-illustrator G. D. Ehret stands out in this respect. He conveyed the form of the plant with an unmistakeable lightness of touch; this is especially apparent in his working drawings, where much of his exquisite pencil work is left free of paint. There are many such studies, drawn in order to show (while simultaneously discovering) the botanical make-up of a plant, so that a 'complete' painting was not always necessary. In the twentieth century, Charles Rennie Mackintosh would sometimes apply paint solely to indicate flower and leaf colour while leaving the rest of the drawing free. To my mind this gives a sense of movement, allows air into the work, whereas many finished, scientifically accurate representations of plants look as if they are trapped in a vacuum. Too often the plant is drawn with an unyielding outline as if under a deadening neon light.

I continued to draw, and wrote in a notebook: 'All the little drawings of 92–93 indicate the growing desire for immersion in the non-human world of plants. This didn't stop me seeing humans in plants, or thinking a mood into a plant. Much pleasure thinking the cool sweep of a stem through the jazz of leaves and berries; the frilly bits; angular forms with petaloid; wavy leaf areas with insistent lines (direction) of stalks and stems. I saw couples in juxtapositions of plants: the graceful with the awkward, the round and jolly with the thin and austere; young with old, not forgetting of course the changing microclimate of our lives, and which surrounds all growing things.'

And I wrote about becoming acutely conscious of the 'strata' of generations, of three lives at pivotal points. 'My mother, now 77, is having to readjust her daily life so that she doesn't collapse with exhaustion; my 17 year old daughter is experiencing new freedoms, making her own decisions and longs to travel; while she in the middle, aged 46, starts to wonder what life has been about so far and what is to follow . . . into old age.'

★ ★ ★

Chelsea Physic Garden, London's once 'secret' walled garden founded in 1673 for the cultivation of medicinal plants, opened to the public in 1983, and when in 1993 I read about a new one-year botanical painting course to be launched there the following January, I knew at once that I should apply. I would at last learn a technique of watercolour painting for a specific purpose, and learn basic botany. The course was to be led by Anne Marie Evans.

Anne Marie came from a distinguished French family and had studied painting at the Bath School of Art and Design at Corsham. She was not herself a botanical artist, which meant that she never gave demonstrations, preferring instead to give us guidelines and showing us the work of the great botanical artists of the past. Anne Marie was blessed with a warm, generous nature but she believed in discipline and instilled in us the importance of drawing a plant accurately in pencil before capturing its aesthetic qualities in paint. Accordingly, she stressed the need to understand aerial perspective (in fine art the bluing of distant landscape) and to apply paint in thin layers so that each additional layer could be carefully deepened towards shadow, magically creating a 3D effect. 'Darker!' she would say, as she walked around the room looking at our work. 'Darker!'

I was very excited and wrote to my mother enclosing details of the course and told her of my new passion. I hoped that she'd be pleased. Our relationship had not been easy: discontent on my side, tactlessness on hers. There had been years of destructive emotional turmoil caused by her affair with a woman my own age, but she always came to life in the company of artists. She knew many whose work now regularly sells at auction under the convenient and to me deadening label 'Twentieth-Century British Art': Roger Hilton, Rose Hilton, Patrick Heron, Bryan Winter in Cornwall, and in London William Scott, Frank Bowling, Sandra Blow – and Elisabeth Frink. I was in my teens when she first took me to Lis's studio in Fulham, a harsh, light-filled space thickly splattered with white plaster and smelling of Gauloises. I was struck by her white hands as she worked on her sculpture. Sandra Blow's studio further up the Fulham Road seemed to me dimly lit and dominated by a cast iron stove and immensely long flue. I looked at her large abstract works incorporating sand and charcoal, noted her repeated use of the diagonal arc. She and Lis would come to our parties at home, where my mother displayed their works in a lively mix: oils next to drawings, big next to small, high and low. It didn't matter. Preciousness was not part of my mother's make-up.

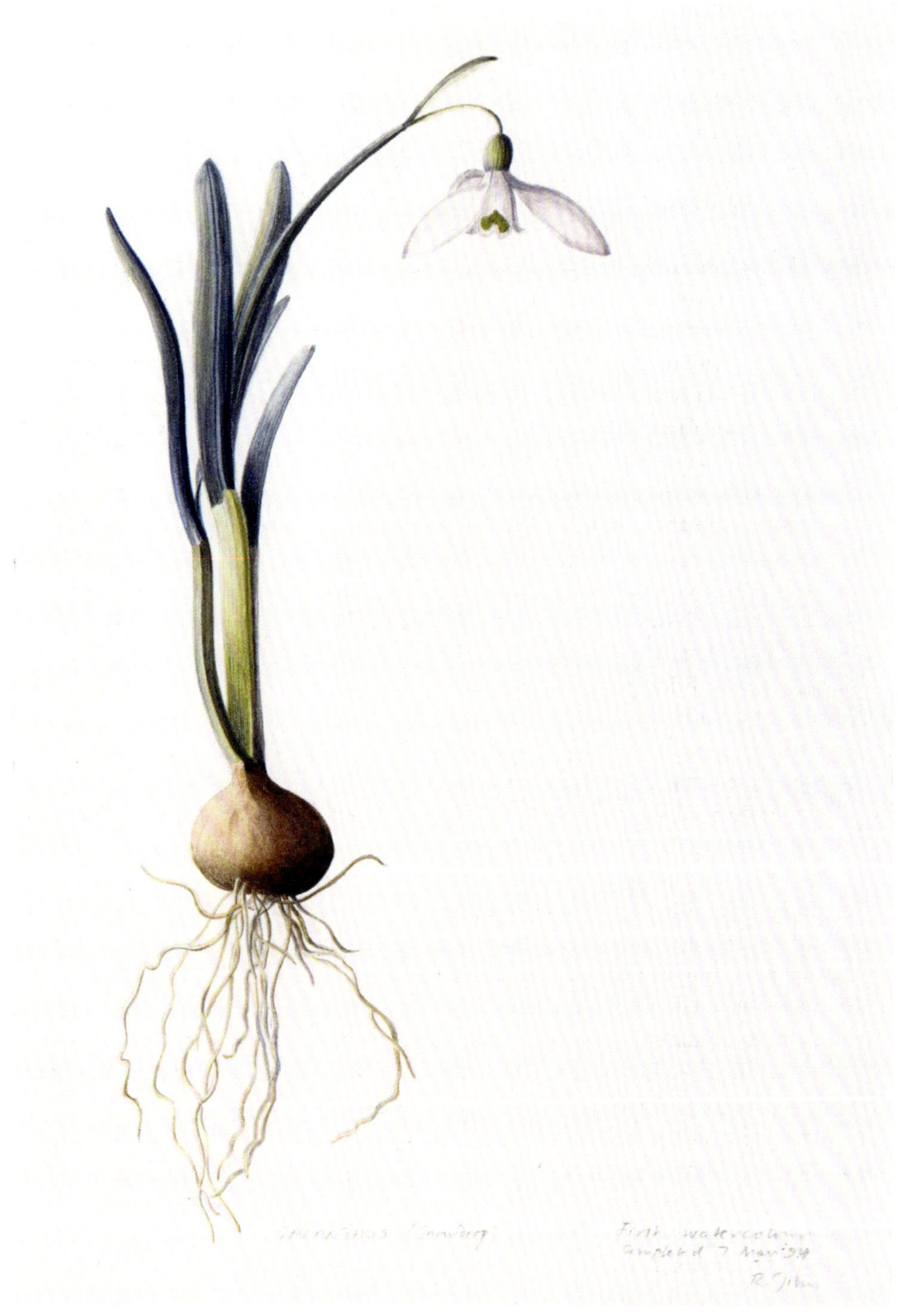

Snowdrop (my first watercolour), March 1994

I told her that every time I walked down Flood Street to the Physic Garden I felt a strong sense of satisfaction that what I was doing had always been inevitable. I'd walk past Rossetti House, where we'd lived in the late forties, and where my brother Phineas had been born in 1950, past the spot where a dingy privet hedge once grew. A great-aunt – her name was Luli – used to joke that it was a magnet for passing dogs and that I'd tear off the leaves and hold them up saying 'pretty flower'.

In March I wrote to my mother again:

> The course is proving wonderfully exciting . . . Last week we did the first two stages of watercolour painting (there are 6), practising on a snowdrop (!), having first drawn it in great detail as if it was a piece of engineering. Also made a visit to the Botany Library of the Natural History Museum where we pored over original Redoutés and Ehrets and work done on Cook's voyages. Visits are planned to Kew and the Fitzwilliam Museum. In two weeks we do two full days of pen and ink technique with a very scientific lady. It all sounds rather lightweight when you describe it, but it's a vast and very complicated subject, botanical painting, and I never ever feel bored or stupid.

With the help of the Order beds in the Garden, I learnt to distinguish between the two major classes of flowering plants, the dicotyledons and the monocotyledons (the smaller class characterized by blade-like leaves, for example the lilies), and to recognize the different characteristics of plant families. In the botany lectures we learnt to categorize the plant kingdom on ever-decreasing scales. I was easily thrilled: the revelation that a thorn is a modified branch (as in hawthorn), a spine a modified leaf (gorse) and that a prickle – the correct term – is comparable to a hair (rose) had me marvelling all the way home on the top of a bus. I felt faint relief too that I was merely brushing the science of botany.

As the course progressed, the work became more and more demanding. I was learning to paint in a very exacting manner – no doodling, no splashing or bleeding colours – and the technical brilliance of previous botanical artists meant that we aspired to an impossibly high standard. It was very easy to despair: to paint a leaf showing reflected light on a curved green surface while depicting its veins was my idea of a nightmare. Each time I started to apply paint to a drawing – work always began in pencil – a kind of fear overcame me. It was the same mix of fear and resolve that I'd felt when seated at the piano in front of a new piece of music to learn for an exam. But that required endless repetition, playing a phrase over and over again. With watercolour, no second chances, and it felt as if I was attempting the impossible. Added to this, there was no knowing how long a plant would last in water before drooping, and a bud might start to open or a flower start to drop its petals before work was completed. I soon found that it was a matter of risk – I'd plunge straight in without sketching, or making studies – and it took a long time to gain confidence or to feel even faint pleasure in the results.

On 7 April I wrote again:

> It's not that bad, but hard at problem times like Easter and Christmas, when
> I really feel very desolate indeed. I could have gone away but chose not to,
> and got lots of work done sitting in the kitchen with the grill on to keep
> warm. I had a whale of a time at the Spring Gardening Fair at Olympia and
> got talking with some very lively horticultural types. Reading through a
> catalogue of 'Hardy Ferns and Ivies' I decided I would suggest to the nursery
> that I illustrate their ivies as described in 'cream and green marbled and
> spotted leaves', 'an irregular yellow splash shading to pale green', 'heavily
> blotched and speckled cream' (and so on). I envisage a series of ghastly abstract
> paintings! Kandinsky and Klee are the two artists I find the most exciting at
> the moment – especially Kandinsky. I like asymmetry and the diagonal too
> (that's Japanese) and I wish to develop some ideas with all this in mind.

On the night of 23/24 April I had a most vivid dream. A landscape of black mud, a strange
taste in the mouth as I walked through it. A tortuous track, glistening black. Then, high
above the stormy landscape, a vision: a branch of star-shaped flowers, burnt orange colour,
waved in the wind against dark mauve storm clouds. I knew at once what this symbolized:
rescue, hope. The feeling of joy filtering into a scene of desolation stayed with me.

The last letter I wrote to my mother on 6 May was to tell her that I'd just successfully
mixed the blues of forget-me-not and bluebell. 'I am now on very intimate terms with
the surface geometry of the pineapple, and the anatomy of rosemary, scabious, hyacinth
and delphinium flowers. Hot stuff!'

The following week I was at work on the paulownia flower, mixing its mauve-blue
colour, when I felt a hand on my shoulder: 'Your daughter is on the phone.' Immediately,
a taxi was called at the Garden's expense and I rushed to University College Hospital
to find my mother in bed after suffering a heart attack. She had been staying with me
and was spending the day with my daughter, Iona, seventeen years old at the time and
with the day off school. Iona had coped with the emergency, called an ambulance and
accompanied her grandmother to hospital.

MARY JOHN

It was a great shock when my mother died a week later on 21 May. She was seventy-
eight and had not found it easy living alone in a remote cottage in Wales – she was
naturally gregarious, hedonistic – and, as with so many women of her generation,
widowhood had coincided with the onset of old age. She became increasingly
antagonistic and would say, 'I feel like an old dog that's had its day', forgetting that
many friends admired her for her outspokenness and generosity. I wrote about her,
immediately after she died, spontaneously, whatever surfaced without effort. I wanted

to capture her atmosphere, her sounds, her indomitability as well as her free spirit. This is what I wrote.

My mother died as she said she always wanted to go – 'with a bang' – and with an abruptness that was characteristic of her. 'Ye gods!' she'd say in exasperation, or 'You don't mean it!' or to change the conversation, 'Have another drink!!' She'd look at herself in the mirror and despair. 'Don't I look terrible,' she'd say, as she patted and ruffled her hair. 'Don't I look like the wrath of God!' and she'd give a great sigh. She often sighed – loud, gusty sighs of impatience, boredom, irritation.

She was famously tactless. 'I don't really think,' she explained, when I'd become exasperated with it all. 'I just say what comes into my head.' And so it was with her singing. She'd sing two lines of a song or little ditties that flew into her head as she moved around the house.

I'm an airman, I'm an airman
And I fly fly fly fly fly
Right up in the sky, ever so high
The sparrows they can't catch me
No matter how they try
Cos I fly fly fly fly fly fly fly fly fly

She learnt that from Caspar, who was a captain and naval pilot when they met and married during the war, in 1944. She used to play 'A Life on the Ocean Wave' on a wooden flute.

She never much cared for naval formality; when Caspar became First Sea Lord he had to visit foreign navies from time to time and I helped her organize herself for official trips abroad. In 1962 they flew around the world in a Comet (the first commercial jet airliner). 'MUM'S SHOPPING LIST FOR AUSTRALIA, NEW ZEALAND, HOLU-LULU [*sic*], SINGAPORE, FIJI AND AMERICA' I wrote in red biro on a scrap of paper that I found in a suitcase of letters after her death. 'Tweed perfume. Lipstick. Black dinner shoes. Walking shoes. Thin din. gloves – black? Tampax. Bra. Mascara. Pyjamas. Suspender belt. Thread beads.' Those thin dinner gloves – there was some trouble in New Zealand over them; she'd apparently gaffed by wearing the wrong length, or was it that the gloves shouldn't have been black? Hat, stockings, high heels; the dress always troubled her. On an official visit to India she was photographed wearing her hat back to front. In Canada she realized she'd left her handbag behind just as the aeroplane was taxi-ing for take-off – a motorcyclist was dispatched to retrieve it. In Rome, they were given a motorcycle escort through the city for their audience with the Pope. Dutifully veiled in black she bent to kiss his hand and received a 'great biff' on her nose with the huge papal ring. 'Poor Mary!' she'd say whenever she recalled the event, as if resigned to things going wrong, even when she thought she'd got it right. It was a relief for my father that all went to plan when she launched the submarine HMS *Finwhale*, the only time she spoke in public.

She could never be bothered with naval timing. The aim was to always arrive five minutes early, so any special 'do' such as a royal banquet in London inevitably gave rise to dreadful panic as she suddenly realised *the time*. I would do her face, zip up her dress, fasten her necklace, see her into the shining black car that waited outside our house like a thundercloud. After that it was just a question of following protocol. Dressed in 'longies' made up for her from material bought at Primavera, a shop in Sloane Street specializing in abstract patterns on silk, she would tell us afterwards what a beautiful skin the Queen had. It was something that really struck her . . . as it has many others. At one of these banquets she was seated opposite the wife of a visiting African dignitary who was wearing a gown printed with portraits of the Royal family. This meant that every time she moved, their faces were contorted into frightful expressions. Mary could barely keep a straight face herself that evening. She always delighted in life's surreal moments.

When she was seventy my mother moved back to the cottage that my parents had long ago bought in Wales, where she could forget skirts once and for all. She lived all year round in trousers, trainers, striped top or jumper, blue denim jacket with lots of pockets, neckerchief, beret. She would occasionally wear a full cotton skirt in summer with socks and shoes. Her kitchen became expressionist: nothing was hidden, nothing was arranged, nothing was thrown away or wiped down. Here she sat for hours smoking her roll-ups and reading the newspaper, a rounded, maternal figure at the midst of washing up, leftovers, rubbish buckets, cat and dog food, wine bottles, screwed up paper bags, *Spectator* and *Oldie* magazines, jam jars, greasy frying pans and scented geranium cuttings. A friend commented that you never knew whether it was breakfast, lunch or dinnertime. 'Bang it in the oven,' she'd say to anyone hesitating over the preparation of a meal.

She was a very good cook and learned the knack of leaving lunch to cook itself while drinking with friends in the local pub. At home in Barnes where we grew up in the 1960s, Sunday lunch was part of life. Lively, quarrelsome, all ages, we'd sit down to roast beef at teatime. The wine never ran out and friends stayed on till evening, when dancing might erupt to our 45s. When visiting admirals came for dinner – this happened fairly regularly as it was the First Sea Lord's duty to entertain once a month – she would cook rather daring dishes for the time – *moules marinière* and *coq au vin* from a recipe given her by Rolande, a tiny French lady living in the Lot et Garonne. She would light the brandy – whoop! – and do a little jump.

My mother always had a dog. Edwina, absurdly named after Edwina Mountbatten, was a neurotic brown-and-white Shetland collie who bit people's ankles and refused to be walked by anyone other than her. Later she found Nell. Nell was a black-and-white Welsh border collie who had been maltreated and so would cower or slink away from anything that moved. But those collies ran like hares. It was an exhilarating sight and walking the dog was 'a must' in Mary's daily life. After Caspar died she acquired her first male dog, a Jack Russell named Billie. He was eventually run over, so she got Bertie. Bertie was her last dog. He menaced the neighbourhood, killed a kitten and chased sheep – an unforgivable crime in sheep country. His bark hurt the head. She adored him. 'Given him some character,' she said. Bertie outlived her by several years.

My mother listened to music. She loved the drama of tragic opera and Wagner's *Ring*; Beethoven; dashing piano music and old jazz. She loved above all the female voice; Richard Strauss's 'Four Last Songs' and Berlioz's 'Nuits d'Eté' would send her. *'Marvellous!'* she would say with unusual emotion. She would play this music when I stayed with her in Wales and I will think of her every time I hear 'Four Last Songs', and cry.

She formed very strong attachments to women, certain friendships dominating all others for years. 'Men!' she would say, or, just as her mother had said, in a flat, unimpressed tone, 'That man', not bothering to use his name. Latterly 'men' became 'fellows'. 'What's that fellow's name?' She was very particular about fellows and became restless and uneasy in the presence of men in grey suits. From time to time she'd befriend a penniless young man, help him in some way, worry about him, give him a tenner. Many jobs at the cottage were done in this way.

She had a habit, when in conversation with people, of leaning forward in her chair and looking intently at their face. It meant that she was giving her undivided attention to what they were saying – her hearing was not so sharp – but I suspect it also had something to do with her sculpting days when, encouraged by her friend Elisabeth Frink and the sculptor Uli Nimpsch, she had sculpted heads in terracotta. She was considered very good, but years of family turmoil wore her down and she lost the urge. But she always remained fascinated by people's faces and liked to study the shape of a cheek, the length of the upper lip, the distance between the eyes. Hair too. 'Look at his hair,' she'd say in a withering voice. We were all done in clay, my brother, my sister and I, and made aware of our differing physiognomies. It was very sad for her that the head of her son, whom she adored, and who'd caused her so much grief, was accidentally knocked to the floor and broken into pieces.

But what of the young woman we children never knew? She would talk sometimes about her work during the war, when she was an ambulance driver based at the Old Bailey, and later working on the canal boats on the Grand Union Canal, transporting steel from London to Birmingham and returning with a cargo of coal, a three-week round trip. In her matter-of-fact way she described negotiating the locks and tunnels, the ordeal of handling ropes in freezing weather and how she was being courted by Caspar when he was on leave from the Navy – all of which has been entertainingly described by her fellow 'boater' Emma Smith in her books *Maiden's Trip* (1948) and *As Green as Grass* (2013).

She talked a little, but not much, about her unhappy upbringing. She never knew her father, Stuart Vanderpump, whom her mother, Margaret Cullen, had married in New Zealand. Margaret had sailed there in 1912, intending to find better prospects for the family – she was the eldest of twelve, their father a baker and confectioner. Stuart Vanderpump was interested in theosophy and the teachings of Krishnamurti. Very soon after Mary was born in 1916 her father began to suffer delusions and stopped communicating with his wife; she described his condition as 'a nervous breakdown' and committed him to an institution where he lived for the rest of his life. As soon as the war ended, mother and daughter made the six-week sea voyage back to England, where, to get over her shame at a failed marriage and finding herself a single parent, Margaret wasted no time in finding work and eventually built up a successful clothes business off Bond Street specializing in handmade silk blouses and Swiss-made suits for women.

Mary spent a lonely childhood in boarding schools and at the age of fourteen was sent to a Belgian convent, her mother believing that the Catholic faith and learning French would stand her daughter in good stead. Mary always claimed that she was uneducated: she summed up the level of teaching at the convent by describing a geography lesson in which a nun pointed a cane at the world's capital cities on a blackboard. In about 1933 she went to Berlin to learn German and made friends, but after eighteen months events forced her to return home. Her unhappy childhood, coupled with the discovery that her mother had hidden the truth about her father's mental state – she never forgave Margaret for this – caused her to rebel. We grew up with a mother who had turned against her own mother absolutely and without guilt, and who wore clothes that were an insult to her mother's fine sense of dress.

THE HOUSE BEYOND

After my mother's death, I began spending long periods at the cottage. It was in a poor state and I had to sort things out while at the same time completing my course.

'Ty Draw' – Welsh for 'The House Beyond' – sits twelve miles inside the Welsh–English border at the edge of the Berwyn Mountains. It is border country in every sense, where hills rise to mountains and fields merge with open pasture above the tree-line; heather moors stretch westward to the grander landscape of Snowdonia while eastward into England lies the Shropshire plain. (Continuing in a line due east, across Staffordshire, Lincolnshire, Holland, northern Germany and Poland, no land rises above 600 feet (180 metres) until the Urals in Russia.)

The cottage faces a dramatic escarpment named Craig Orllwyn. We name it 'the Ridge', while Mr and Mrs Breeze, dairy farmers living closer to its base, call it 'the Rock'. It was formed during one of the oldest named geological periods, the Ordovician; six miles away another volcanic escarpment forms the ledge over which the highest waterfall in Wales drops 240 feet (73 metres). There is the feeling of a landscape with an eventful past; wooded valleys and rivers are strewn with huge mossy boulders; rocky outcrops and hills change shape as you travel the labyrinthine lanes that connect isolated farms with villages: a flat-topped hill gradually becomes rounded; a long unbroken slope on the skyline disappears as it merges with distant hills.

Welsh is spoken in the village, which gives the feeling of being abroad; this feeling is intensified during hot summer months, when the hills turn brown and under a blue sky the landscape seems to change atmosphere, to become foreign.

The timing of my mother's death could not have been more significant. In one sense it was very moving; it was as if she had offered up the cottage at the very moment I needed a place close to nature where I could work. But it was also as if she had not died and left the cottage: I cooked where she'd cooked, slept where she'd slept; heard her voice, expected her to walk through the door after walking her dog over the fields and put on the kettle. There were moments when I thought I should leave, but instead of rising to the old antagonism, I'd make myself think of her wonderful cooking, her delight in making everyone laugh when playing her home-made tapes which cut skittishly from jazz – Fats Waller, say – to Rubinstein, to a heart-stopping Mozart aria; of evening sessions of *vingt-et-un* when her face lit up, and of her love of horse racing . . . how she'd jump up and down if a horse she'd backed was close to winning. I thought of her humour, her chivvying. It never became impossible for me to stay on: I was by now safe in the world of plants and wrestled instead with hawthorn and blackthorn, with tangled grass and leaves and the eternal problem of nature's green.

★ ★ ★

In that summer of 1994, I made a study of five species of the Leguminosae. This vast family appealed to me because much of it provides food and is economically useful (all peas and beans, lentils, alfalfa, clover). The Leguminosae bear irregular flowers described as 'papilionaceous' – think 'butterfly' – and in some species the stems are 'winged'. Naturally I began to think 'flight'; *Lathyrus* suddenly appeared to me to be flying across the page. I made numerous pencil studies of these 'winged' plants, lovely to draw and curiously liberating.

During a conversation with the biologist Rupert Sheldrake, who had made a study of Leguminosae in India, he suggested I devote work to plant families and call the project 'Meet the Family!' This prompted much mirth, and I jotted down a list of plants growing around the cottage under the heading 'Relatives!' I coupled the pretty honey-scented lady's bedstraw with rampant, clinging goose-grass; spotty-leaved lungwort with hairy-leaved borage; spiralling honeysuckle with tough, independent elder; frilly rowan with thorny blackthorn.[9] But it was too daunting to embark on a grand project at this early stage. I attempted only a fearfully difficult coupling of ash with lilac – cousins, if you like, in the Oleaceae family; having observed their behaviour in the garden, I noted that they shared a

---

9 The families Rubiaceae, Boraginaceae, Caprifoliaceae, Rosaceae.

propensity to spread themselves effortlessly, the ash by self-seeding, the lilac by sprouting suckers. The difficulty was to paint the numerous tiny florets of the lilac flower in subtly darkening violets and mauves so as to portray the fall of light across the flower head. I failed at this, but later that year I made a painting of an altogether different character in the same family: symbol of peace, oil-rich, biblical, the olive spoke to me of pure goodness. I've painted around twenty olive branches, and one now rests in a drawer at the National Museum of Wales.

★ ★ ★

One day at the Chelsea Physic Garden I met the botanical artist Gillian Barlow. We fell into conversation and she invited me back to her flat in Pimlico where she promised to show me her paintings.

A flight of steps led down to a door which opened into a book-lined passageway. Gillian worked at a table in a room with a window below street level; there was a bed, and a plan chest where she stored her paintings. A cosy study was lined with books floor to ceiling; at the back a kitchen, and a yard with an outdoor loo. I felt immediately at home. Gillian opened the chest and one by one dropped her paintings on to the bed, the only free surface. I looked in some amazement at the sheer quality of the painting. This work was highly skilled and took long hours – days – of solitary concentration, testing physical and mental strength. We went into the kitchen where she cooked on an ancient speckled enamel gas stove, the kind that stood on legs, older even than mine. Bread and cheese, a bottle of wine. What was her story?

Gillian had attended the Slade and later lived in New York where she began to concentrate on painting plants for an interior decorator. Needing the money, she remembers selling the paintings 'as a job lot'. Not long after we met she was given a solo exhibition at Spink, art dealers in St James's. It was heartening to walk into the gallery on a snowy December night and see paintings of spring- and summer-flowering plants and an exquisite group of small works on vellum. Gillian became an RHS gold medallist and a valuable and much-loved teacher at the Chelsea Physic Garden. Today she undertakes commissions for Kew and works on a regular basis for the College of Arms, where she is a heraldic artist specializing in decorative borders of plants and animals for grants of arms. She would sometimes call in while crossing London on her bicycle, carrying her vellums rolled up in a bag, and we'd have long and sometimes sharp discussions about 'bot art' and the problems of plant representation.

When I despaired of leaf painting I asked Gillian if she would give me a demonstration. We used an ivy leaf. I watched her tiny brush strokes follow the rise and fall of the leaf's dimpled surface, carefully darkening the shaded parts and leaving the vellum bare where light had caught the surface (later to be toned down with the faintest wash). Veins were defined as if nestled in a valley. Within minutes the surface of a leaf had appeared from empty space, like magic, and I saw at once what to do.

II

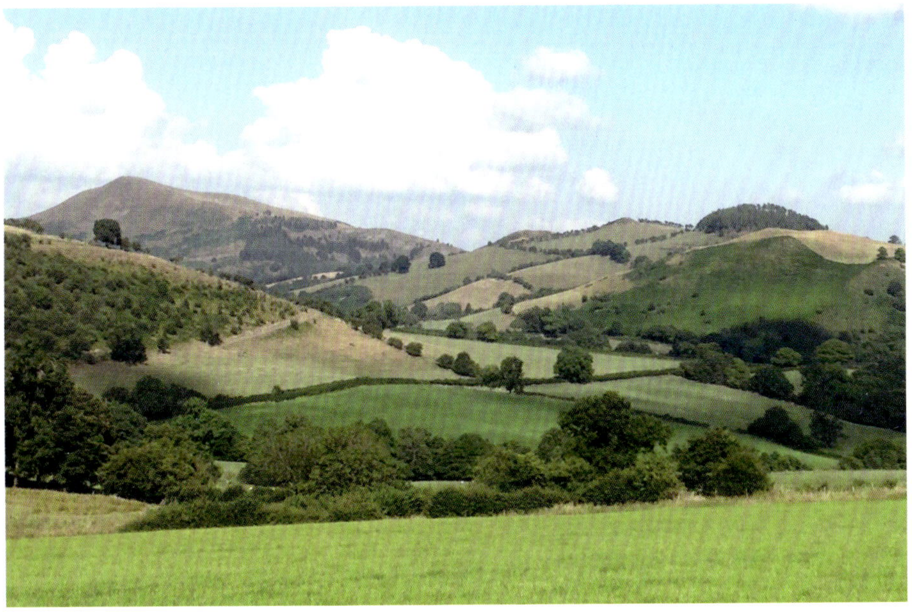

Summer in the Berwyn foothills

1995

I spent the long hot summer of '95 in Wales, discovering new details in the landscape and getting ever closer to the trees and wild flowers of the lovely Berwyn country. I was experiencing so many new sensations that I began writing notes and diary entries to accompany each new painting and to keep up with my thoughts.

★ ★ ★

I find I'm dividing the living from the dying, the defined from the undefined. Take a fern. It speaks to me like this:

LIVING	DYING
Greens	Browns
Symmetry	Asymmetry
Uniformity	Abandonment
Predictable	Unpredictable

The two states perfectly illustrate Pablo Casals's dictum: 'Fantasy with Order'. In musical terms, the living fern is mathematical, contrapuntal, Bachian: it is highly ordered and fearfully difficult to paint successfully. In its dying state, the fern is being released from its structured existence and becomes fantastical in shape: disordered, asymmetrical, rococo; the relentless green gives way to yellows and browns. The question is whether to paint the abstract in great detail with impeccable technique, or with a loose brush/arm. Within the pattern created, there must be areas of dry paint and wet paint.

AUGUST

Long summer grasses are collapsing along the bank. I pull out a handful and twist them into a knot. In an instant I see an object that I want to paint. I take another,

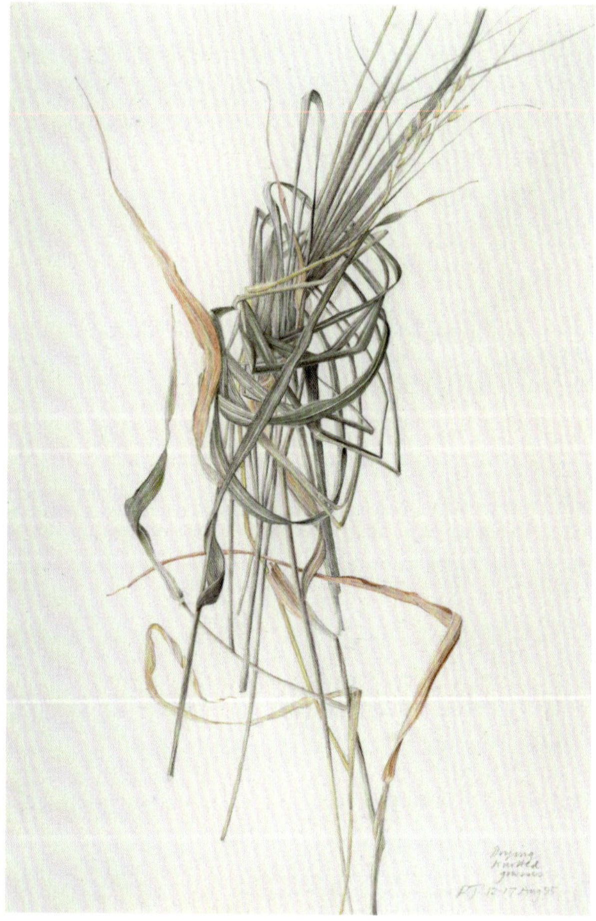

Drying knotted grasses, August 1995

bigger handful, which takes six days to map, to define the blades of grass, first in pencil and then in thin layers of paint, and as I work I trace a single straw-coloured stem through the knot, which I elect a thread of gold. A memory comes back: the delight at seeing a nineteenth-century Russian dress embroidered with straw, which was used as a substitute for unaffordable gold thread. Straw-work. The drying knot of grass, now fading to dusty greens and coppery browns, takes on a metallic look and I begin to think 'sculpture'.

SEPTEMBER

An apple tree had been planted over the spot where Ida's ashes are buried. That autumn it was heavy with red apples which made a lovely contrast with the silvery tree lichens: the indeterminate forms of old age contrasting with the rounded forms of youth.

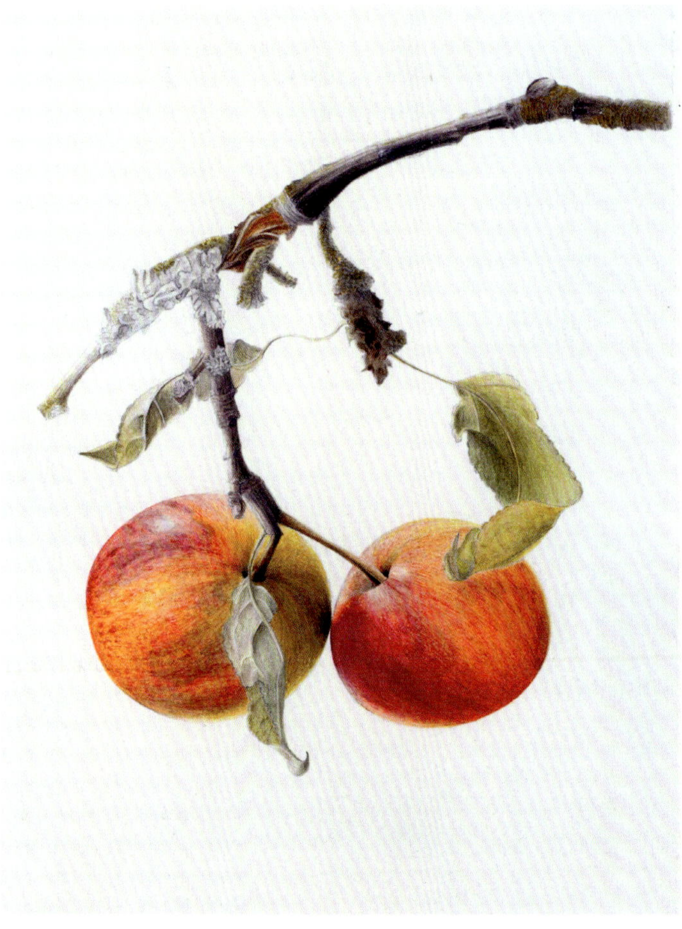

Apples on a branch, September 1995

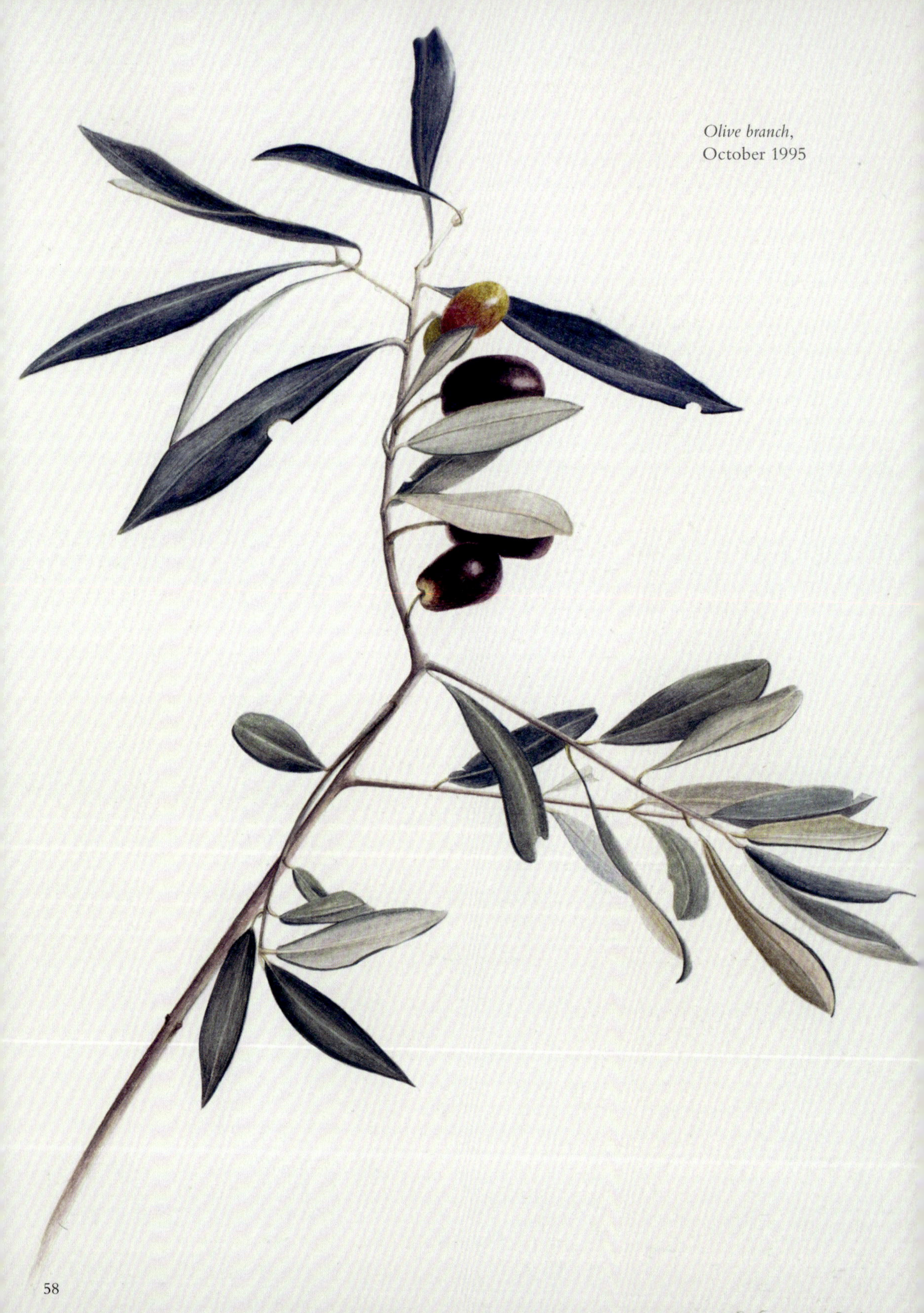

Olive branch,
October 1995

OCTOBER

I began painting my first olive branch sitting outside in warm October sun in the South of France, and finished it indoors during a thunderstorm. It did not worry me that the warm light changed to a thundery gloom; it made it more exciting to paint. Back in London, in November light, I painted another olive branch from the hundred-year-old tree in the Chelsea Physic Garden. I was so enthusiastic about my subject that I did not stop to think that I had laid it on the table upside down: the olives in the painting are defying gravity. I showed these with eight other paintings at the Alpine Club Gallery in an exhibition of work by students who had completed the first botanical painting course. A barrister and a solicitor each bought an olive branch. I commented that lawyers must like olive branches. 'Yes,' came the reply, 'but they're not good for business!'

1996

JUNE

Having spent the first half of the year curating an important exhibition of my grandfather's drawings, which I had assembled in groups to reveal his habit of working in series, I returned to Wales to catch summer's long light days, when I could begin work at 5 a.m. and continue till 8 at night.

As I walked around the garden a brave fennel shoot emerging from last year's brittle old stems caught my eye, and I embarked on a subject that seemed to metamorphose as I painted it. Whatever I began seeing – a fantastic sea-going vessel, or fabulous winged creature – there appeared a strong forward movement. I dared to add a wash – I did not know how to do washes – to imply this forward movement, and panicked, so I started a second version. I learnt very quickly how the eye 'adapts' to 'seeing': the plant has only slightly altered in appearance – I'd chipped off some earth – but I am noticing more detail, measuring distance, adjusting angles. A new experience.

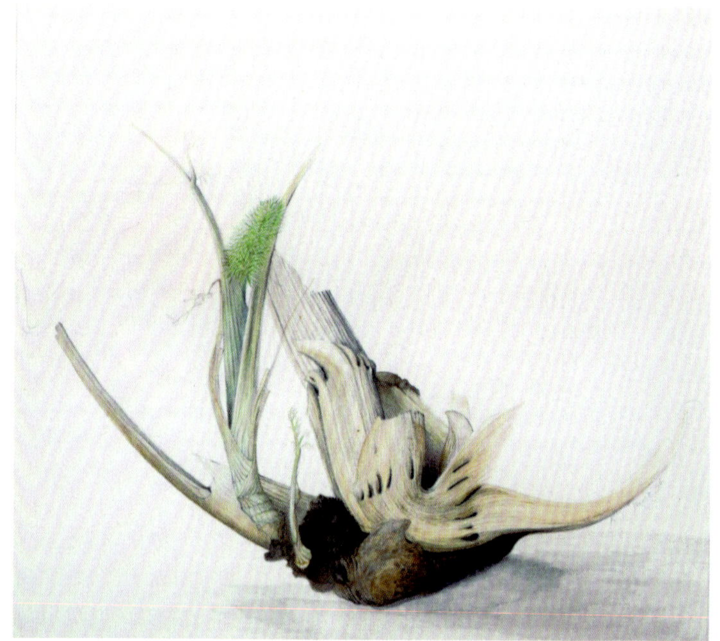

Old fennel stems I, June 1996

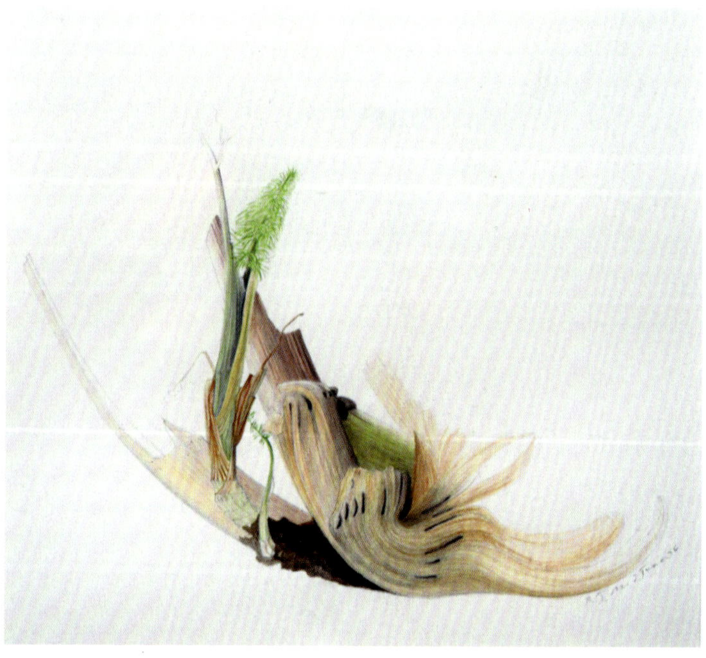

Old fennel stems II, June 1996

AUGUST

I loved alternating the upright stems of grass with their falling, twisting blades. It was not until I saw bluebells in flower the following spring that I recognized the ghostly form of the seed head in the living plant.

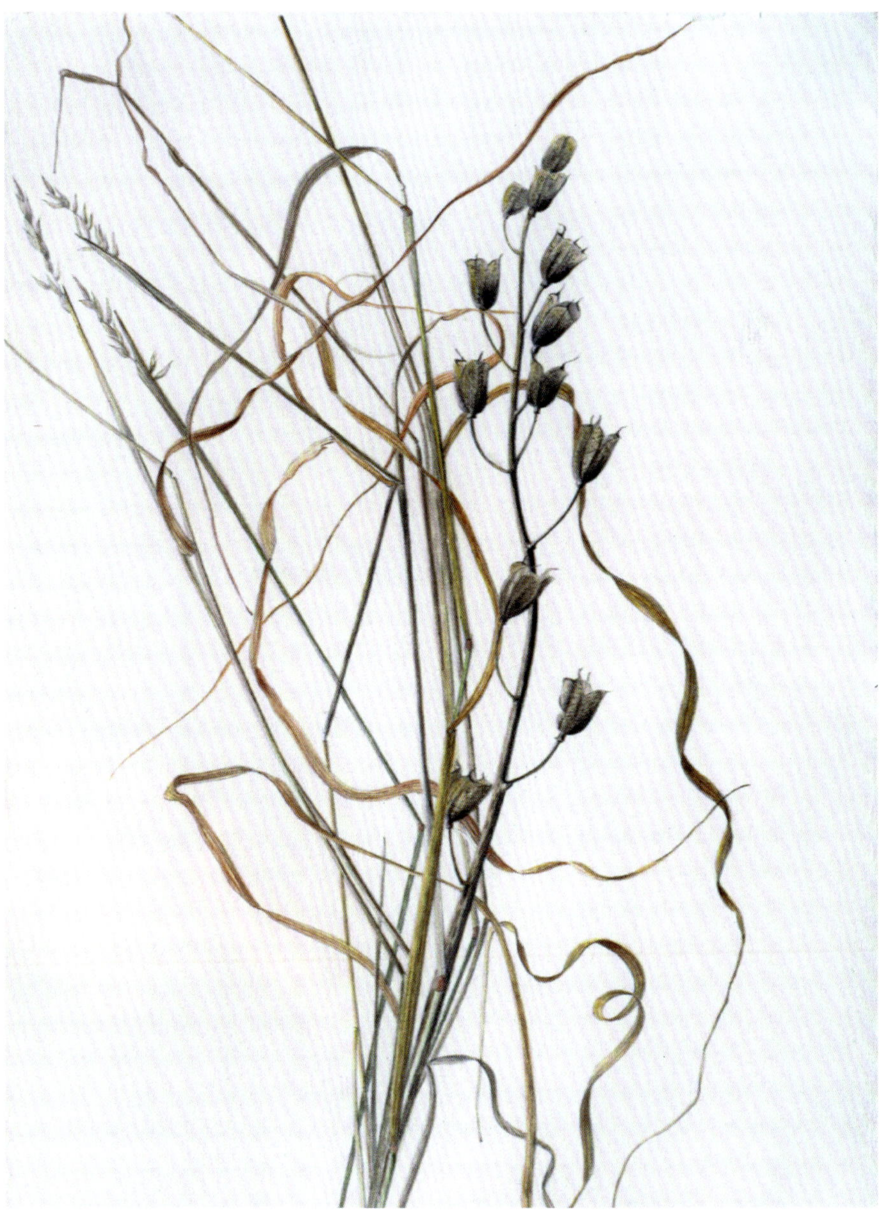

Bluebell seed head and grass, August 1996

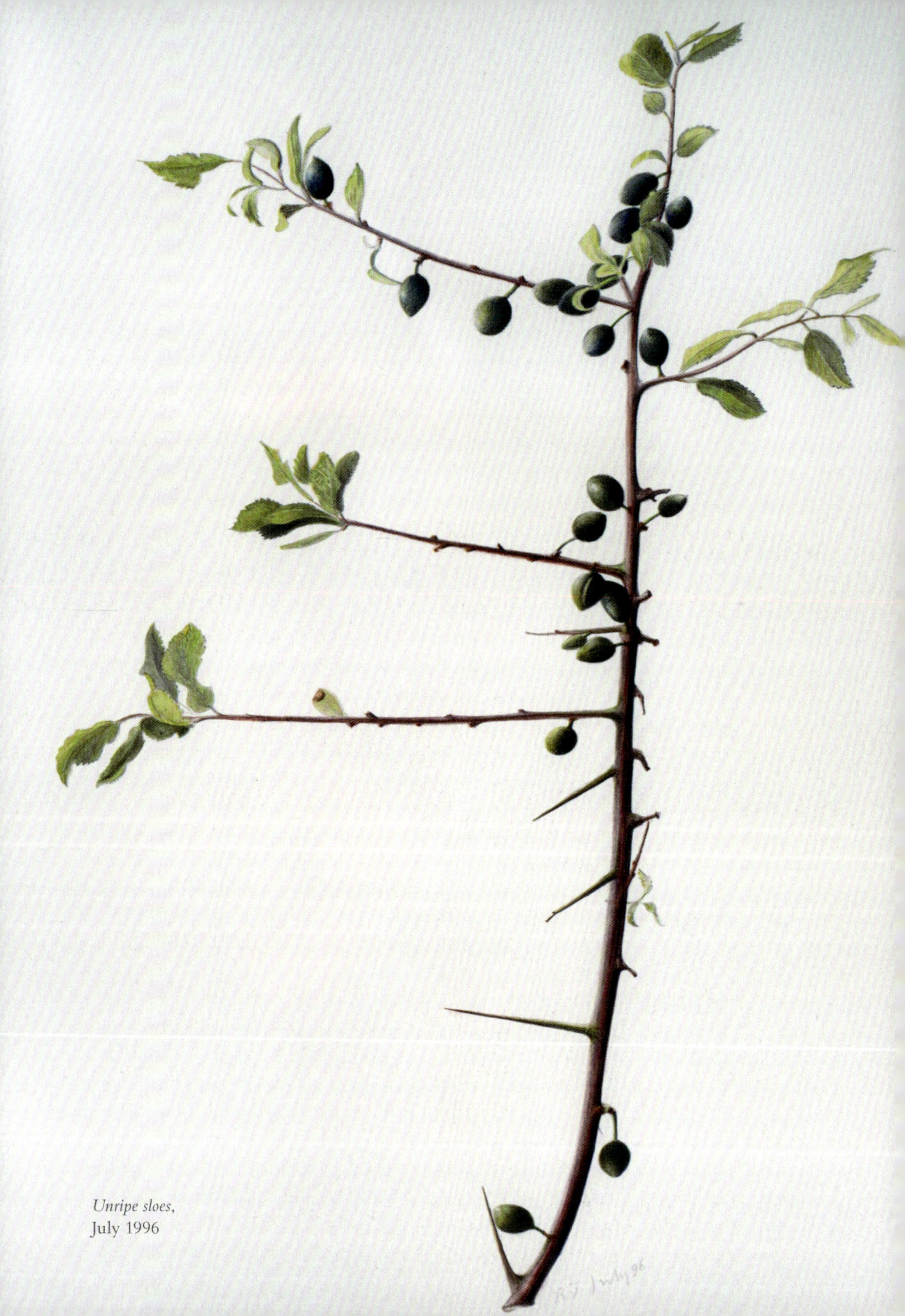

Unripe sloes,
July 1996

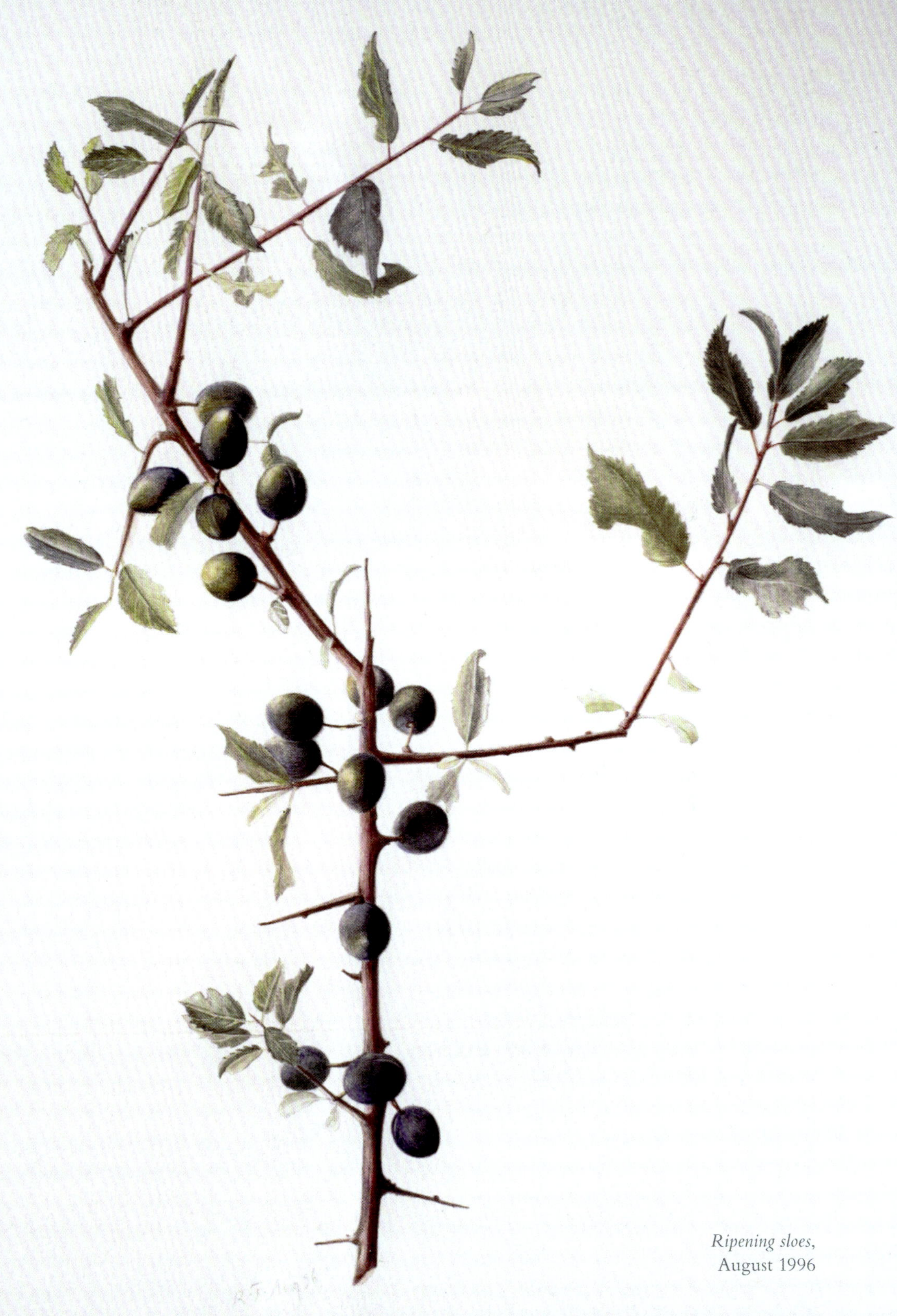

Ripening sloes,
August 1996

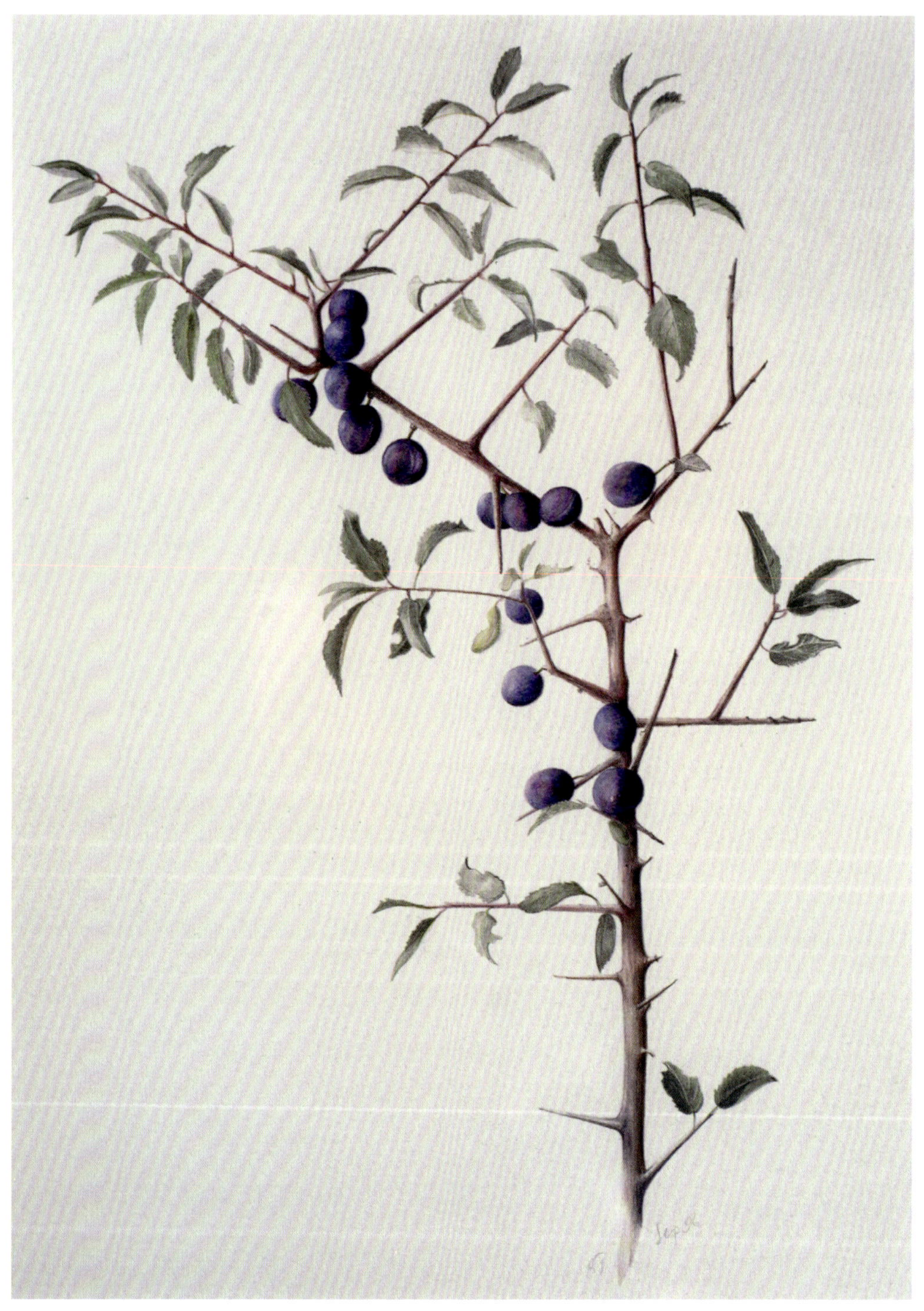

Ripened sloes, September 1996

SEPTEMBER

There is no field hedge without blackthorn in these hills: spare, gauche, a maze of right-angled stems and thorns horrible to contemplate, it becomes distinguishable from its companion, hawthorn, when it is the first to flower in early spring. Blackthorn's fruit appears as a small, hard, unappetizing green berry that, over summer, slowly swells into the inedible blue-black sloe, prized for flavouring gin and memorialized in poems by Dylan Thomas and by Gerard Manley Hopkins in 'The Wreck of the Deutschland'.

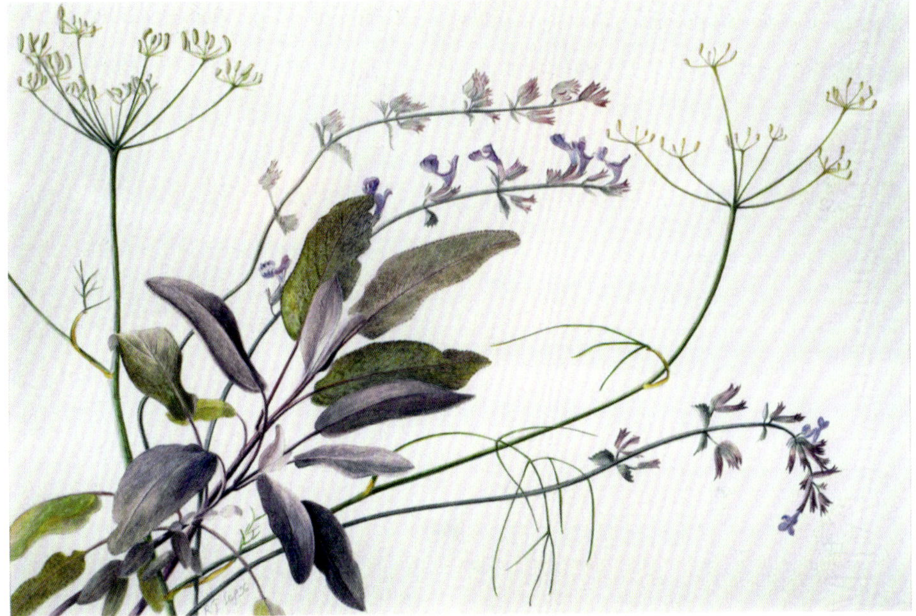

Fennel, sage, catmint, September 1996

A spray of plants appears to me to be suspended, but not still. It is as if a gentle current of water, not air, sways the plants.

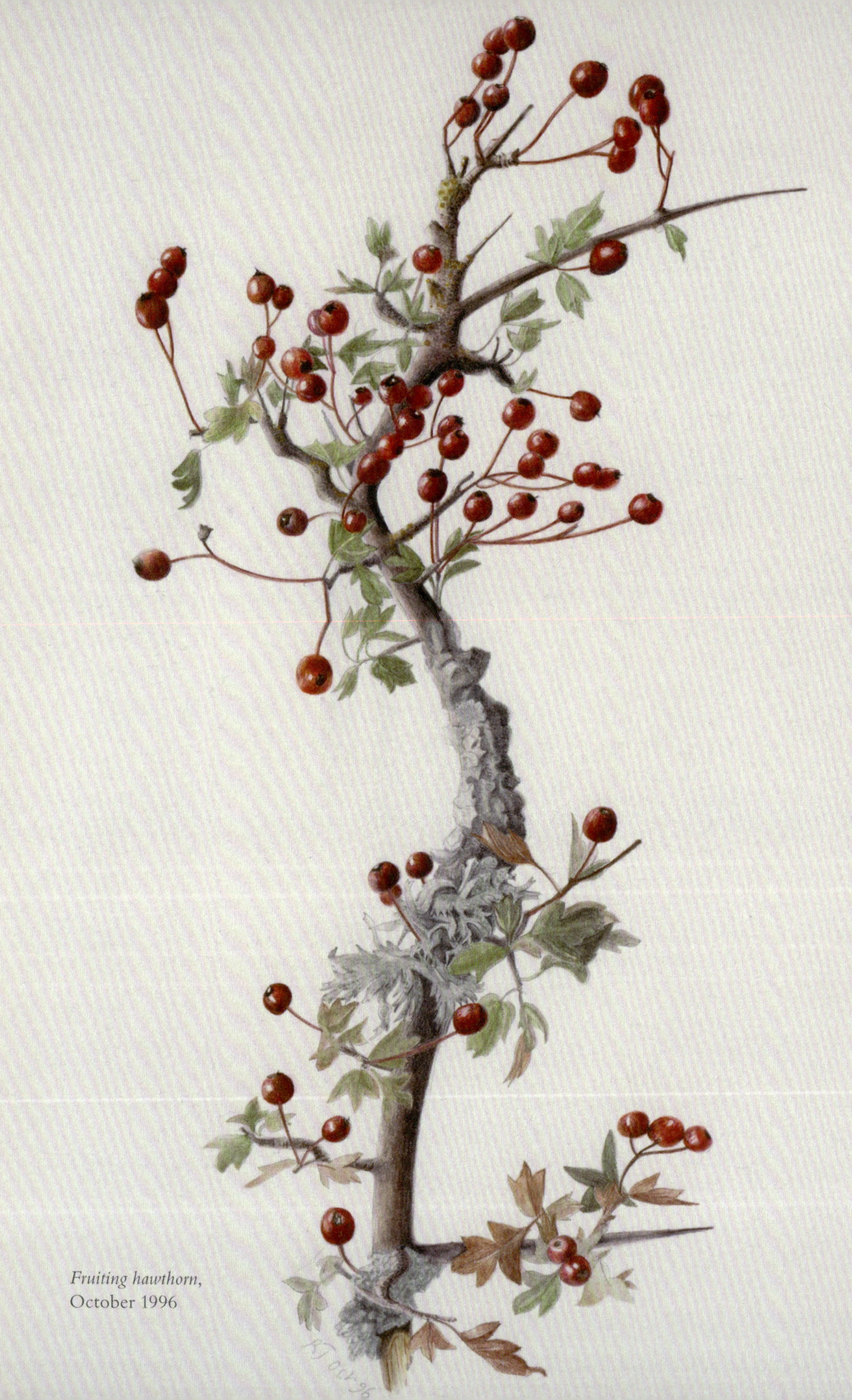

Fruiting hawthorn,
October 1996

OCTOBER

A hawthorn tree growing by a stream was thick with red berries sparking upwards, as if on fire.

★ ★ ★

A dream: Running. How I ran – blissfully, in slow motion and at great speed, over grassland, skirting tree tops. An unexplained energy, a hidden power, never tiring, but running . . . in long, long strides . . . and came to a stop staring into the eyes of Lucian Freud: clear, blue, steady, without fear. No need to interpret this dream: I had met Lucian years ago when I was drawing plant details. He showed me the painting he was working on at the time – the view from his Paddington studio, *Waste Ground with Houses* (1970–72). I looked at the heap of rubbish, then at the painting – I admired the bleak reality and wondered how it was possible to paint decaying rubbish over a long period of time. I understood nothing about painting in oil and was too in awe of the artist to ask. Years later, I happened to walk by his oil painting *Two Plants* in Tate Britain. I was at first stunned . . . then bemused by the simple title which belied a complex intertwining of stems and leaves, all greens and browns, which filled the entire canvas: living leaves, dead leaves, shiny leaves; large and small, each leaf individually painted. I could not understand how it was done, until I read that it took three years to paint (1977–80). This made a mockery of the rules pertaining to botanical art, whereby leaf curl can spell the end of a painting in a day. Watercolour does not allow a reworking.

★ ★ ★

The exhibition of my grandfather's drawings had opened at the National Museum of Wales that summer, and afterwards travelled to Spink in London, and on to the Royal Cambrian Academy, Conwy, on the North Wales coast, where it opened that November.

Conwy is built on a hill at the mouth of an estuary opposite the island of Anglesey. Encircled by turreted walls and dominated by the ruins of its massive thirteenth-century castle (eight towers, four turrets), steep streets lead down to the water's edge and at its centre is Plas Mawr, a magnificent Elizabethan merchant's house. The drive to Conwy was spectacular; I never tired of crossing the mountain ranges of North Wales. I would occasionally stop to take a walk and think of Turner and the English watercolour artists who, prevented from journeying into the Alps during the wars in Europe, had travelled here in their quest to capture the beauty of mountain scenery and the drama of ever-changing light and weather effects.

At Conwy, it had been decided to turn the exhibition into a family affair. I was asked to contribute the work I'd done over the summer, which would hang in a separate room with works by Gwen and a cousin, Tamsin John. I strongly resisted the idea. 'Never! Never!' would I exhibit alongside my grandfather and the idea of exhibiting was far from my mind anyway. But I gave in under pressure and on the crowded opening night all reservations vanished as, one by one, the paintings sold.

1997

31 JANUARY

I have been in intense and exhausting contemplation with leaves and stems, light and shadow; with changing tone and colour; with round forms, sharp forms, abstract forms. Here is my devotion. A meditation. Thinking the plant.

I don't think I have revealed to anyone the experience of the last two to three years. When I work alone I exist differently. And when someone comes along, or the

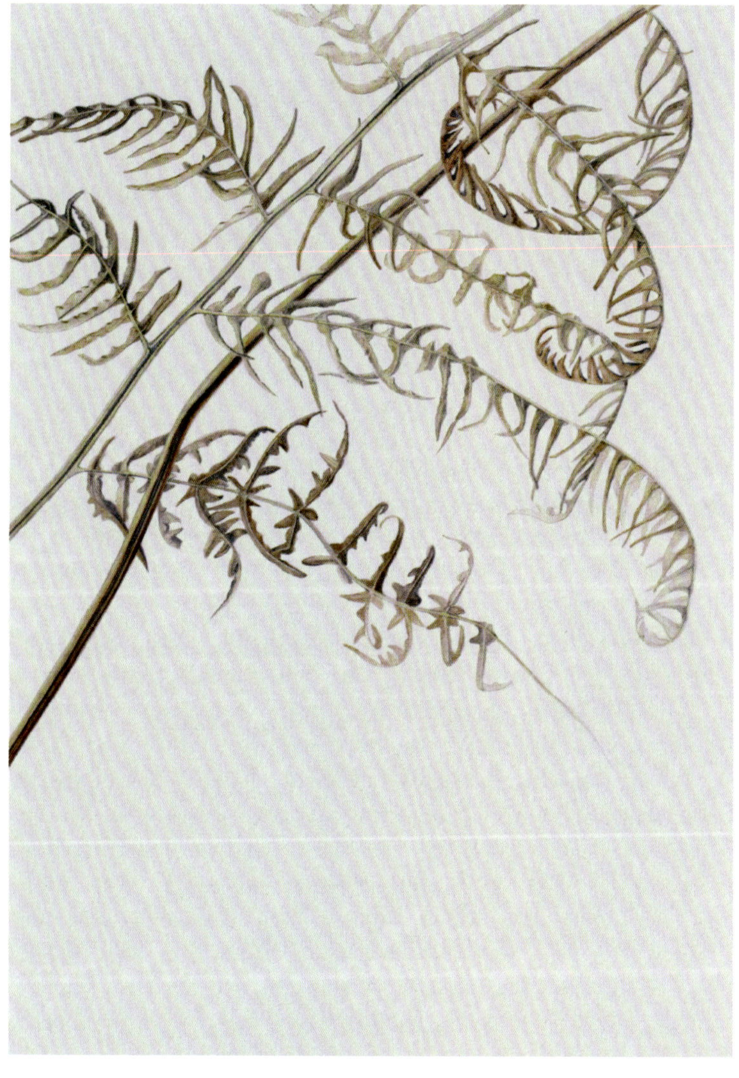

Dried bracken, magnified, February 1997

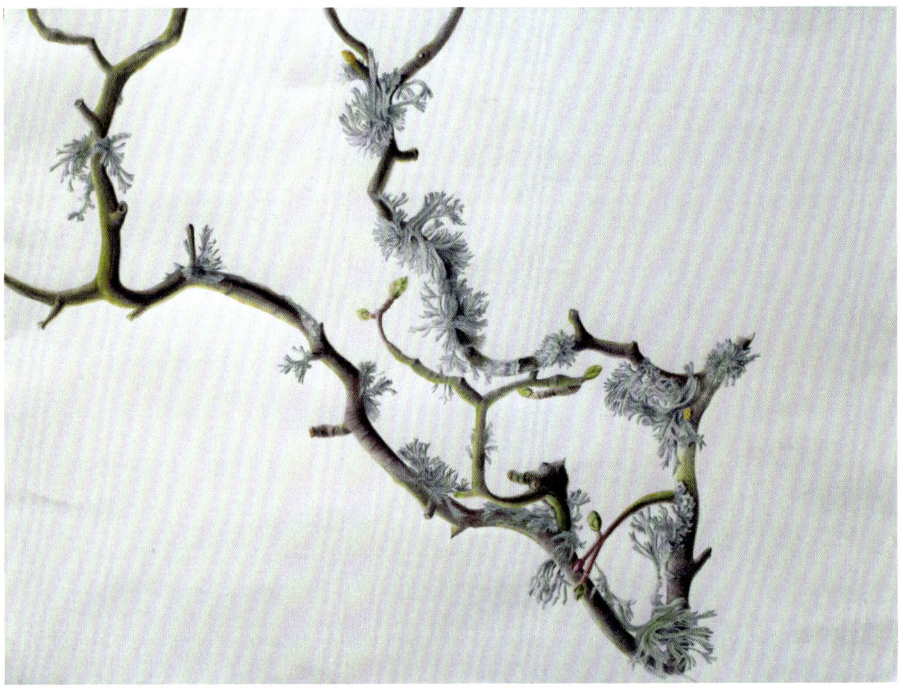

Lichens on sycamore branch, March 1997

phone rings, I am no longer that person. I become material, feel mundane. Have to speak in sentences, which is difficult.

★ ★ ★

Spare, bleak February. The hedges and banks are frilled with dead bracken; striped, curling, broken bracken. I place a frond beneath the magnifying glass and something very beautiful is revealed. I draw what I see through the glass, and as I paint in brown monotones the bracken seems to float and partly dissolve in space; becomes atmosphere in which I discern wisps of smoke metamorphosing into some unidentifiable underwater plant. I am losing my way, but the strong diagonal of the stem keeps me on course.

In March winds I am walking over tired grass beside rushing water. At this time of year the tree lichens are bright and visible; the soft rain sets them winking among the bare branches of an old sycamore tree. I jump up to snap off a branch and decide on the spot that this is to be my next painting.

I had no idea how I would mix the silver-grey or paint the individual strap-like thalli which grow in dense mats. Sycamore branches lack grace; curved when young, they zigzag with age. The most difficult painting to date.

A sage bush planted by my mother had grown leggy with age. I propped the cutting in a glass of water and for two days I could not get started. Then at night, in low electric light, I looked across the room and saw at once my next painting. Perhaps it was the firelight playing on the leaves, the sense of being locked in with bad weather outside. The form took shape in the dim orangey light.

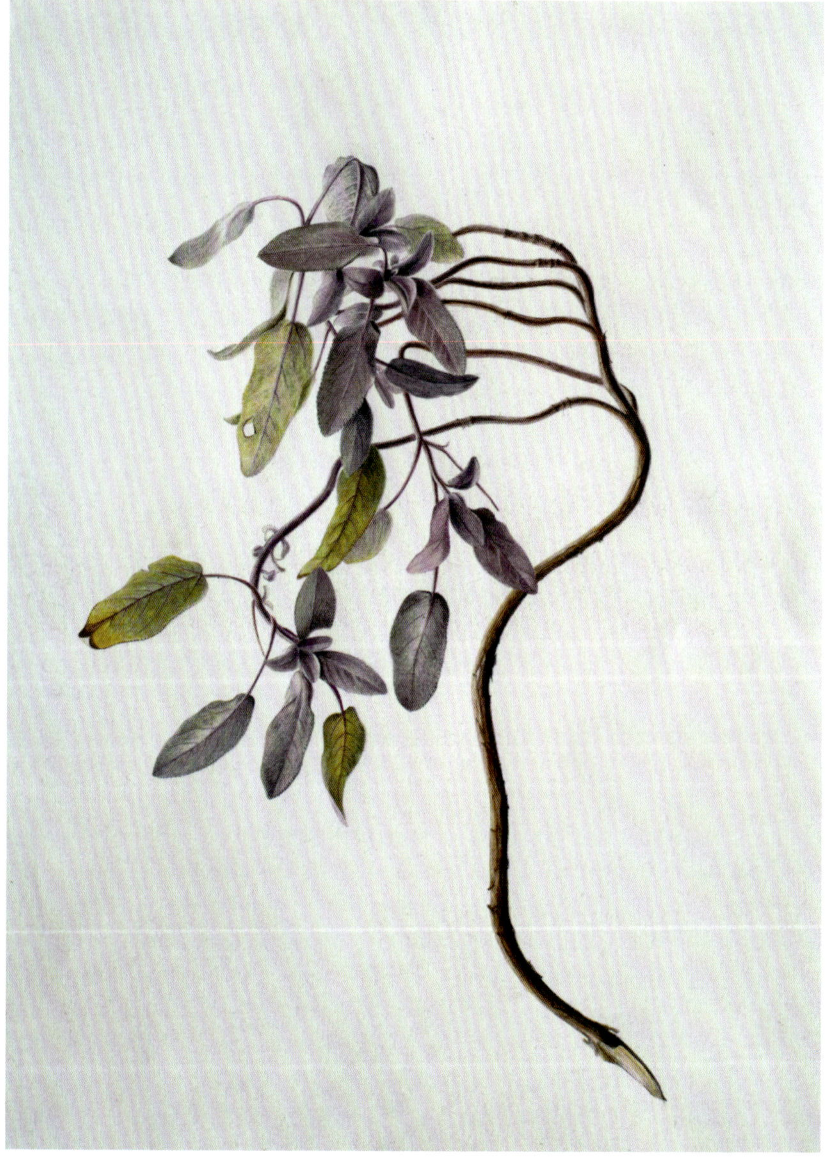

Purple sage, March 1997

APRIL

Walking along the river, a broken branch lying in grass seemed to leap up at me, a living filigree in green and silver animating dead wood. What was that netting? As I painted, the image of a female torso emerged: thigh, torso, nipple, armpit. The 'netting', I later learnt, was created by insects living beneath the bark.

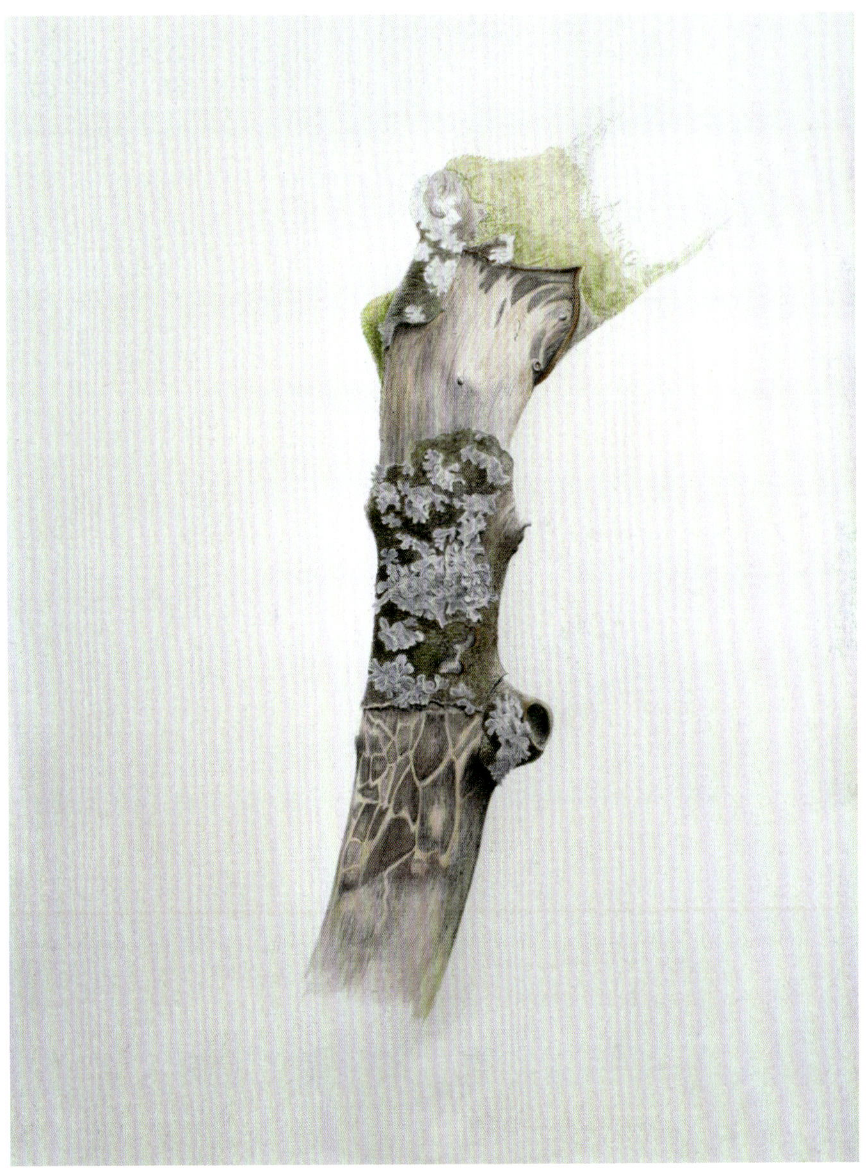

Fallen branch, April 1997

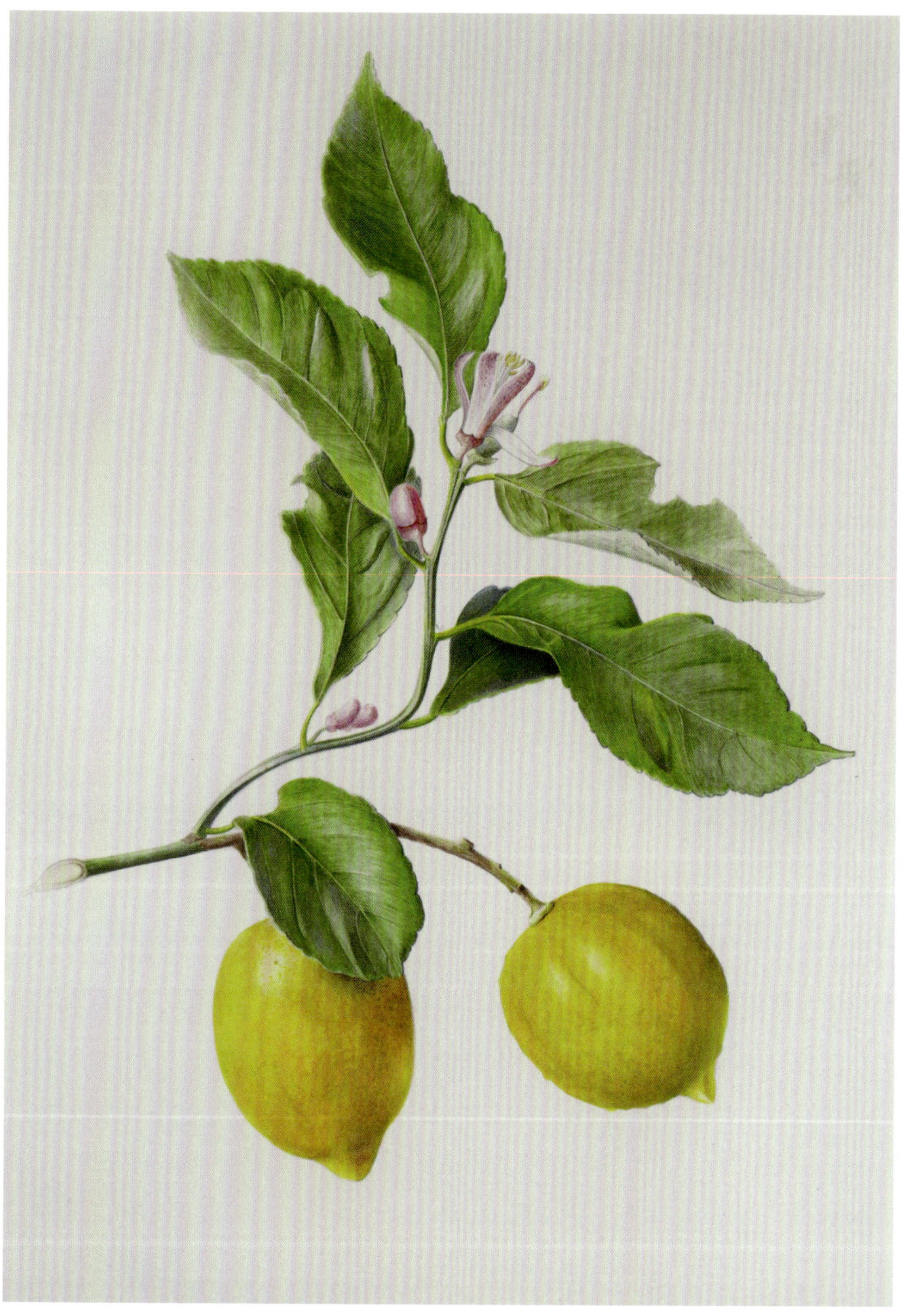

Lemon branch, May 1997

MAY

SOUTH OF FRANCE

The bold round shape of lemons, the antithesis of calligraphic grey-green lichens. I mixed minute quantities of differing yellows, taunted by the way this colour deepens to an ochre in the southern evening glow, and turns bright lemon yellow in the morning light. I was learning so much about yellow that I soon became 'yellow blind'. I moved on to the leaves, and then the unthinkable happened: I dropped a brush loaded with green oxide on to the naked paper at the top right. Horror! Green oxide is an opaque, staining pigment impossible to remove from paper. There was only one course of action, or so I thought: since I could not conceive of turning the green stain into a butterfly I dabbed some opaque white over it. Never mind the poor result . . . the bright lemons hold the eye.

JUNE

A world become simple, severe; a feeling of serenity. In Richard Fortey's *Life*, his book about the history of life on earth, there is a passage describing the four-thousand-million-year process of bacterial slime coagulating into mats, and ultimately into man. It seemed miraculous, and I begin to see everything in the environment as a miracle. It is a miracle that I am *walking* . . . along a *path* . . . to a *garden gate* . . . to get in a *car* . . . to drive down a *lane* . . . to a *village* . . . to buy a *loaf of bread* . . . in a *shop*. The ink on the page of this book is a miracle. The green covering of the landscape appears suddenly to look newborn. The centuries-old ash and oak trees in the landscape appear as fluff; mere windblown fluff atop 480-million-year-old rock.

The country is bursting with wild flowers, but I have no desire to paint them. Instead I return to the old sycamore tree by the stream and take a lichenous branch home to examine under a magnifying glass. What I see is unearthly, strange . . . other-worldly. I become irretrievably lost in the growth pattern of *Evernia prunastri* (oak moss), and embark on a series of magnified details. I am transfixed: lichens are a symbiotic marriage of algae and fungi which lichenologists have divided into three main types – bushy, leafy, crusty – giving them the most exotic-sounding names: bushy *Evernia* and *Ramalina,* leafy *Parmelia* and *Xanthoria*. Crusty *Graphis scripta*, so named for its resemblance to an ancient script, forms on smooth tree bark as if on paper. Many lichens cannot survive in polluted air, and I think 'How beautiful!' The thicker the lichens on stone, heath, tree, the cleaner the air. A vivid image comes to mind: back in the years before the Industrial Revolution, a solitary horse and rider are travelling through a landscape speckled russet, orange, yellow; blue-green, grey-green, white. I am in celebratory mood, but an eerie calm persists. Looking through the glass gives the impression of peering into still, clear water – and I feel I am intruding into a secret world.

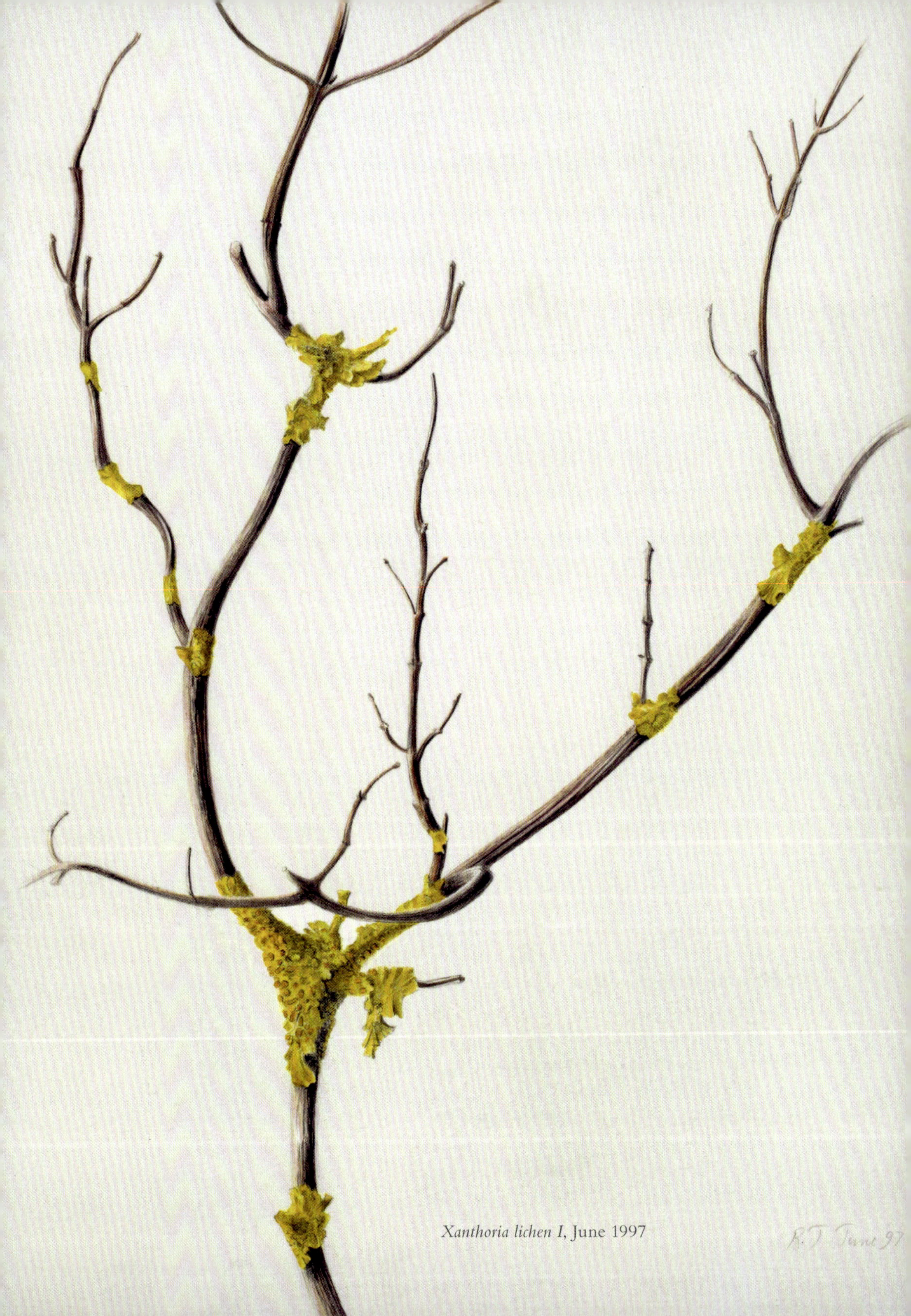

Xanthoria lichen I, June 1997

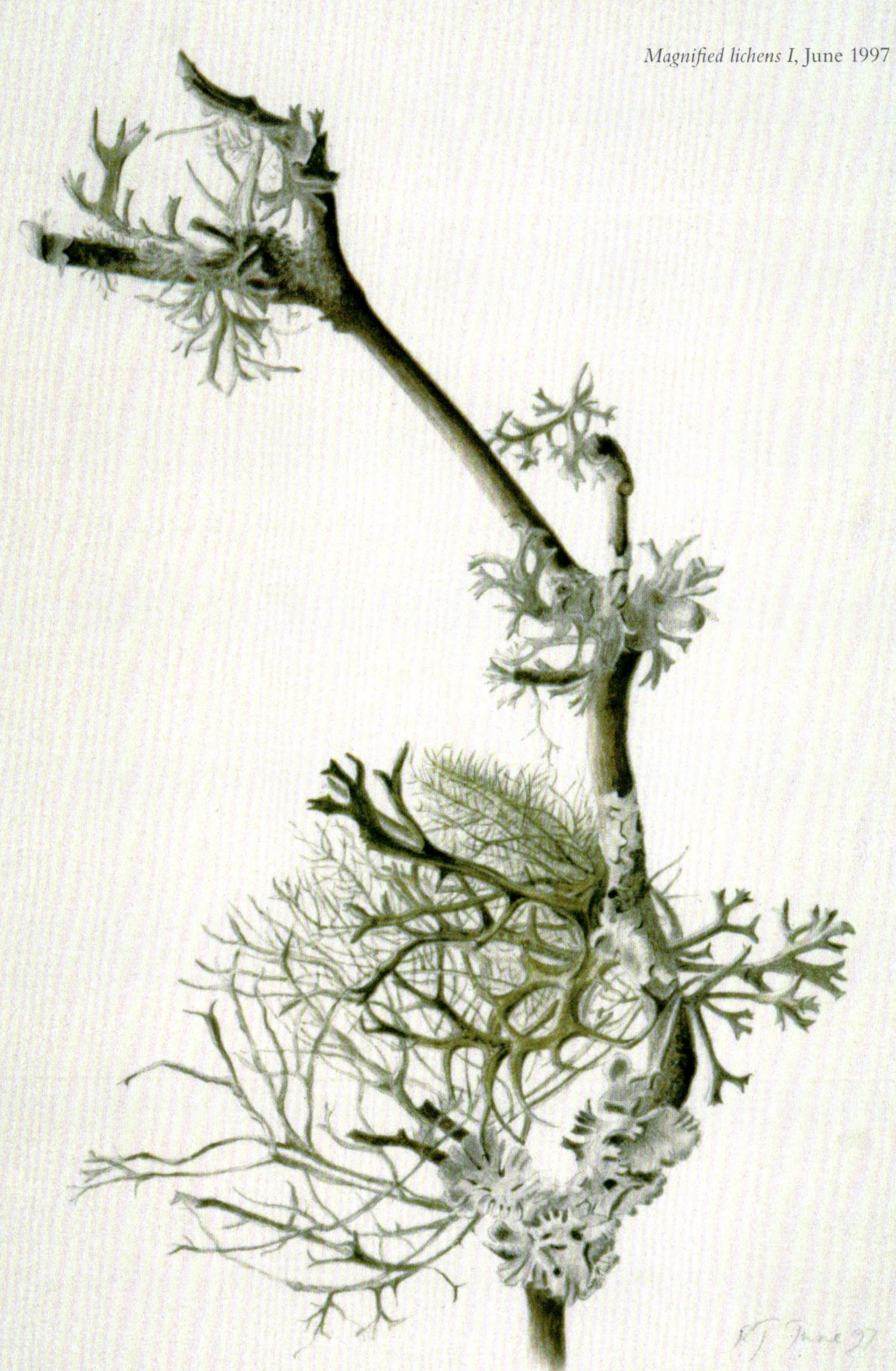

Magnified lichens I, June 1997

MIDSUMMER

Cold, cold, cold. Began work at 6.30 a.m., while a cock pheasant stood in the field squawking as if he had hiccups. I am in awe of the foxglove. It grows singly or in pairs; in groups or in vast colonies, as we humans people the earth. Explored the area between Llansilin and Penybont. Narrow wiggling lanes. Sudden views of bare rocky hillsides sloping into grassland, which disappear into dense groves. Cream, brown and black cows grazing. Sheep. Everything dripping wet, lush. Long June grasses, trailing dog roses, vetch, campion. An abandoned farmhouse, a track lined with ancient box. A cow giving birth in a field. I was travelling through a tapestry.

JULY

And now I'm travelling through the hills of the English/Welsh border to a remote property on the edge of the Black Mountains. A friend has asked for a painting of a plant that she can associate with Charity Farm and its owner, my cousin Ben. It is a bleak, windswept place overlooking the great sweep of the Olchon Valley. Wall pennywort is growing out of a drystone wall bordering a stream. I sit in front of the wall looking for a long time at the plant and decide I must include the stone. Nothing happens. I am spent, cannot face another plant; cannot adjust to painting a life-size plant after the complexities of magnified tree lichens. I walk around the house. An old knife is lying on a table. Something makes me want to try and paint it, perhaps because in Ben's world – down to earth, rustic, no frills - a good French table knife had a lot more going for it than wall pennywort. It is stained steel with a bone handle, bought in a flea market in Paris.

I've never painted flat abstract pattern before. Here are stains and light bouncing off steel. It seems I am painting a thunderous sky with gaps of blue. This is total freedom within the narrowest of spaces. Freedom with order. I feel liberated, and it occurs to me that I am liberating the knife from the context of the still life. French, Italian, Spanish, Dutch; how many still lifes feature a single knife lying on a table next to food?

In the months that follow, everyone wants a knife painting.

AUGUST

Sultry heat. A thunderstorm, evening. The setting sun unusually bright as thunder becomes louder and lightning streaks through a slate sky. I stood in the garden, listening to a live broadcast of Beethoven's Ninth – L'Orchestre Révolutionnaire et Romantique. Very dramatic. Bryn Terfel's entry made me shiver. I am painting a handful of mixed grasses for friends living nearby. I am exhausted, but the thunderstorm re-energizes me and I have to work fast as the light is fading.

22ND AUGUST

Daughter Iona, ever loyal, arrives on a coach to be with me on my fiftieth birthday. We drive to Llanarmon down the long straight drover road lined with bent hawthorn trees. We watch a rainbow swell and brighten in the valley below. We are looking *down* on a rainbow.

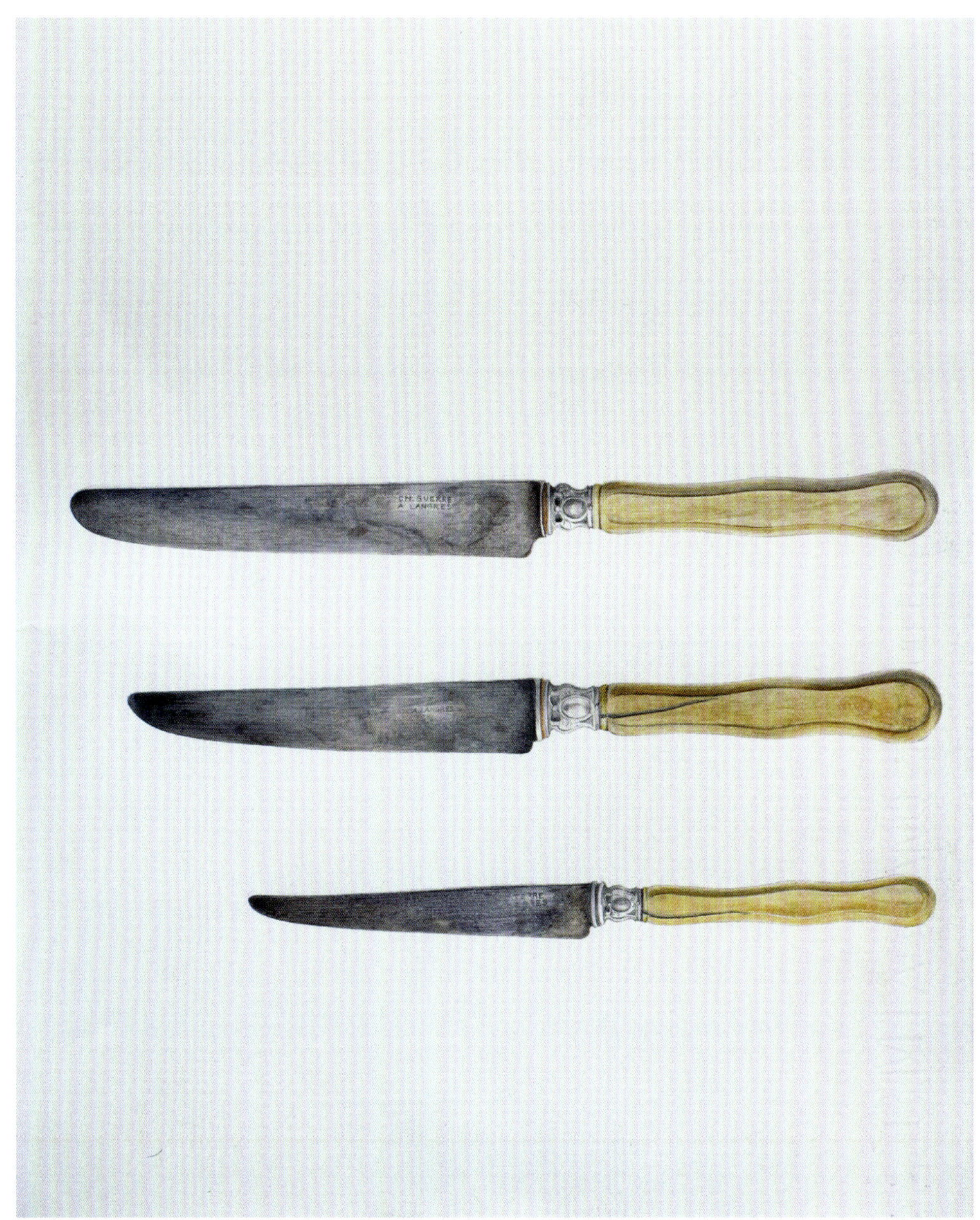

Three old French knives, July 1997

SEPTEMBER

A gold-pink morning; at 7 a.m. a three-quarter moon high in the sky. In the garden, the eglantine rose has blown down, filling the air with the apple scent of its leaves. Nearby, the scent of jasmine; in the hedge, honeysuckle, and walking through the cottage, wood smoke; all this in a small patch of unprotected hillside ringed by fields of grass. Collected sloes and yellow *Russula* fungi.

OCTOBER

Balmy autumn days. Picked rowanberries, wild plums and sloes. Made sloe gin and bottled the plums in vodka. Finished a painting of hawthorn, at once pretty and vicious.

   Dazzling sun. Walked up Elen's way above the little church of St Garmon while the bell tolled. Collected hawthorn branch for second painting. Towards evening, after working, everything seemed still, clear. The only sound an isolated birdsong

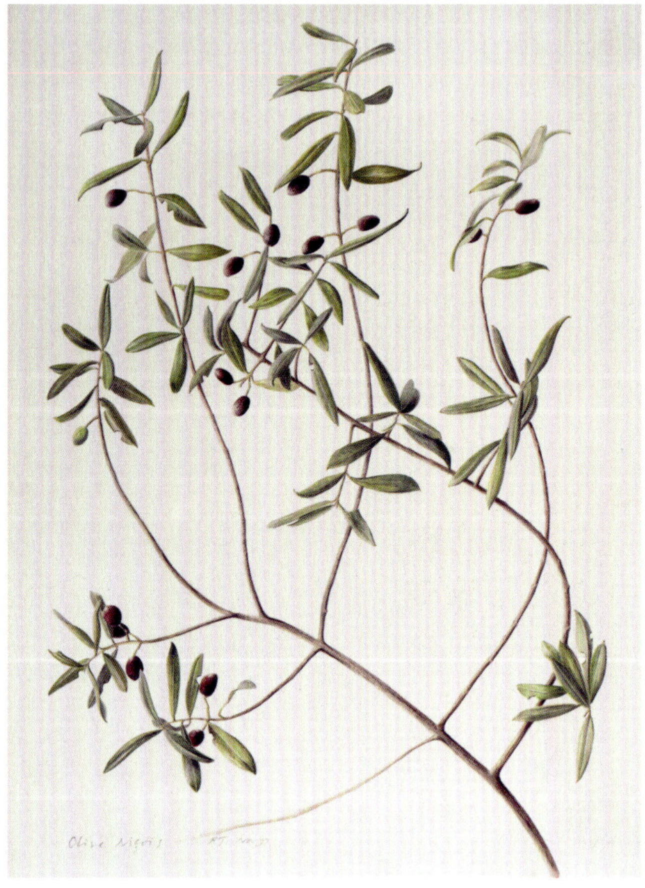

Olive niçoise, November 1997

echoing loudly in my head. After a week's solitude country sounds sharpen, carry new meaning.

2 NOVEMBER

My aunt Poppet's funeral in Ramatuelle, in the South of France. Nerves, emotion, surprises. The start of new friendships. I travel home on the high speed train from Provence and on to Waterloo with a branch of olive *niçoise* sticking out of a plastic bag, leaving a trail of olives in the Paris metro as I run through the tunnels between trains. I sit in my London flat in November gloom painting the olive branch, reliving the days surrounding the funeral – the sparkling blue sea and sky, the kindness of friends, the church service and procession to the village cemetery – and since this is olive-harvest time, I start another painting of a pair of branches from the hundred-year-old tree in the Chelsea Physic Garden; it is a fatter, more luscious species of olive.

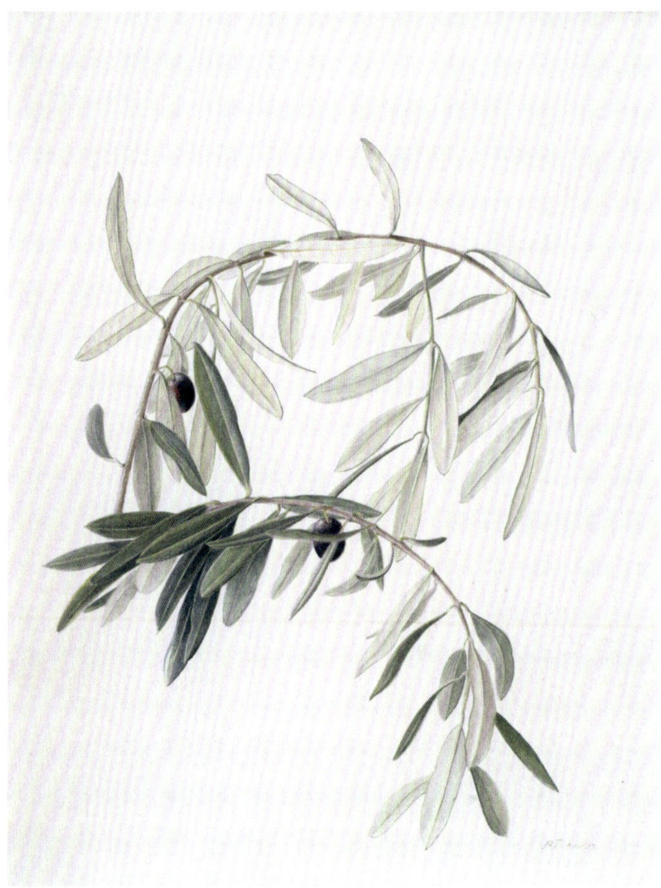

Olive branches, November 1997

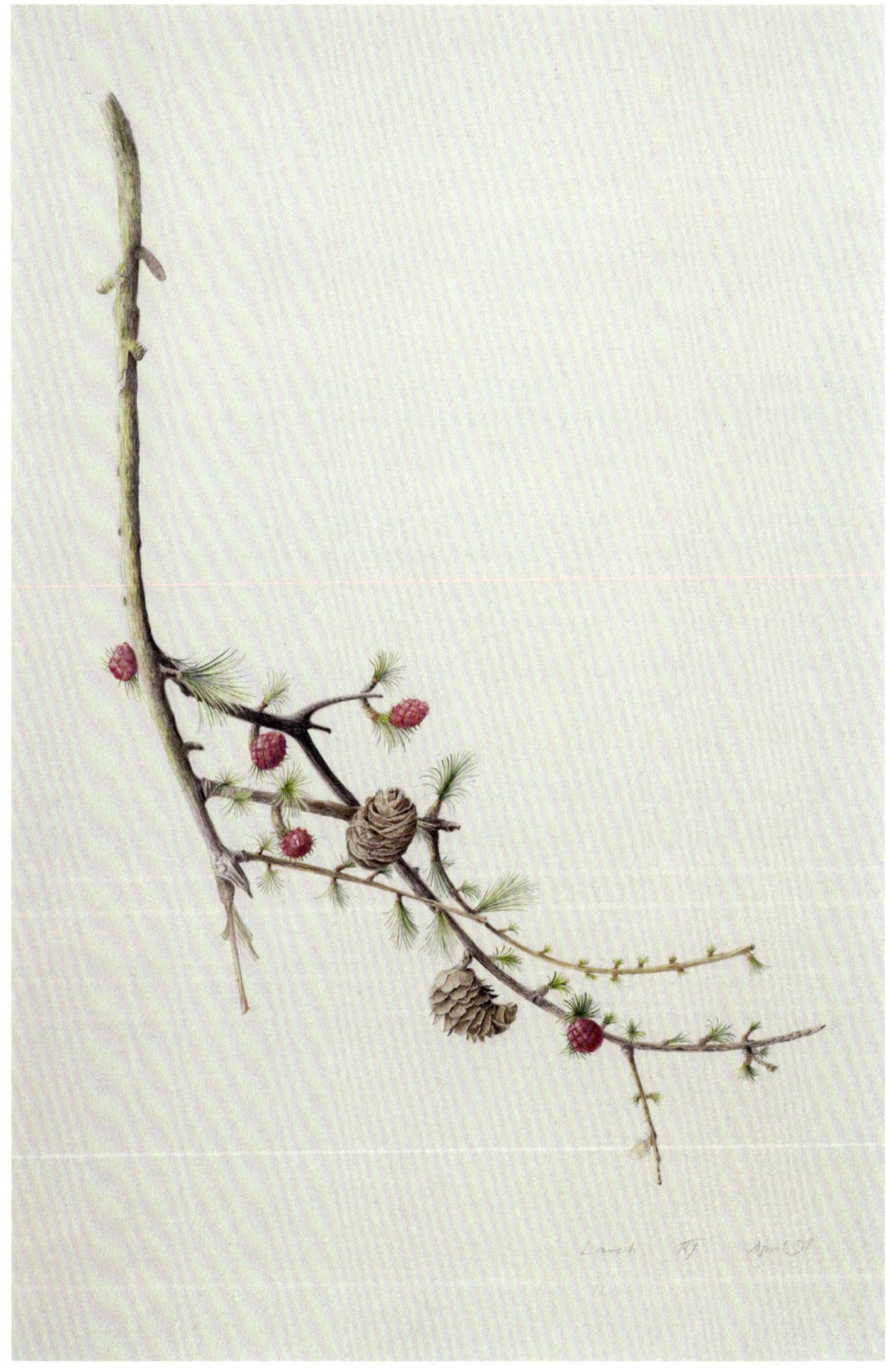

Early spring larch, April 1998

1998

MARCH

The wind has blown and snow has fallen. Illness. Wind whistling through end windows, which are falling out. Days like these precede greater resolve.

Clocks forward and now there are lambs in the fields, primroses, and blossom on the wild fruit trees. It's as if we are emerging from a dark cupboard and I feel a disorienting rise of energy.

Work begins for an exhibition at the Lefevre Gallery in May 1999. The Lefevre Gallery, established in the 1920s, has dealt mainly in Impressionist and established twentieth-century artists, but over the years has occasionally given exhibitions to little-known artists. This gives me the opportunity to show the world that a botanical painting does not have to be a polished watercolour of a tulip.

APRIL

A blackbird singing outside, Webern's music inside, at equal volume. More snow, and north winds. A white Easter.

I have never peered into a larch tree before. At this time of year little raspberry-pink cones are forming along the sad downward sweep of its branches – all greens and browns – a surprisingly cheerful note in a tree associated with melancholia.

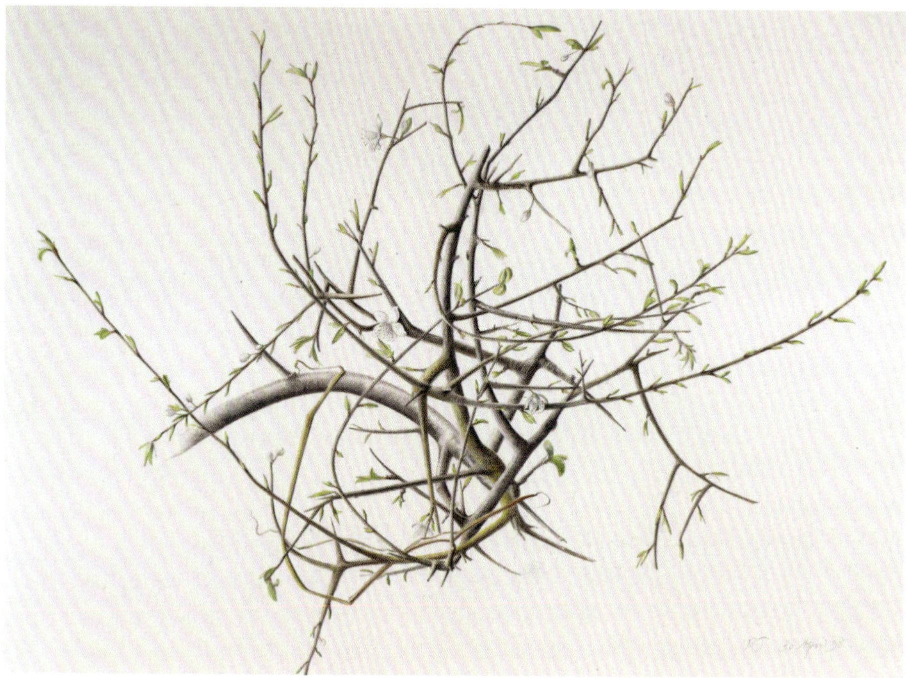

Spring blackthorn, April 1998

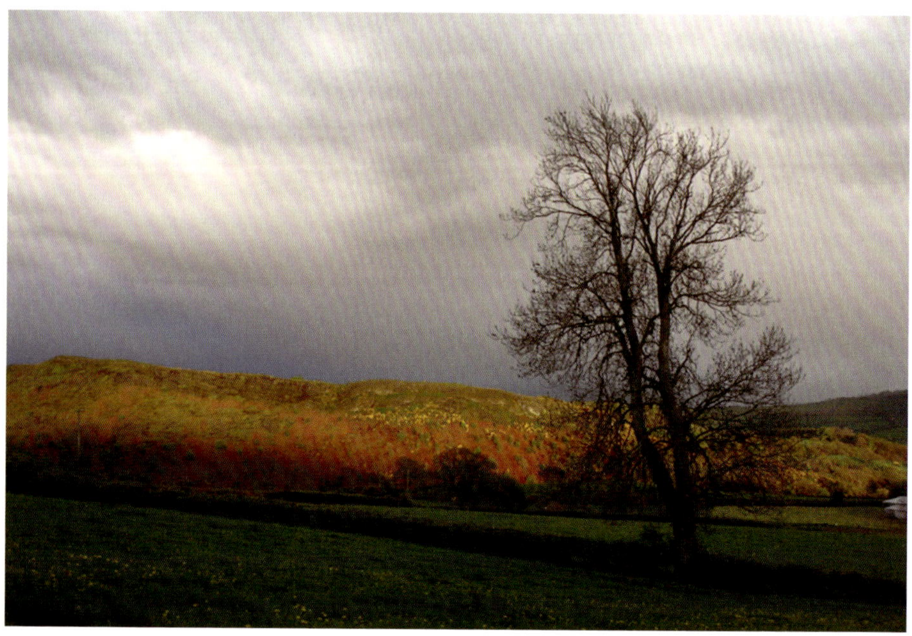

The Ridge lit by setting sun, April

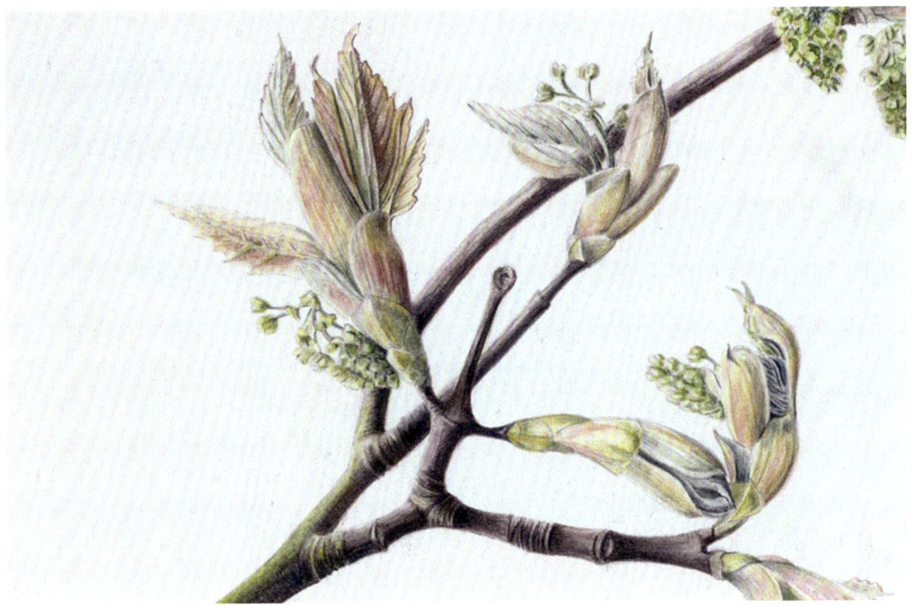

Sycamore flowers unfurling (detail), April 1998

Astonished by the range of pastel colours on sycamore buds, a tree I've always associated with the dull summer green of its leaves, though, viewed from a distance, the tree seems to rise from the ground like a green cumulus cloud and becomes a thing of beauty.

Walking at the foot of the Ridge, a thicket of blackthorn blazing with green sparks seemed to be leaping from the ground. A few white flowers had opened in the fierce maze of branches. I was immediately seduced.

13–27 MAY

SOUTH OF FRANCE

The other day while working on the leaves of star jasmine, *Trachelospermum jasminoides* – about forty, each one at a different angle and a different shade of green – I suddenly wanted to break loose and paint a single fantastical leaf. Botanical accuracy is under threat. But I am not ready to abandon *order* for fantasy.

I am at work on a flowering olive branch, seated by an open window. The evening warmth is intense. A gold light fills the room. Nightingales sing. A dog begins to howl as the sun drops below the pine trees . . . now a wood pigeon cooing . . . the scent of pine intensifies . . . everything now still, concentrated. The tiny white olive flowers stare back at me. The world beyond seems vast.

JUNE

Returned to summer in Wales. Ever-changing greens speckled with the whites, blues, pinks, purples and yellows of June flowers; the promise of blue skies; heat; scents; the call of the curlew; long, light days.

A sleepless night, kept awake by mental notes on the colour progression of ripening fruits. Take green–red–black: growing in the wild around here are elderberry, blackberry, bilberry, damson, plum and sloe; in southern France, grape, olive and fig. All of them swim around my head as I picture the green – clear and bright, the unappetizing acid green of hard, unripe fruit, best mixed with blue and yellow, or by adding lemon yellow to green oxide for a thick, opaque green. Then comes red, which is not strictly red at all, but a pinky, rose doré, flushing to tawny-wine red, a sign that the fruit is nearing edibility before turning 'black'. This is anything from maroon-black to purple-black and which, on sloes, plums, grapes and figs, is frosted with a light cobalt-blue bloom. An olive branch displaying the greens-reds-blacks of ripening fruit among its silvery evergreen leaves is an interesting contrast to a spray of ripening blackberries, the dull mid-greens of its deciduous leaves becoming scorched with bright reds and yellows as autumn advances.

Wild rose tangled in hedging is a common sight in summer. The flowers appear bright and fragile against the dark mass of leaves and thorns, but they pale in the mist of white paper.

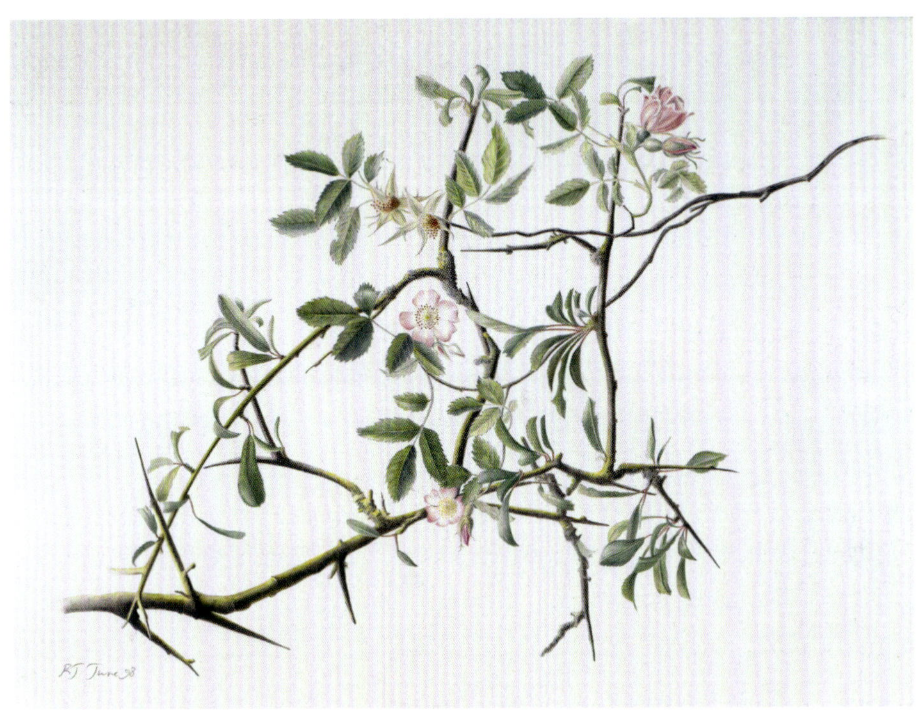

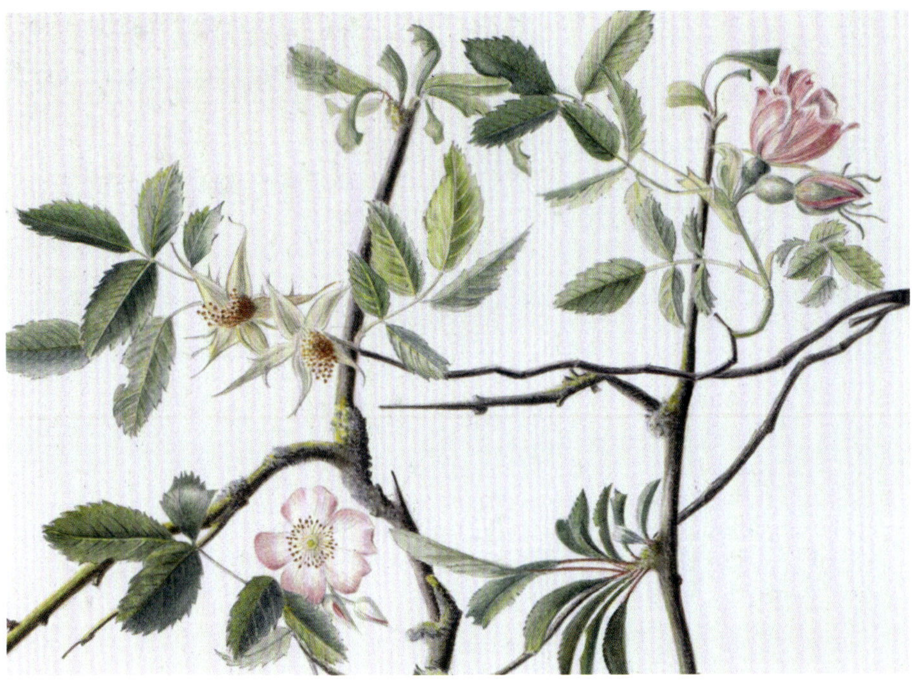

Dog rose tangling with blackthorn (and detail), June 1998

Certain images leap out at me. The principal components seem to be an asymmetrical arrangement of line and matter, lightness and darkness. These are the four basics. To analyse:

> *line* = playfulness (movement)
> *matter* = a still presence
> *lightness* = emergence
> *darkness* = recession

The resulting rhythm is dependent on the juxtaposition of these four components. The composition will sing by carefully applying colour and tone.

Every subject creates its own atmosphere, its own vitality. I like to present the plant afloat in its own 'ether' in the infinity of space. This is the blank paper. Within this space air is moving. A breeze. A gust of wind. I recall the moment of seeing. The tree lichens swaying in the wind, their colours deepened by rain. A nearby stream rushing over rocks and stones. Now the image of seaweeds swaying in sea currents . . . a submarine bush . . . I see the lichens as corals of the air. The fantasy entrances me.

★ ★ ★

At this time, and purely by chance, I met Honor Frost, pioneer in marine archaeology and deep-sea diver, who had spent years working in the Eastern Mediterranean, and long before had attended the Central School of Art. I asked her if she had ever heard of a rare blue coral that I had read about, to which she replied that she'd like to see my source. I sent her a photocopy and she wrote back to say that the author was garbling, and enclosed some tantalizing descriptions of different corals from her unpublished paper, 'Gilgamesh and the Sea':

> 'Black coral' (which is a false coral) has thorns. Both true and false corals can look like plants although they are both colonies of animals. The true corals, *Madreporaria*, are stony. Those used in jewellery are tree-shaped and grow upside down from overhanging rocks, or the roofs of caves. In colour they range from red to pink. With the exception of one white variety from Japan, this jewellery coral is found only in the Mediterranean . . . Coral trees never die. Black coral is known as the 'Plant with a Thorn' . . . and looks like a tree, but it grows upright from rocks to a height as much as 2m . . . and while living it has the pliability of green-wood.

The Plant with a Thorn. So here I was in the landlocked fields and valleys of the Welsh border country painting thorn trees and lichens, thinking corals and seaweeds.

I met Honor at her apartment in Welbeck Street, furnished and decorated on two floors in deep undersea colours. She had inherited a collection of modern British art, among which was a Lucian Freud and a number of paintings by Stanley Spencer, which she'd hung in the dining room. In a dark cupboard she stored an oil painting of a girl in a blue dress by Gwen and a rare watercolour of Irish peasants by Augustus which she showed me with a torch, as if she was shining a light on hidden treasure under the sea.

She showed me slides of coral trees, and we discussed with much amusement the best way of painting seaweeds, which would have to be kept in seawater once plucked from the sea. Honor loved to talk and urged me to go to the Natural History Museum to see the corals she'd described. I stared at sea whips and sea pens (quills), and the sea lily, an animal resembling a feathery flower. I was entranced and felt I was on some kind of quest, but I wasn't at all certain where I was going.

But one thing I did know. I was close to realizing my long-buried ambition to paint on vellum. I told myself that I wanted to make that leap from silver to gold, that it would no longer be a question of defacing an expensive surface, but conjuring a jewel-like form from within the void: a 5 × 7 inch (13 × 18 cm) void, for I had set my heart on making my first image on the piece I'd bought so long ago and which, in retrospect, had terminated my short-lived attempt at painting nature as jewellery. This time I wanted to be fully prepared.

★ ★ ★

A friend, Caroline Cuthbert, arranged a meeting with Romana McEwen, widow of Rory McEwen, whose work on vellum she was willing to show me at her home. Caroline had curated the 1986 exhibition of Rory McEwen's work at the Serpentine Gallery, where I saw his work for the first time. I was dazzled by the technical brilliance and beauty of his flower painting and kept asking 'How?' How was it possible?

I felt like a child being given a longed-for present when Romana handed me his unfinished work to examine. To be able to see where his exquisite brushwork trailed off was far more exciting – and less daunting – than looking at the framed works on the walls.

My meeting with Romana that June coincided with a visit to Paul Getty's collection of historic book bindings and illuminated manuscripts housed in his specially designed library at his home in the Chilterns. It was one of his open days and vellum manuscripts dating from the twelfth century had been laid out on tables without glass protection. I had only ever seen such manuscripts locked beneath glass in the British Museum. This 'close-up' was a bit sudden, a little unnerving. I noted the cockling, the wavy edges, the worm-holes circumnavigated by a monk's handwriting; the sheer labour and control and patience of the inscribers and illustrators; their devotion, their dedication. This was daunting, and I was relieved to come across Fincham's *Pond Life*, an unfinished vellum manuscript dated *c.*1938 lying open at a pair of folios extolling the virtues of scum and slime, handwritten and exquisitely illustrated with amoeba and algae as seen through the microscope.[10]

Fincham's description of an amoeba named slipper animalcule had me smiling in sympathy: 'It is a strange looking little fellow about 1/500th of an inch long and difficult to draw, as it is constantly dashing backwards and forwards in search of food, and seems to expend energies out of all proportion to its size.' This 'little fellow' fed on putrefying matter, so helping to purify the water for 'higher forms of life'. In an introductory note Fincham explains: 'With the aid of a microscope, much that appears corrupt and useless, is revealed as a world of fantastic beauty. Some of the worlds I wish to survey are: pond water, scum & slime, blight, snails, moths, thorns, stings, nettles, mildews–fungi, poison–hemlock, nightshade, snakes, flies, gnats, spiders & cobwebs, frost, tiddlers, worms, etc., etc.'

He only completed ten leaves.

I had a brief word with Paul Getty; he was a shy man, and I knew he had a fine eye. I told him that I wanted to start working on vellum. He spoke in a very soft voice, and with a faint twinkle said, 'They say that vellum is always trying to get back to its original shape.' This was comic and I knew then that the world wouldn't end if the skin began undulating while I painted on it.

Four days later I was on my way to the Welsh hills, armed with my 5 × 7 and some offcuts from William Cowley Parchment and Vellum Works, sole UK supplier located in a cluster of shed-like buildings off the M1 at Newport Pagnell, where I'd gone for further enlightenment and to order a supply.

That afternoon in the cottage I took a scrap and started to doodle abstractly. I wanted to find out what it felt like and how paint would behave on its surface. That took some doing. As a botanical painter I was not used to thinking in blurs and undefined shapes, but I soon discovered I was able to manipulate the paint in ways I'd never thought possible. Unlike paper, which is stained by colour, paint sits on skin and can be pushed around or lifted off so that barely a trace remains. I later discovered the disadvantage of this: great care has to be taken when brushing layer on layer because each application of paint can move the layer below and in no time the paint looks curdled. Once the technique of layering is mastered, the final effect is brighter, deeper – some would say harder – than watercolour on paper.

21 JUNE

Something bright and defined against mauvy greys has appeared in the 5 × 7 inch void. Walking around the garden, the sight of crimson rose petals scattered over purple sage leaves brought back a memory of an idea I had experimented with before.

---

10 *A Book of Observations on the Plant and Animal Life inhabiting Pond Water*, illuminated by Hjalmar Fincham, Wormsley Library, Buckinghamshire. He had been a pupil of the calligrapher and illuminator Graily Hewitt (1864–1952), who had enrolled at the Central School of Arts and Crafts in 1900 and later held courses there for nearly thirty years.

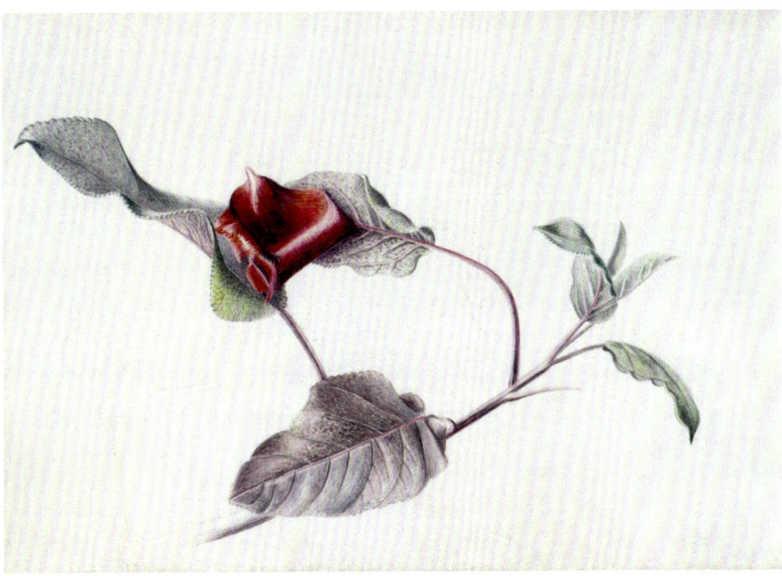

'Guinée' rose petal on sage (vellum), June 1998

I had seen an Indian tapestry in which fallen flower petals had been woven on to huge tropical leaves in a scene of unrestrained jungle growth. I loved the idea of capturing a disintegrating flower in its last moments of fleeting jewel-like brilliancy. When I'd seen a chestnut tree's flowers scattered in their thousands all over the leaves, I'd made a few studies and reserved the idea for the future.

I cut out a spray of sage holding a single petal from the 'Guinée' rose. I liked that: a transient coupling necessitating swift execution. I painted the splash of red in deepest indigo-darkened crimson through to faint vermillion and rose doré against sage leaves stippled with violet and grey, blue-green, yellow-green, grey-green. The mental tightrope I was walking gave me little time to agonize over what I was doing. If anything I thought of my parents, who had grown a 'Guinée' rose in their London garden – my childhood garden – and later planted it against the cottage wall in Wales, where it thrives in unforgiving winter winds and intense summer heat. I had little interest in gardening, but this scented rose represented continuity and beauty and was a minor triumph of my parents' erratic gardening techniques.

★ ★ ★

I am in no hurry to continue working on vellum; the moment must feel right, unforced. I return instead to the series of magnified lichens growing on different trees, this time selecting a branch of rowan which has an elephant-grey bark. The rowan tree, or mountain ash, grows on rocky mountainsides at precarious angles, its vermilion-scarlet berries against late-summer blue skies an unforgettable sight. Strange to think that this same tree thrives in city streets, trunks straight up, backdrop of concrete and brick.

26 JUNE

Evening. A succession of rainbows dip into the June-green domes of ash, oak, sycamore. White-gold sun in west, mauve clouds, grey sky. An opening of cobalt blue streaked with white jet trails. Sunlight on far hills, sunlight on the nearby barn. On the window pane, rain drops. Through the raindrops a mesh of bright green fennel. In the fennel a pink rose. Beyond the rose a streak of silver in a pewter sky.

Two pink rose petals, tear-shaped, caught in the mesh of fennel, painted.

JULY

Late night. A desolate feeling listening to the sounds as I write: a lone fly jetting around the room, wind blowing hard around the cottage and moaning through a decayed window; rain against glass, rosehips knocking against glass. Five minutes have passed. There is silence, wind and rain gone.

AUGUST

Grass to walk on, herbs to eat, roses for romance, trees for atmosphere. These four growing things make the garden here.

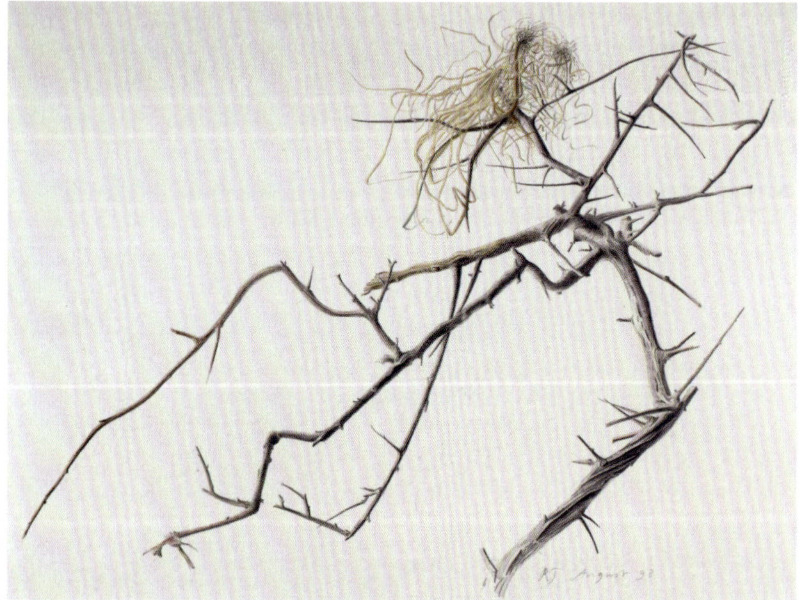

Tuft of grass in blackthorn, August 1998

A harvest moon – full, orange – rising over the Ridge. Wild raspberries by the lake.

The yellow and blue of advanced dusk, when electric light inside yellows and the light outside blues. A most beautiful hour.

Amber/grey; brass/pewter. The tones of old master drawings.

On the Berwyn heather moors, a branch of gorse had been leaning close to the ground in its death throes, but at home I positioned it upright. Weathered and cracked with age, a few ghostly spines remained, while bright green moss and silvery lichens sprouted happily from the branch.

No fresh young branch of gorse would have so much to tell.

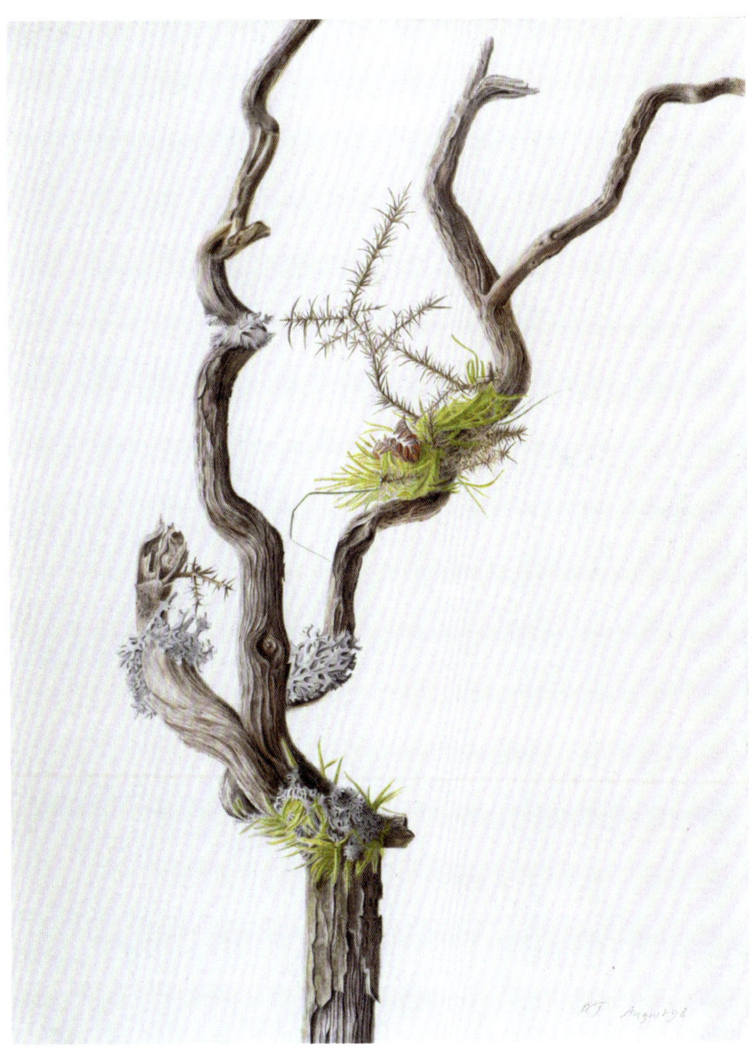

Ancient gorse, August 1998

22 AUGUST

The light today from dawn till dusk began grey, then slowly brightened with sunrays and silver clouds before dulling to a chill gloom. A second brightening towards evening brought spreading blue sky, heat, and sunlight over hills.

The idea of working in the traditional steady north light of the artist's studio sends a cold shiver through me. I work indoors, always, but I want to be dazzled by sunlight from time to time, see the sun alter the colours of nature as I work, observe the effect of dimming light on a plant, watch colour and shadow deepen. No plant in nature grows in a steady north light.

Extreme exhaustion this month. I know now why artists let everything go around them. Gwen once wrote in a notebook, 'Drawing and painting is as tiring as housework.' I was so surprised by this that I copied it out. How right she was. No tyrannical 'interior' for me. To clean is to disturb the atmosphere. The cottage is alive with spiders, flies and moths. Cobwebs in all corners, around windows, across beams, ceilings, books. A long, mottled brown slug lost on the stone tiles inside the door, left open all night as usual.

SEPTEMBER

Each picture is an emotional reference point. I have been tempted to give some paintings non-botanical titles but it is best not to enclose the subject in meaning. Leave it free.

To paint without concern for *how it is*. But the plant says, 'This is how it is.'

Picked up a blackthorn branch from the field floor, and knew at once that I wanted to paint it. I decided that it should be my second painting on vellum, hoping that the restricted colours would make it less daunting – I'm still at a very early stage. As I painted, the windblown grass seemed to flower from the branch, softening the ruthless thorns and right angles.

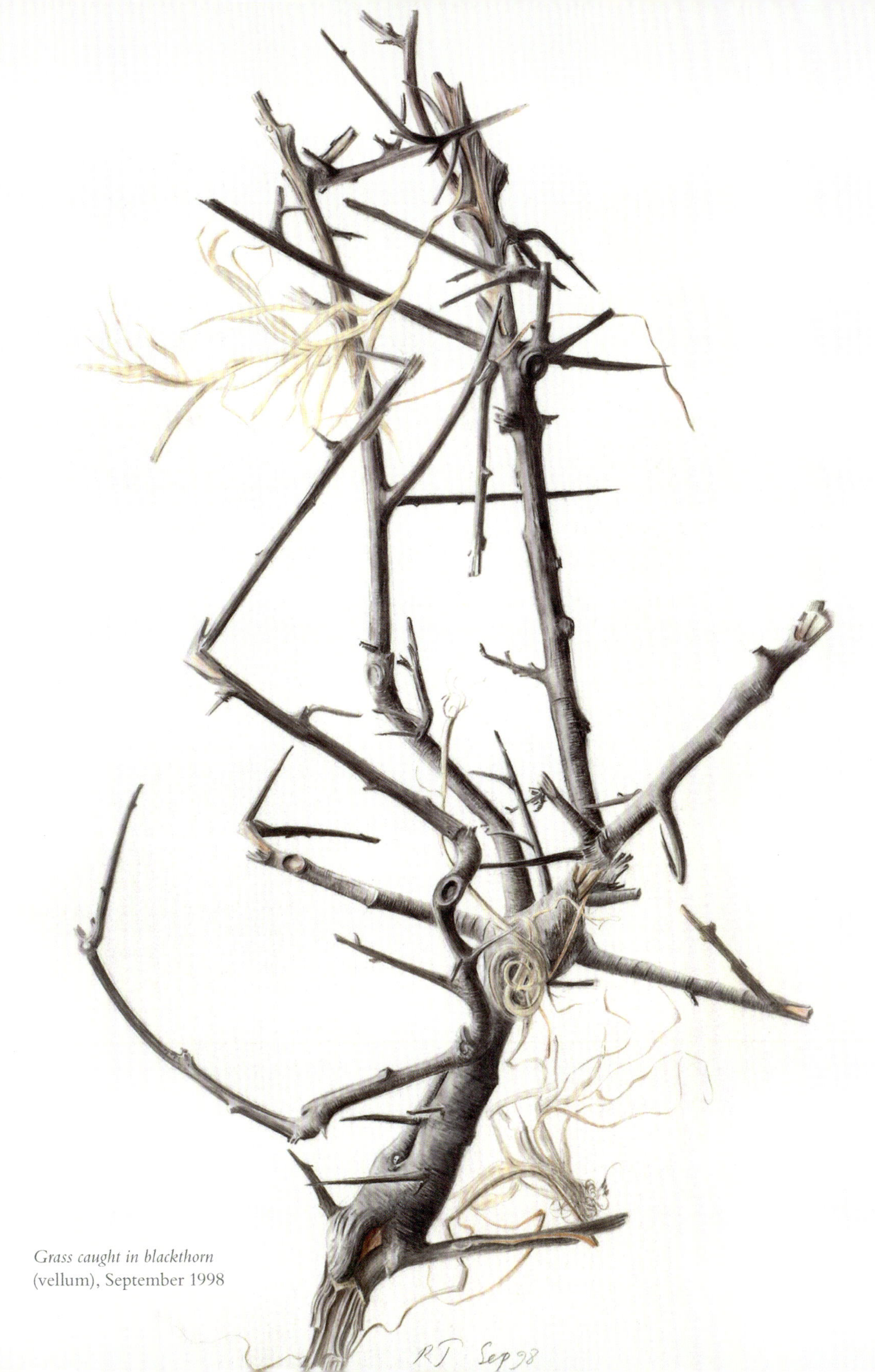

Grass caught in blackthorn
(vellum), September 1998

The most exquisite wild flower grows in grass. The harebell looks fragile, but it is a sturdy, long-lasting sitter, the buds continuing to open for days. Sheep had bitten off the tip of the stem. The colour is fiendish to paint: at a distance in open air the flower is light blue; at close quarters indoors the blue appears to be now violet, now mauve. In reproduction the flower will appear purple.

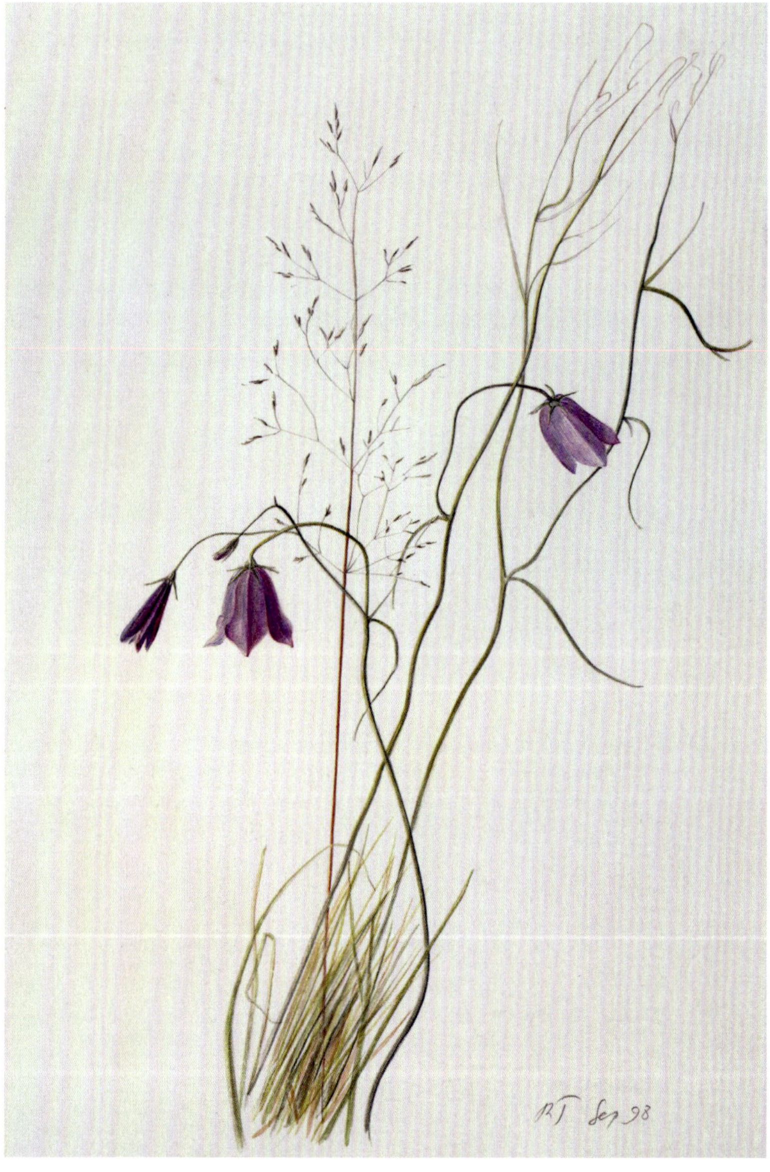

Harebell in grass, September 1998

OCTOBER

The end of another six months working at the cottage. Extreme isolation; long periods
without human contact. But such is my contact with plants that I formulate new ideas
about how to portray them inside the paper rectangle. There are three ways:

> The subject speaks for itself. In this case, minimal interference: e.g. a
> single leaf, painted as in a full-face portrait.
> The subject is composed to create rhythm across form and colour. With
> this, some interference: e.g. dying leaves against living leaves; a stem
> at a diagonal through leaves.
> The subject becomes unscientific. This involves interference to a greater
> degree so as to render the subject hard to identify: e.g. abstract surface
> pattern in an isolated detail with no recognizable outline.

NOVEMBER

One subject began speaking to me long before I succumbed: a dying blaze of peony
leaves coupled with cool, living sage leaves. Rose doré and ochres cooled by terre
verte and violets.

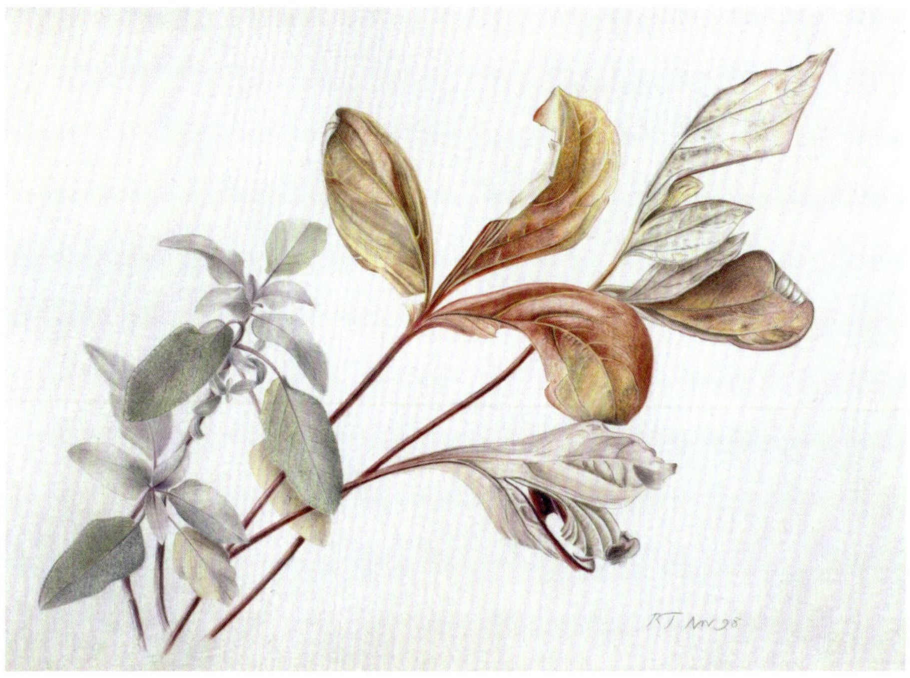

November peony leaves with sage (vellum), November 1998

DECEMBER

The grey-flowering green-tipped zigzag of lichens sprouting on a sycamore branch
nagged me for days before I gave in and chose vellum; this meant I could indulge in
many hours of hairline definition. I had some difficulty with aerial perspective.

In a strip of hawthorn, three elements excited me: the frilly lichens catching the
light, the khaki-green lichen holding shadow, the lethal thorns.

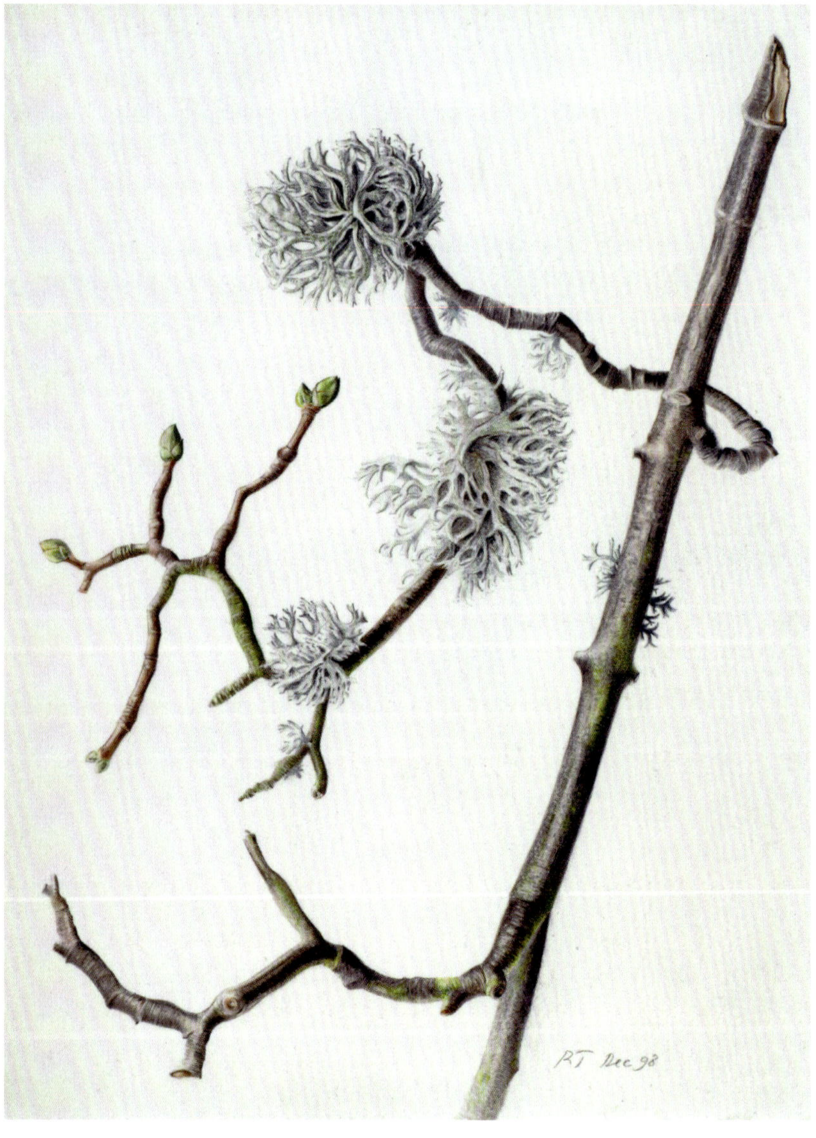

Lichens on old sycamore (vellum), December 1998

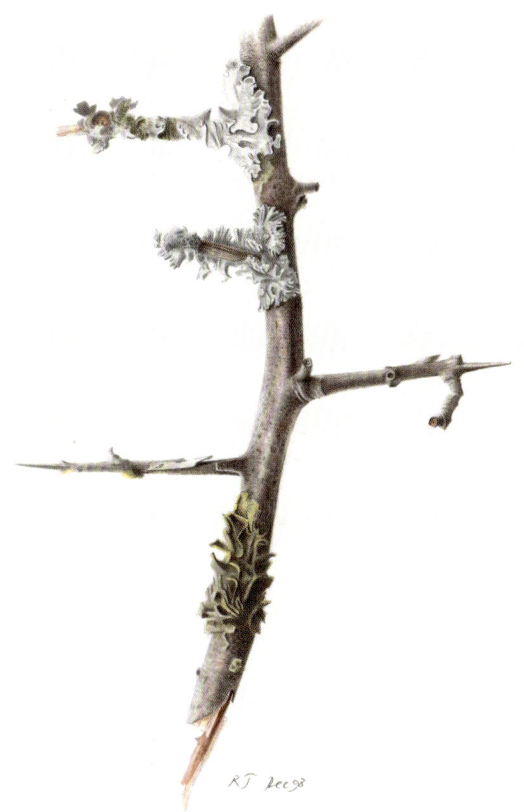

Magnified lichens on hawthorn, December 1998

1999

Nature's green presents the greatest challenge to the botanical artist. Too much green is a disaster – think of a landscape painting smothered in green paint, or, as I have observed in botanical painting, one shade of green mixed for the leaves of an entire plant. But the colour is unavoidable. It is life. The trick is to think of green in three basic shades: blue-green, yellow-green, grey-green. Green leaves change colour dramatically during the course of a day's work. The sun is out, that leaf is yellow-green; a cloud crosses the sun, the leaf has turned blue-green. Was it Gainsborough who created the effect of green by dashing yellow and blue together as he painted leaves on trees? And avoid at all cost the deadly 'mid-green'. Green oxide of chromium is just that; being one of the few opaque watercolours, it can cover anything underneath it, but it will deaden a painting in which green predominates. With these thoughts in mind, I choose subject matter where green is either absent or confined to a specific area.

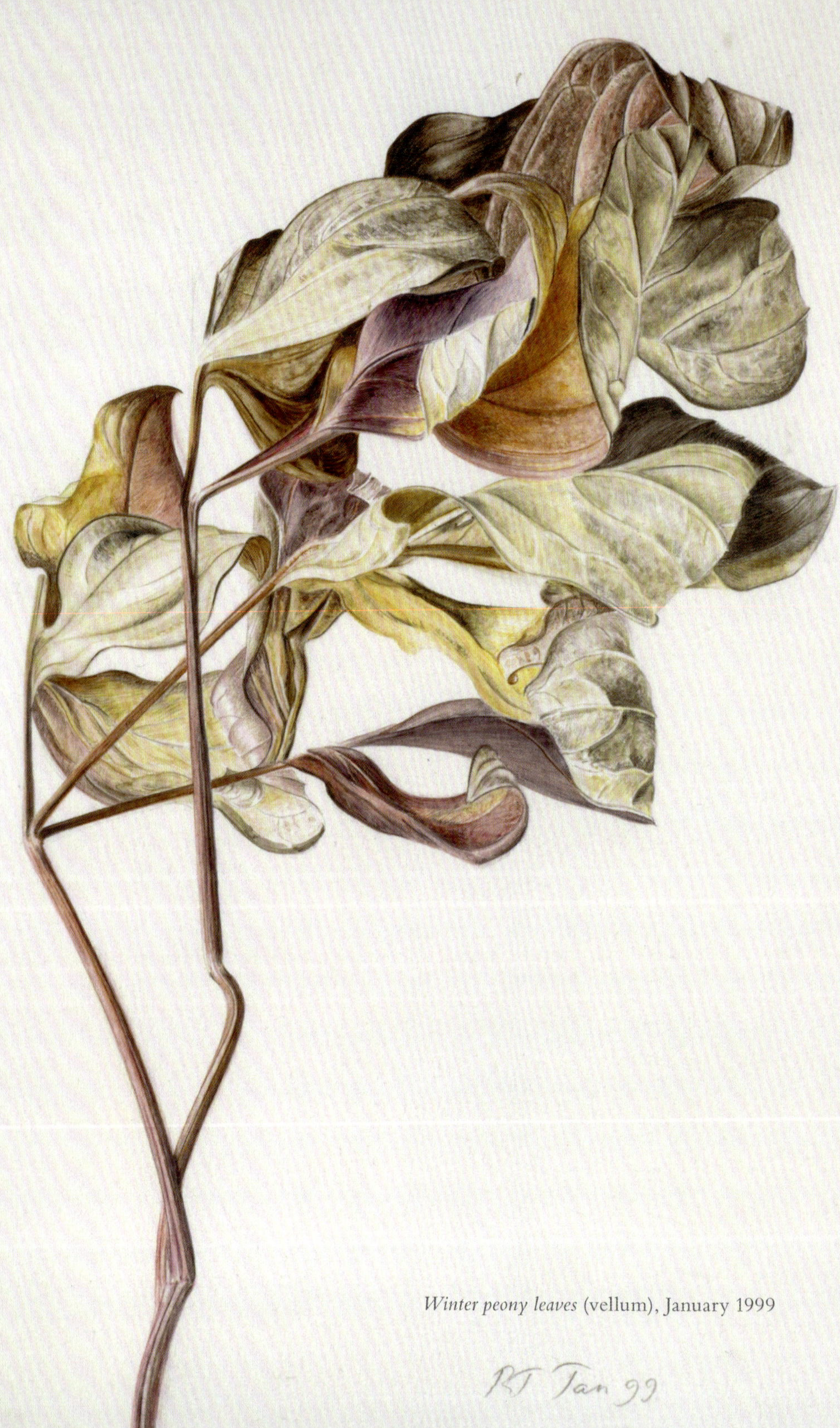

Winter peony leaves (vellum), January 1999

JANUARY

Some peony leaves sat on my London mantelpiece for weeks, their faded colours deepening in the winter light and becoming more attractive. I savoured the prospect of sailing away with them in the New Year. It wasn't long before I was thinking 'faded Venetian' and as I worked on the smooth surface of the vellum the leaves turned to silk billowing in a wind.

Continuing the series of magnified lichens on different trees, I painted two contrasting species of lichen on a branch of larch which I had spotted at a London flower stall, for sale as Christmas decoration.

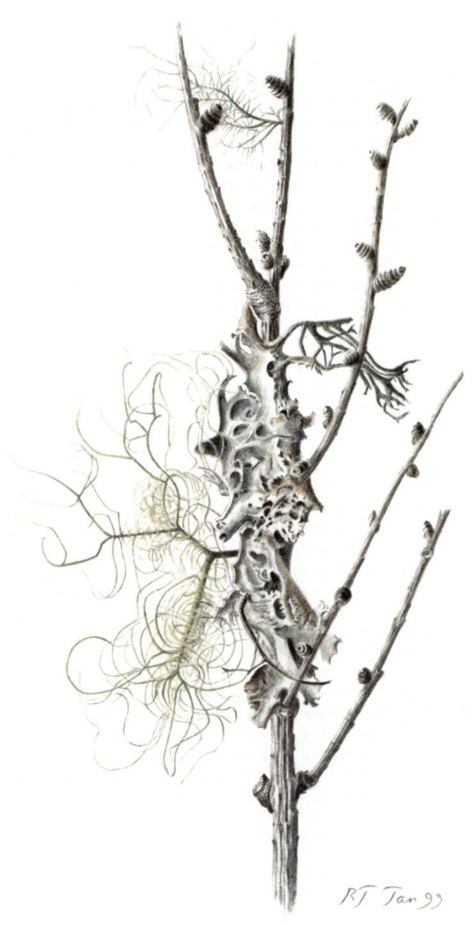

Magnified lichens on larch, January, 1999

From the hedgerow
(vellum), February 1999

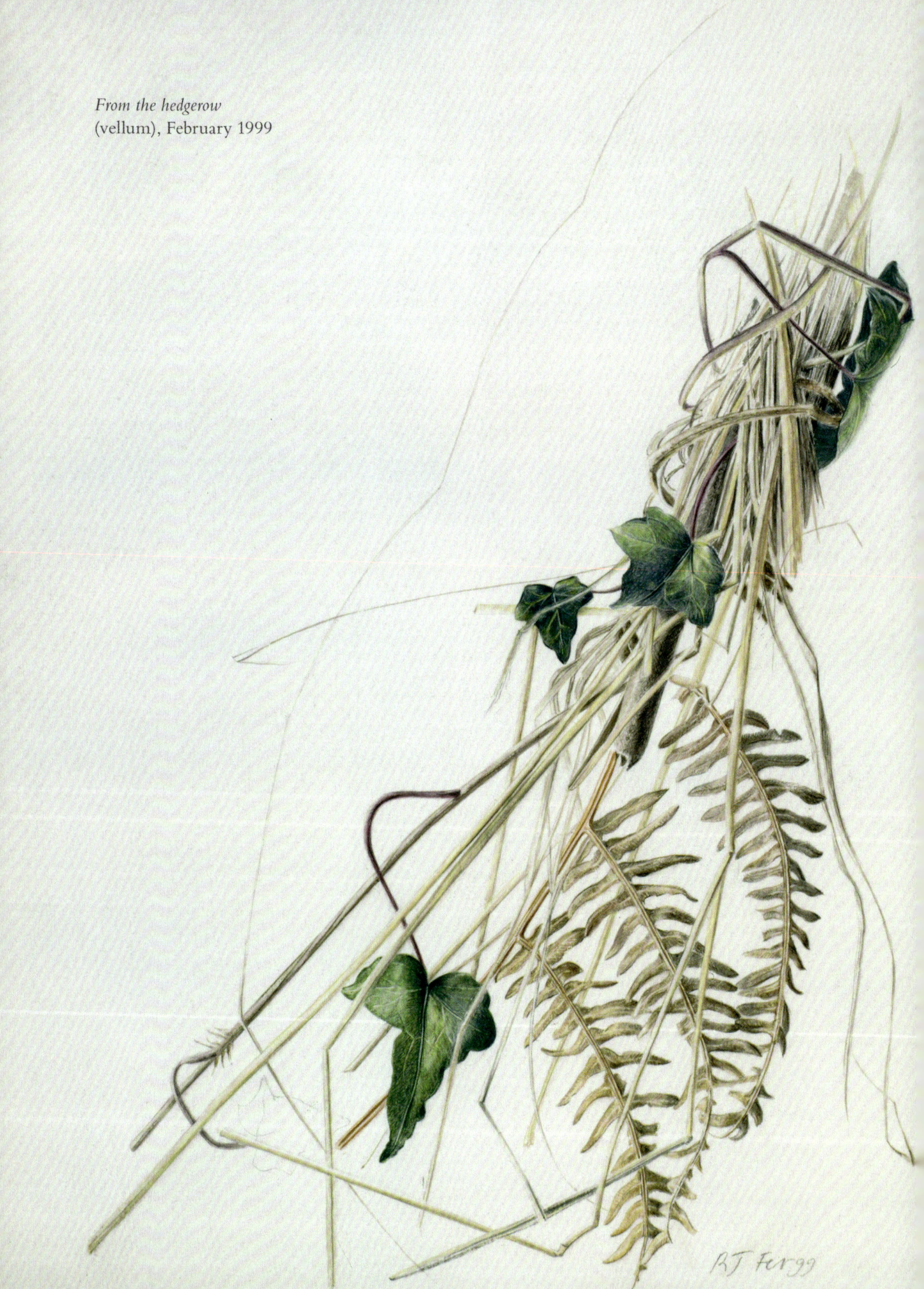

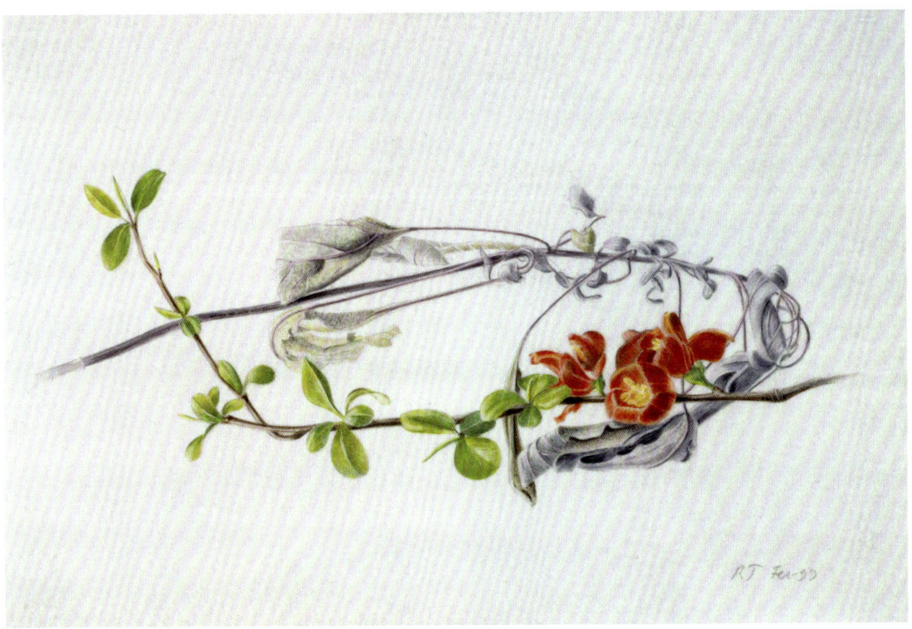

Japonica and dried sage (vellum), February 1999

FEBRUARY

A handful of sparse matter collected from the track suited my mood. I concentrated on the striped broken bracken and deliberately left the fifth ivy leaf, at the bottom left of the picture, unpainted. At my exhibition the following year, someone pointed to the empty leaf as if it was a mistake. I said that I didn't think the picture needed a full stop.

Fiery red japonica flowers with acid-green leaves were bursting through railings in a London garden, an uplifting sight in grey February. At home I put the japonica down by a sprig of crinkled sage leaves, forming a ring that I instantly wanted to paint. The sage leaves brought to mind Chinese cloud motifs. Fire, vapour.

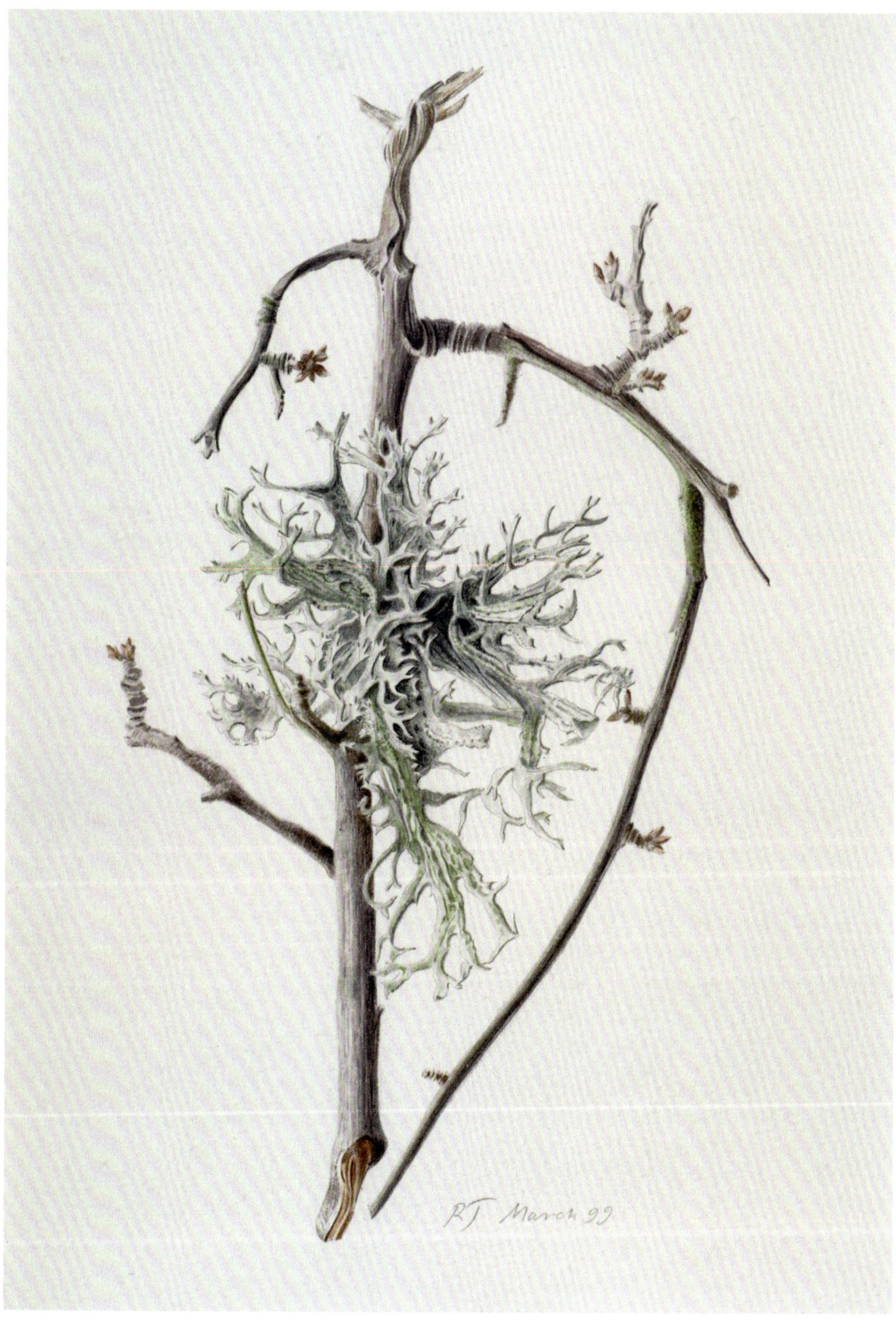

Magnified lichens on blackthorn, March 1999

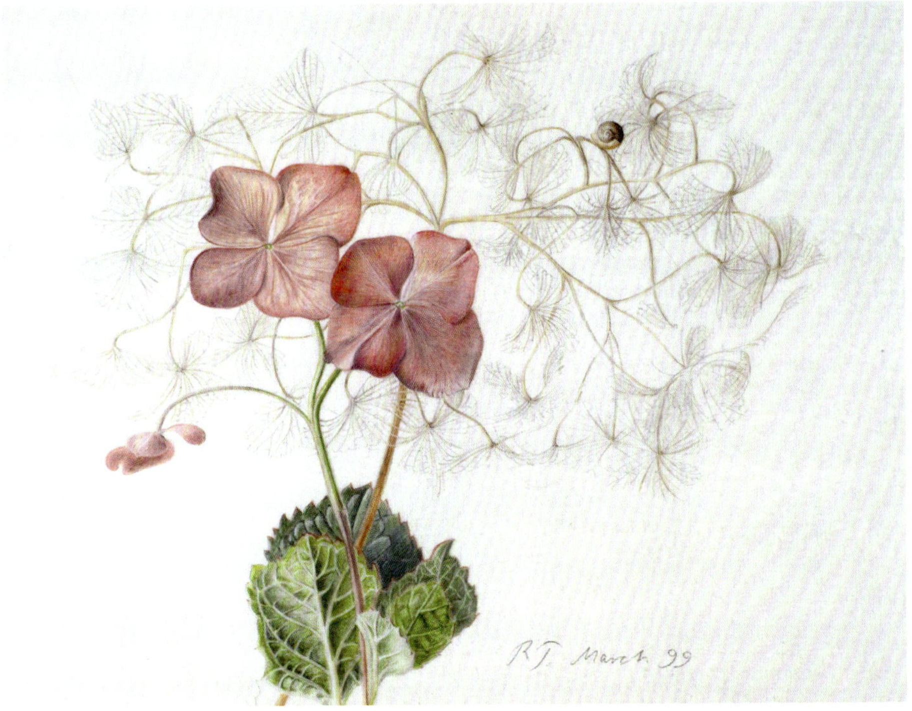

Spring leaves on dried hydrangea (vellum), March 1999

MARCH

A branch of blackthorn appeared to me as a fantastical brooch, and as I painted I imagined studding the lichen with gleaming seed pearls and setting a luscious topaz between the claws.

Two faded rose doré hydrangea florets had survived last year's flowering, becoming papery. A tiny snail was camouflaged in the skeletal remains of the flower head and became visible as I was drawing; the pencil is a remorseless instrument that can uncover and define a detail that a 'flat' photograph cannot.

APRIL

The deadline for the Lefevre exhibition is nearing.

The moment I begin a painting, I embark on an imaginary journey. Every change of direction on the surface of a leaf is to travel it. The graceful arc of a stem running into the central vein is a long receding road all the way to the tip. Small areas become large, concentrated passages of painting. It is difficult to emerge into the pettiness of the everyday world of talk and decision-making. It all seems so mundane. I was greatly surprised when one day, by chance, I read in a newspaper Ted Hughes's account of the effects on him of solitary engagement with fishing. 'When I'm fishing alone – as I come out of it, if I have to speak to somebody, I find I can't speak properly. I can't form words. The words come out backwards, tumbled. It takes time to readjust, as if I'd been into some part of myself that pre-dates language. It doesn't happen when I'm fishing with people.'

MAY

The opening party for Plant Life at the Lefevre Gallery. The terror has passed and in no time I'm at the midst of a deafening crush of people. The paintings have sold out and I'm drunk on margaritas. At home I sway in the arms of a friend before I collapse in the dark of my bedroom, sick as a dog.

'So *delicate*,' people said of the paintings; but how *bold*, how *daring* I felt creating them.

A woman walked into the gallery during the exhibition and said, 'I prefer her cats,' which makes one wonder how anyone could possibly have thought they were looking at the work of Gwen John.

★ ★ ★

I begin work for an exhibition in New York, opening in April 2000.

Ownership transforms the thing possessed in the eye and mind of a new owner. A picture is conceived. A picture is created. A picture is not finished, but abandoned. It lies around in a mundane way. It might be given its first new home: a frame (pity the work that has been locked into the wrong home). Its second home is likely to be a wall (pity the work that is hung on a sunny wall).

A painting affects the atmosphere of its new home. The new home affects the atmosphere of the painting. These watercolour drawings will not 'travel' across a room, preferring to remain afloat in their own space.

JULY

A new thought: millions of people are now seated in front of flickering computer screens all day. I am seated in front of a piece of white paper, similar in size, conjuring an image out of a flat white surface. This is my screen. It does not flicker, but will dim or brighten according to the light. Sometimes I experience a very strange phenomenon: the echo of voices, or music, floating from the surface.

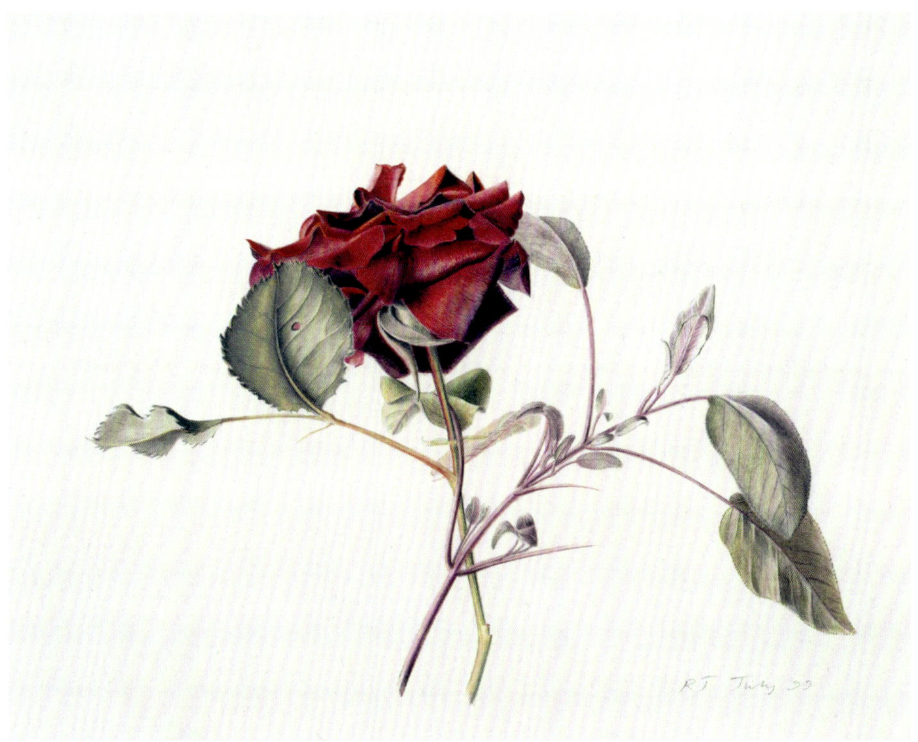

'Guinée' rose and sage (vellum), July 1999

The first time this happened, I had just resumed working on the wave of a poppy leaf, having begun the previous day with the radio on. The moment the brush touched the surface voices floated out of the leaf; it was as if sound had fused with brushwork. This happened over and again with passages of music. From within a maze of lines, or a berry, came the sound of distant music – a fleeting passage of a string quartet perhaps, or, on one startling occasion, the sound of jazz trumpet. So I decided to choose certain pieces of music to work to. In this way I listened to Schubert's piano music, inspired by a line from Alfred Brendel's accompanying text: 'Compared to Beethoven, the architect, Schubert composed like a sleepwalker. In Beethoven's sonatas we never lose our bearings . . . Schubert's sonatas happen.'[11]

I secretly hope for a painting to 'happen'.

---

11 In *Musical Thoughts and Afterthoughts*, Robson Books, 1976.

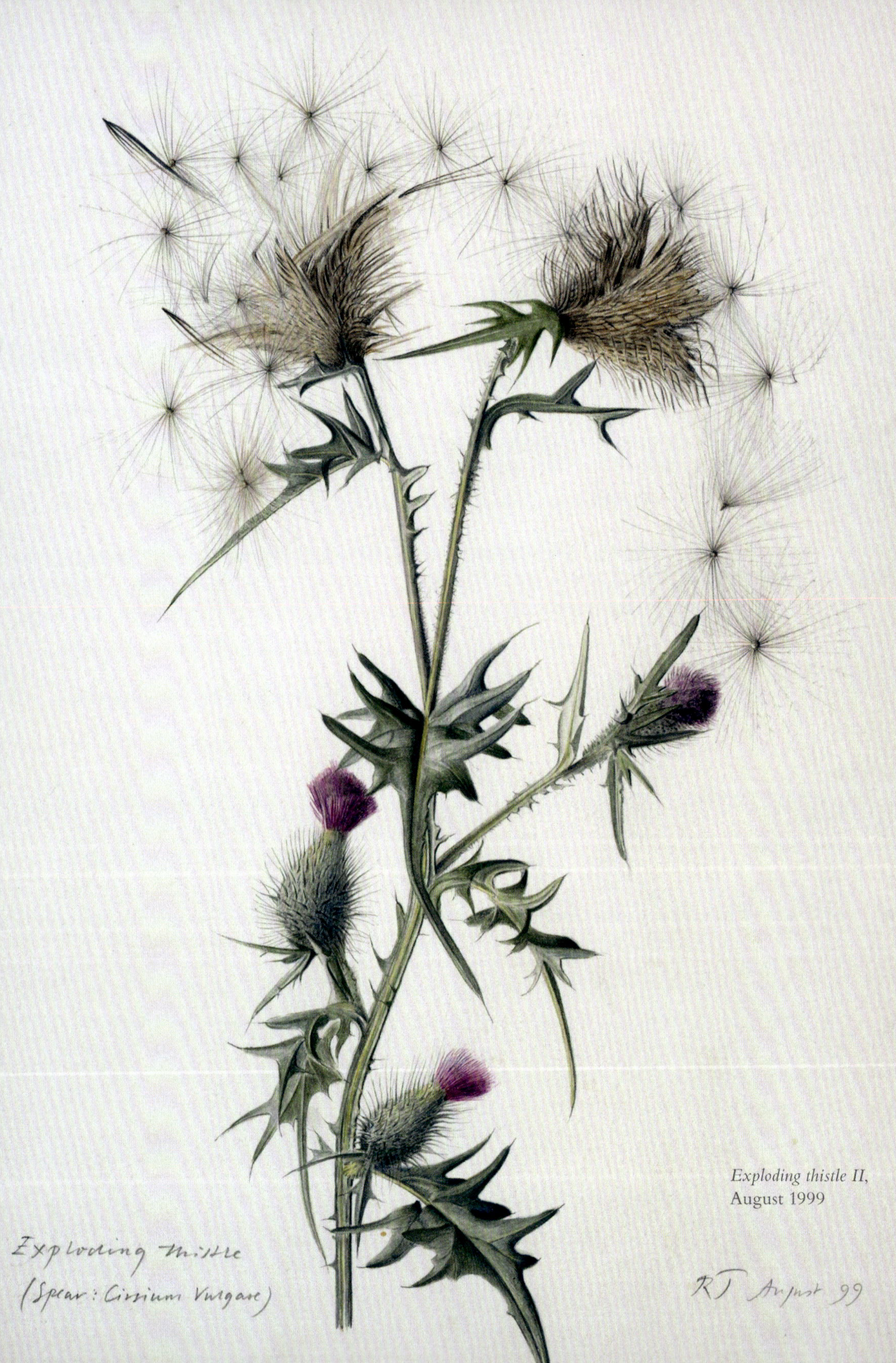
Exploding thistle
(Spear: Cirsium vulgare)
Exploding thistle II,
August 1999
RJ August 99

AUGUST

Some friends with Scottish connections asked for a painting of a thistle, 'the very wasp of flowers'.[12] I chose a tall spear thistle which took an afternoon to draw – the spiny, undulating leaves seemed to metamorphose into some prehistoric beast under my pencil. Next morning I stopped short at the sight that greeted me: the seed-heads had exploded overnight in the warmth of the cottage but the thistledown had not been able to blow away and remained suspended in a chain. I started painting immediately and was soon hooked. The transformation from purple honey-scented flower to dehiscent seed head was lovely to see, so I quickly started a second version, and a third, smaller picture of flower heads.

Walking among the dunes on the north Norfolk coast I picked whatever I passed and drove back to Wales across England with sea holly, gorse, sea lavender, rush and grasses. There was great August heat, but cool Norfolk winds played around the bouquet as I worked.

––––––––––––––––––––––

12 John Clare, 'The Fear of Flowers'.

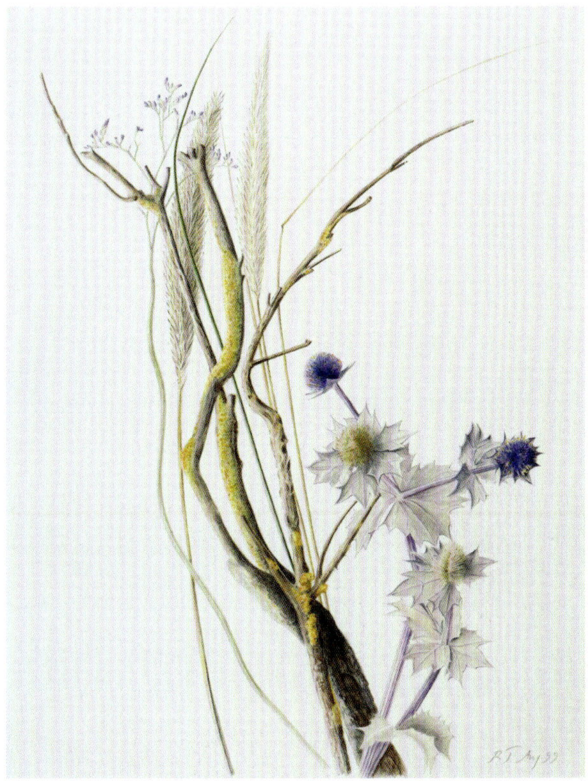

From the dunes, August 1999

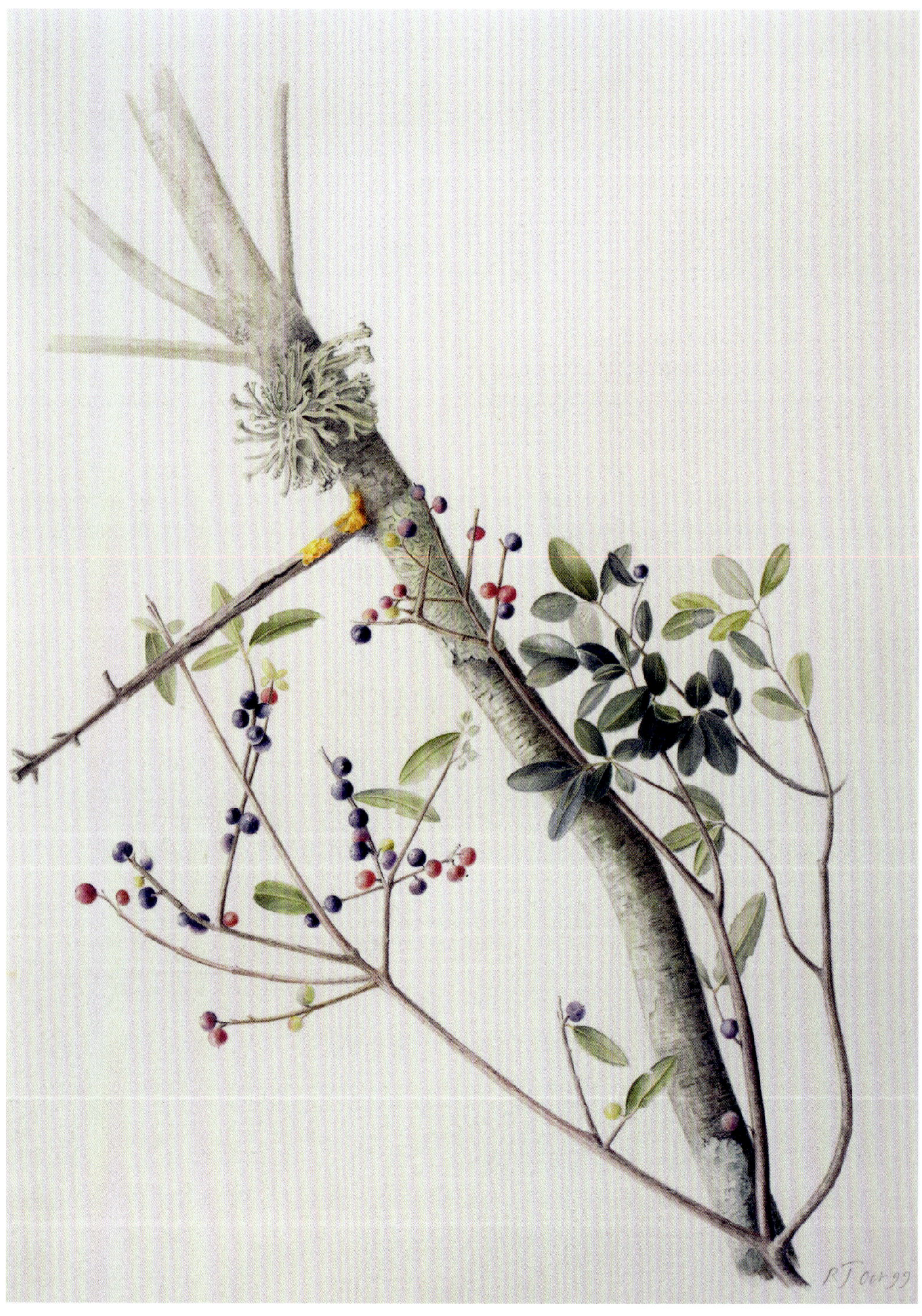

Phillyrea latifolia, October 1999

OCTOBER

SOUTH OF FRANCE

A relative of the olive, *Phillyrea latifolia* keeps company with cork oak and myrtle on the hillsides of southern France. I took a branch from a shrub growing by the long tortuous track leading to Chartreuse de la Verne, a vast Carthusian monastery dating back to the twelfth century. Perched high up in Les Maures in thick forest with precipitous drops to the valleys below, I first saw la Verne when it was a deserted semi-ruin: baking heat, deafening cicadas, tumbled stone walls, monks' quarters overgrown with long grass; not a soul to be seen. I never forgot that day and would return whenever I had the chance, but the renovation, with signs and walkways, shop, café and tourists, has overwhelmed any sense of the isolation the Carthusian Order once sought. The memory of that first visit came vividly to mind as I painted the *Phillyrea*.

NOVEMBER

I ended the century in the company of my old friend, the hundred-year-old olive tree in the Chelsea Physic Garden. The tree had needed a prune, and the head gardener offered me some branches.

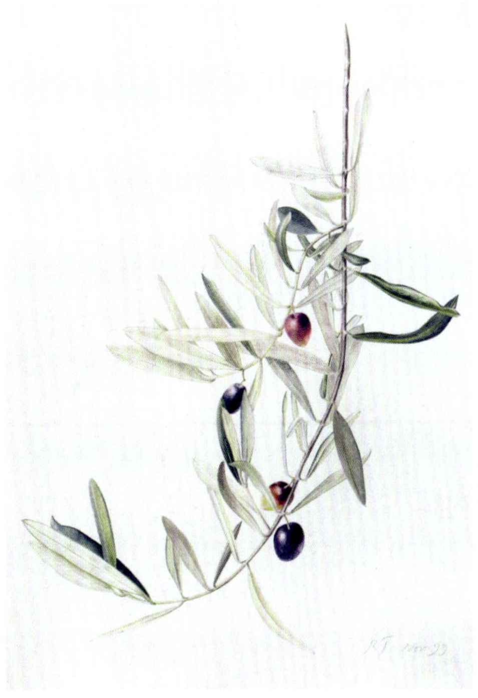

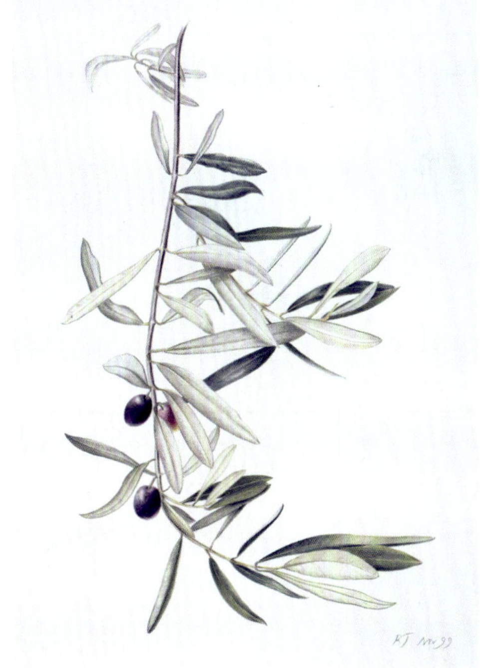

Olive branch I, November 1999   *Olive branch II*, November 1999

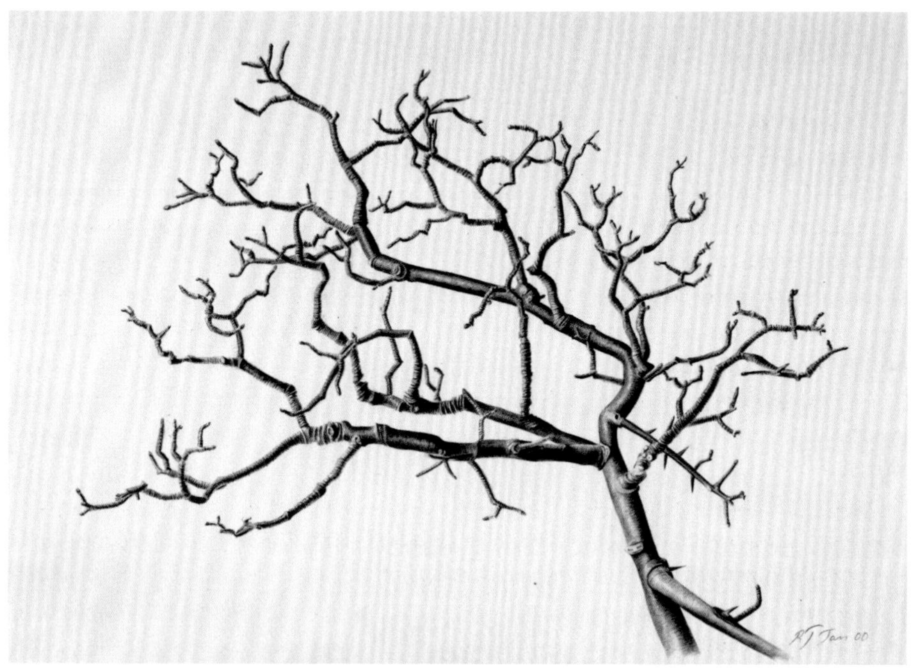

Winter hawthorn, January 2000

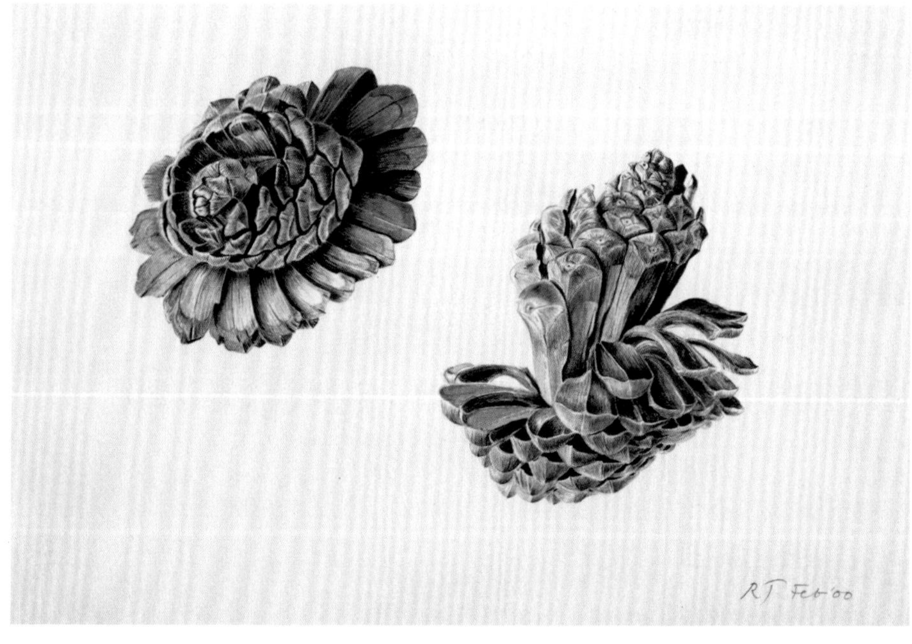

Opening pine cone (two views), February 2000

2000

NEW YEAR'S DAY

As I walked by the waterfall in Pennant Melangell valley the fierce look of an old hawthorn tree caught my eye. The tips of its branches seemed frozen in a zigzag fight against winter winds. I painted in monochrome – Schminke's 'Neutral Tint' – since there seemed no point in mixing a dull mid-brown. Very stark. Great isolation, and perhaps because of this an overwhelming desire to paint a large fantasy leaf. Thoughts of underwater coral becoming airborne as I painted. It is strange how white paper 'alchemizes' in the mind into elements: wind is blowing across its empty space; a strong current of water sways the plant; now it becomes a frozen white-out as I get colder and colder sitting for long hours.

FEBRUARY

The moment I saw a pine cone lying in a drawer in an artist's studio I wanted to paint it. It seemed to have got stuck at the opening stage, and looked faintly comical. The mathematical structure of the cone necessitated very slow work at both drawing and painting stages. The use of monochrome allowed a certain freedom, and as I worked the pine cone seemed to slowly revolve in space.

Woodbine is the name given to wild honeysuckle as it binds itself around tree trunks, thriving in overgrown woods where it has been left to mature undisturbed. I painted a couple that were fused in old age and had been cruelly chopped into a log for the fire. Although I didn't remember at the time, two years previously I had painted a flirty young couple I found in a bower by a stream. But now the pliable, pink stems of youth had thickened and cracked in old age and were unrecognizable.

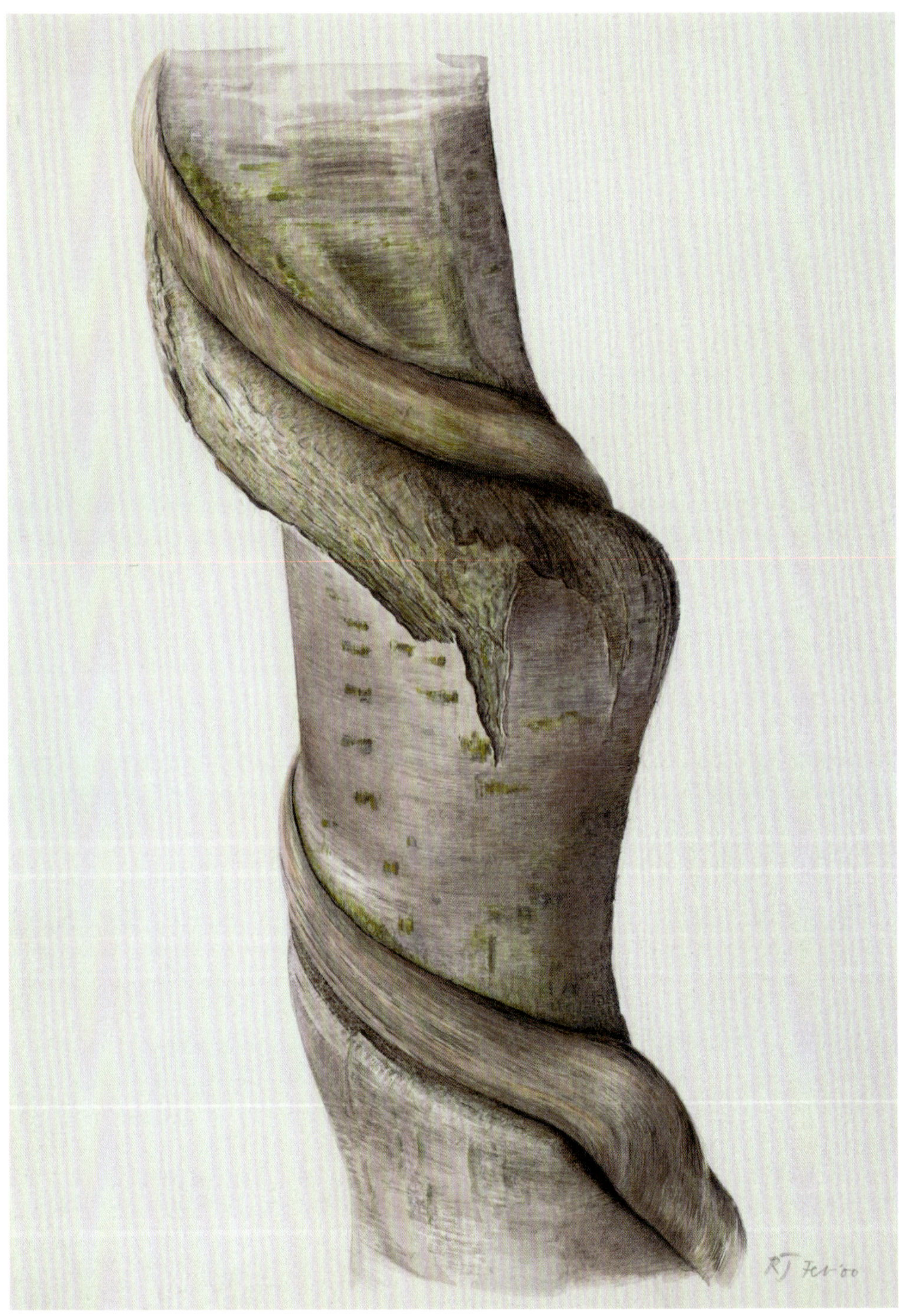

Woodbine (honeysuckle) entwining hazel, February 2000

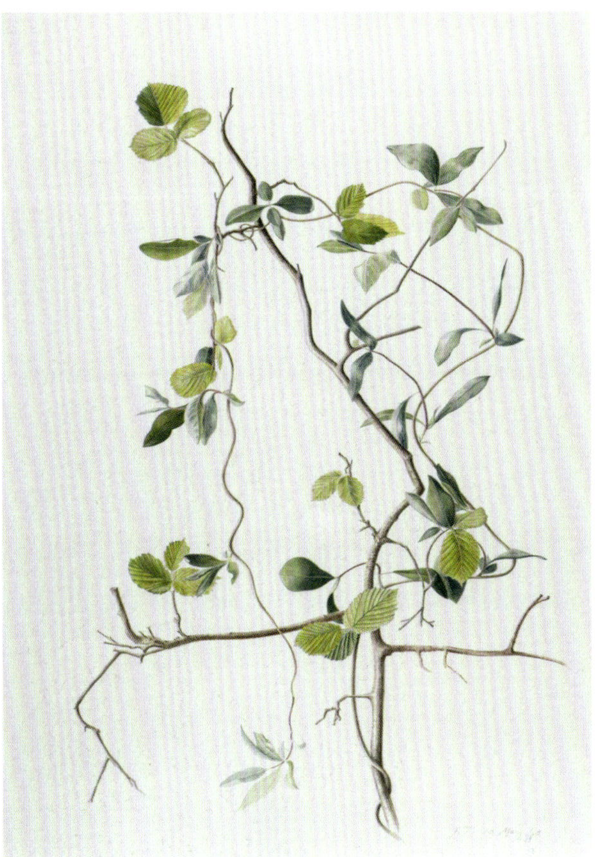

Honeysuckle entwining hazel, May 1998

APRIL–MAY

To New York for my exhibition, 'Plant Life II', at Davis and Langdale, a small, intimate gallery on East 60th Street. Cecily Langdale represents Gwen John in the US and is the author of the catalogue raisonné.[13] A professional to her fingertips, and with a wonderful wry sense of humour, Cecily was the first dealer to offer me a solo exhibition, after she'd seen a portfolio of my work in London, but I decided it was wiser to kick-off on home ground where I had already been selling work (initially to friends in Wales, and at the Royal Cambrian Academy in North Wales and the Albany Gallery in Cardiff). Cecily sold a good number of paintings and after a week in New York I flew down to Oaxaca, Mexico, to stay with the artist James

---

13 Cecily Langdale, *Gwen John: With a Catalogue Raisonné of the Paintings and a Selection of the Drawings*, Yale University Press, 1987.

Brown and his magnificent wife, Alexandra.[14] They lived with their three children in a large old hacienda set against low rounded hills at the end of a long dirt track. A fountain splashed among evergreen plants in the central courtyard. I was given a room last occupied by the artist Francesco Clemente. Double doors opened on to a cactus garden. I stepped out for a wander. Huge, stately, threatening; I couldn't help admiring the cacti, but I would never want to paint one. The garden ended at a whitewashed wall; in the distance, a range of blue-mauve mountains.

---

14   Since writing this I received the tragic news that James and Alexandra Brown had died in a car crash in Yucatan.

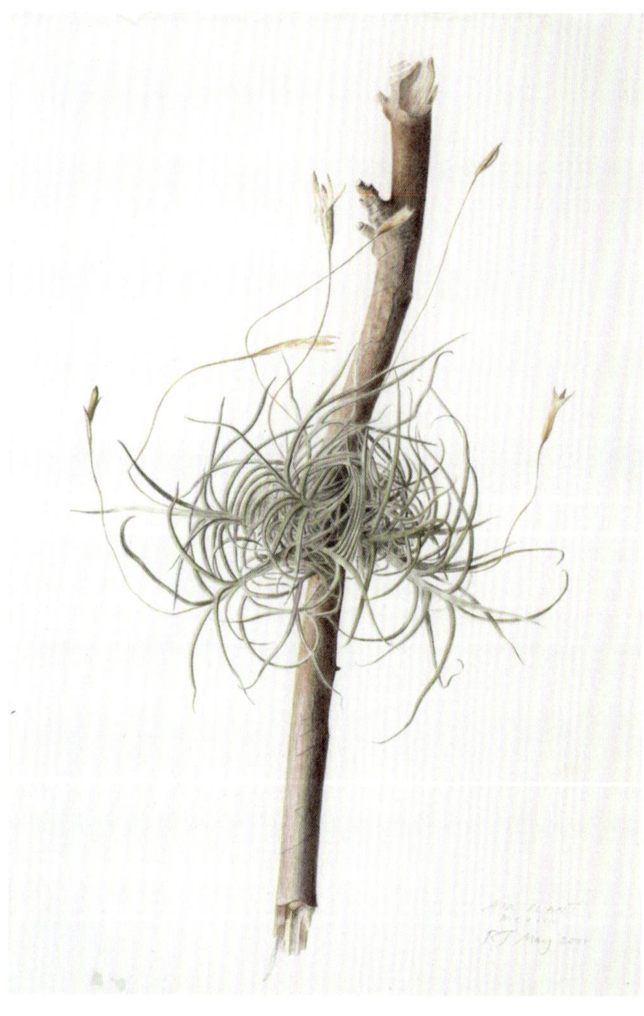

Air plant, May 2000

I walked down an arcade of pink and red bougainvillea and stood beneath a tree with only one thought in my head: this is my first morning in Mexico! I looked up into the tree and to my surprise thought I was looking at what appeared to be tufts of giant lichen. I snapped off a branch and knew at once I had to paint it in the short time I had. It was an air plant – those extraordinary epiphytes that grow without soil, taking their nutrients from the air. Here in Oaxaca they colonized telegraph wires. I spent days tracing the thin grey-green filaments of the air plant; picked out strands bearing dried flower heads; noted the cracked, cinnamon-coloured bark and all the time I had to portray depth and light falling across the filaments. I did not know if I could possibly succeed.

Back home in London I decided it was good enough to frame and hung it on my living room wall. I look at it across the room, feel heat, hear the drone of June bugs and the fleeting sound of a far-off mariachi band. I know too that a mile or so beyond the spot where I painted it stands the Tule tree, a living-cathedral tree that began growing around two thousand years ago.

OCTOBER

In autumn, there are lovely surprises at the edges of woods and sometimes the promise of a meal.

Along the Maenggwynedd Valley the meadows sloping down to the river are speckled with fungi every autumn. Hidden in the grass are brown fairy rings; more visible are the parasols and *Boletus;* the crown jewel is the brilliant orange-red waxcap, *Hygrocybe.*

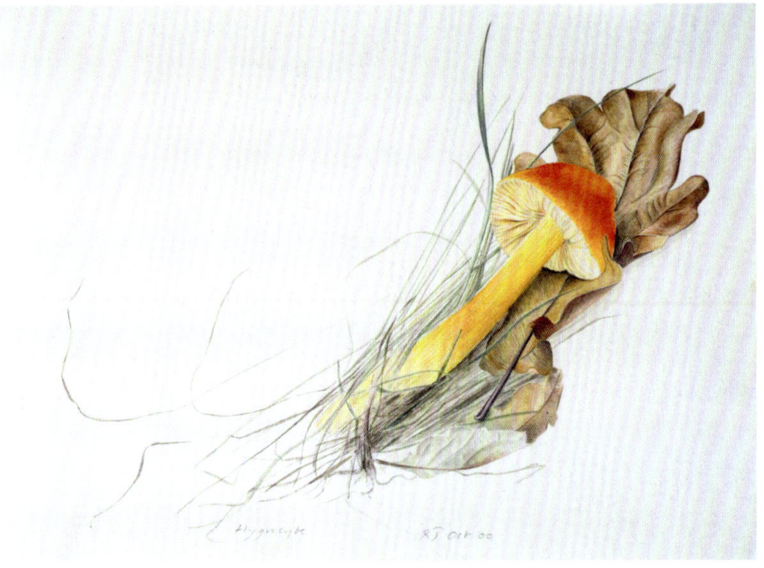

Waxcap (Hygrocybe), October 2000

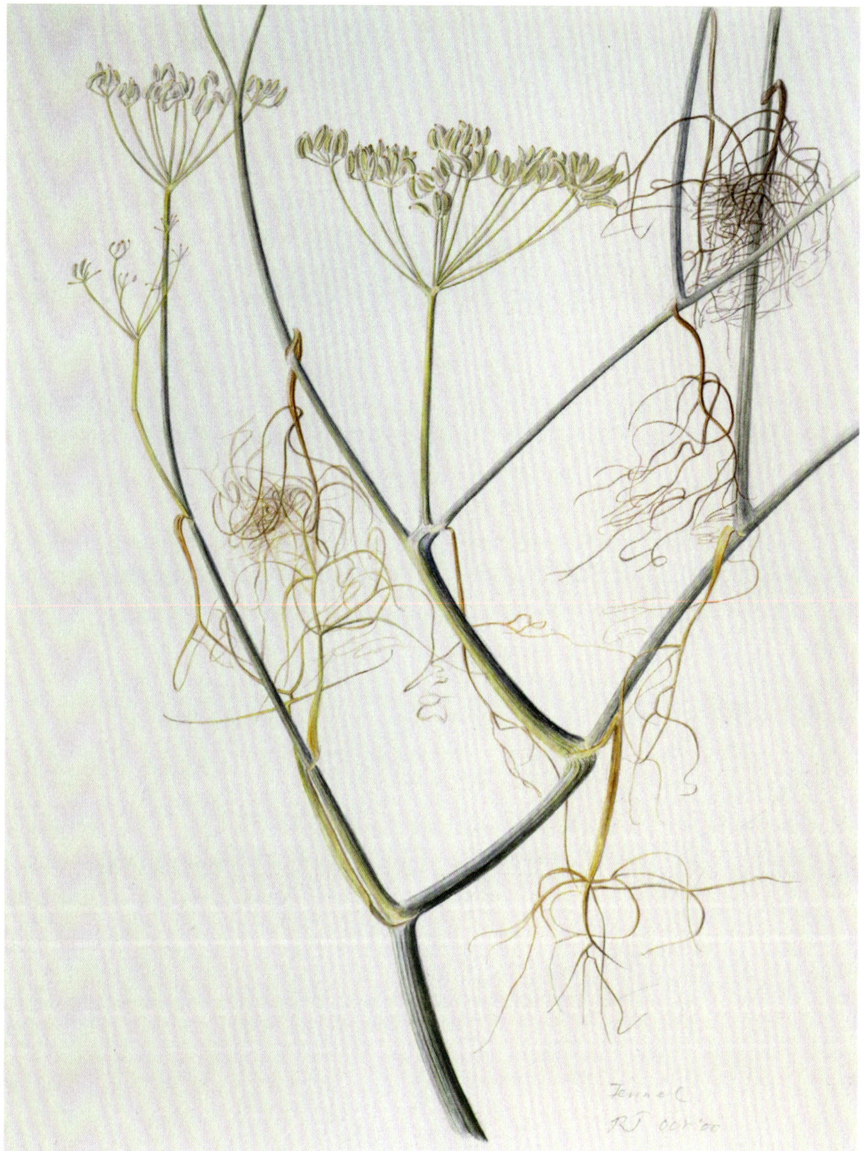

Fennel, October 2000

Every year the fennel growing in front of the cottage reaches a height of 9 feet (2.75 metres). It sways in the wind and is lovely to watch through the window from inside the cottage. It becomes seaweedy in autumn.

★ ★ ★

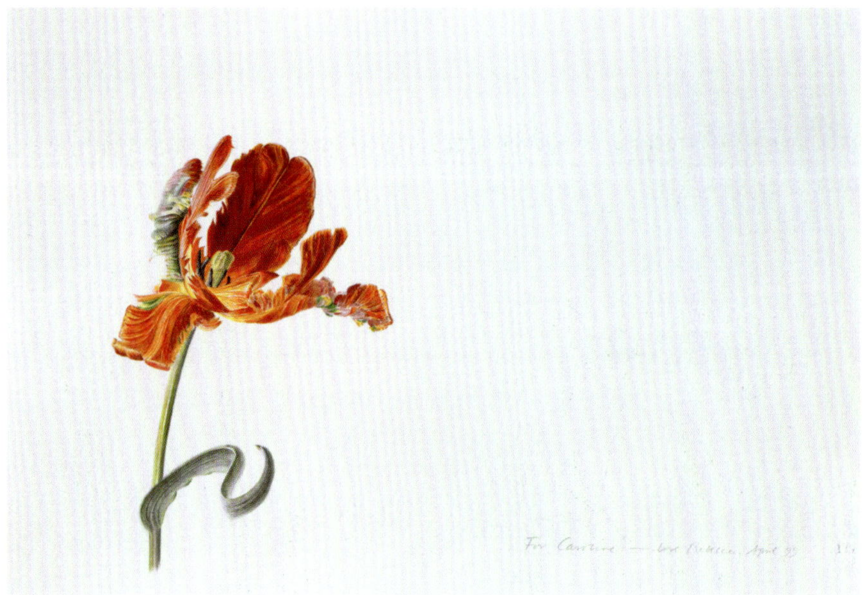

Parrot tulip, April 1999

To paint a plant – a rose, say – so that it is recognizable is to declare, 'This is a rose.' The rose dictates to the artist, and the artist dictates to the viewer. (I think of Michael Craig-Martin's work in Tate Modern; *An Oak Tree* is a glass of water on a glass shelf, which I at first took to be a joke; but the artist is challenging the power of art to confer 'truth' on what we think we are seeing.) To paint a rose as a rose is to revel in its form, to celebrate the beauty of its colour and construction. It is one of the most difficult of all flowers to paint because it is already beautiful, and its construction requires very careful planning at the drawing stage. Far easier to abstract it down, or paint a semblance, an impression. Redouté's roses are miraculous but have lost all meaning through over-reproduction.

Botanical painting – if we are to say 'painting', not 'illustration' or 'art' – is littered with fine watercolours of tulips, lilies, irises, auriculas – flowers with instant decorative appeal that I have deliberately avoided. Why choose yet another tulip? Rory McEwen has given us his exquisite paintings of the flower, and before him countless other botanical artists, not to mention Dutch flower painters and Persian miniaturists. But when a friend gave me a scarlet-flamed parrot tulip to paint, I could not refuse. The tulip is the most painterly of flowers.

And then . . . during the long daylight hours of late spring and summer, when these flowers are in bloom, and I'm sitting at the table before the opening bud of a rose, or a cup overflowing with multi-coloured primulas . . . What company! Why not . . . just this once?

A faithful rendering offers no opportunity for interpretation by the viewer. Today, people confronted with contemporary art need to decide for themselves an interpretation. The greater the incomprehension, the more we are forced to intellectualize, to find meaning. The viewer now decides what he/she thinks or sees.

Having been a slave to accuracy over the previous seven years – think of the love and fear that comes with that: love for the plant, fear of betrayal through misrepresentation – I find I'm wanting to rebel against this tyranny . . . to play a little, abandon a leaf, make up a green, *brush* instead of draw. Technically it is as daunting to loosen up as it is to remain forever in control.

There's no stopping the semi–real images I dream of painting, but the fear of the unknown is too great and I cannot free myself from the greater effort of painting the real. I used to regard the crossover into abstraction as the easy option. Wasn't this a short cut to making 'a picture', a licence to brush paint on paint, so that 'mistakes' could not happen? But now I see abstraction as a natural process. This is nothing new, and nothing I've discovered or experienced these last years is new, but it has been new to me and I remain in thrall to the process.

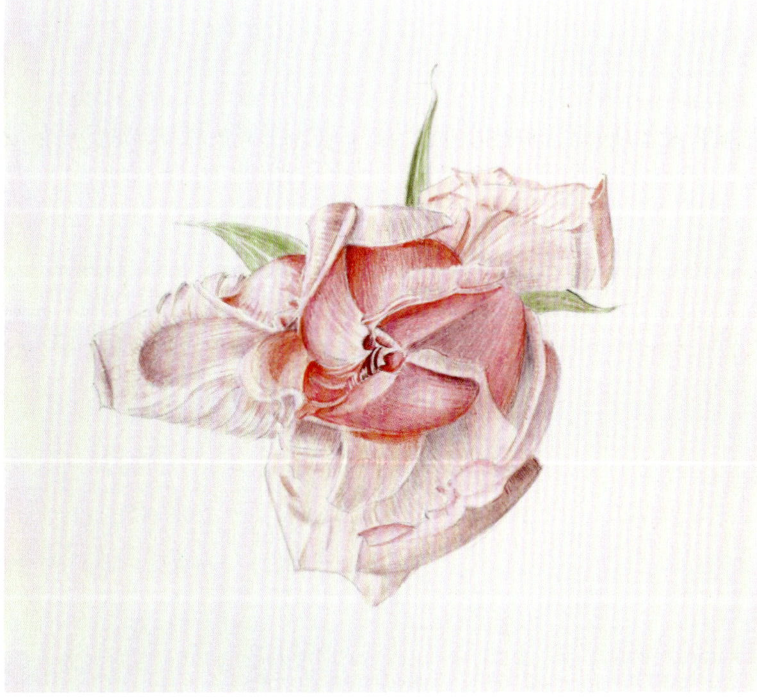

Rosa 'Albertine', June 2001

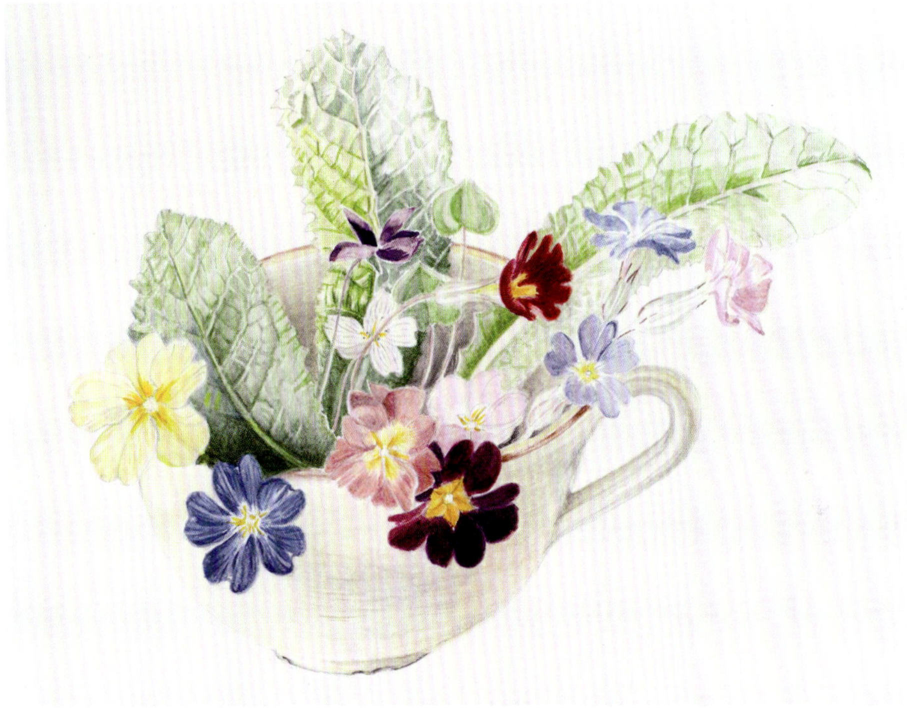

Cup of primulas, April 2010

There have been other processes at work. I have had to adjust daily life to allow for work which often begins spontaneously and which demands a commitment lasting days, intense concentration and a great deal of risk-taking. This means an unwillingness to make quick decisions with friends, to commit ahead. Keats called the state of uncertainty 'Negative Capability', an odd phrase he defined as 'when a man is capable of being in uncertainties, mysteries, doubts, without any irritable reaching after fact and reason'. I like not knowing what I'll want to paint next. That way lie surprises.

2001

NEW YEAR

I begin working towards a second exhibition at Lefevre Gallery, to be held at the end of the year.

On a visit to Lypiatt Park in Gloucestershire I was given some branches of a cherry tree that looked most decorative in its winter jewellery.

FEBRUARY

Walking with a friend in the Maengwynedd Valley. Deep gloom. Rain. Wet lichens sparkled in the leafless trees. I felt immediately inspired. I kept a branch moist with rainwater so that the lichens kept their shape and retained their strongest colour – like a stone in a stream. As lichens dry out they pale and start to curl; once moistened the thalli – strap-like filaments – flick back into shape, startling me with sudden bursts of movement. I inscribed the painting *Lichens on sycamore*; it was a mistake. A visitor to the exhibition at the end of the year wrote in Lefevre's visitors' book: 'Not sycamore! Field maple.' The tree is a close relative of sycamore, but with a more graceful habit.

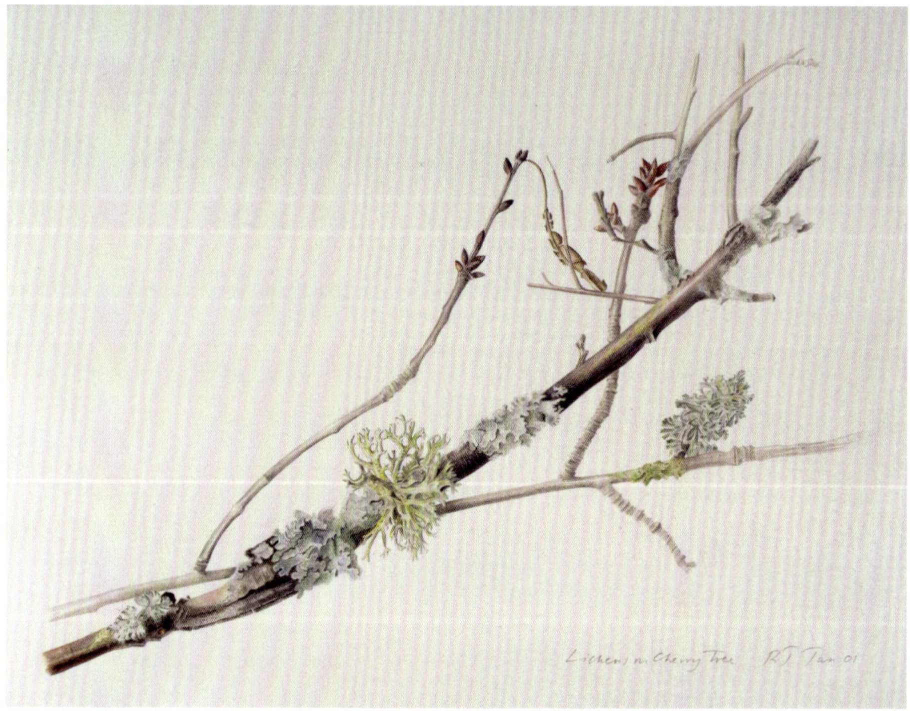

Lichens on cherry tree, January 2001

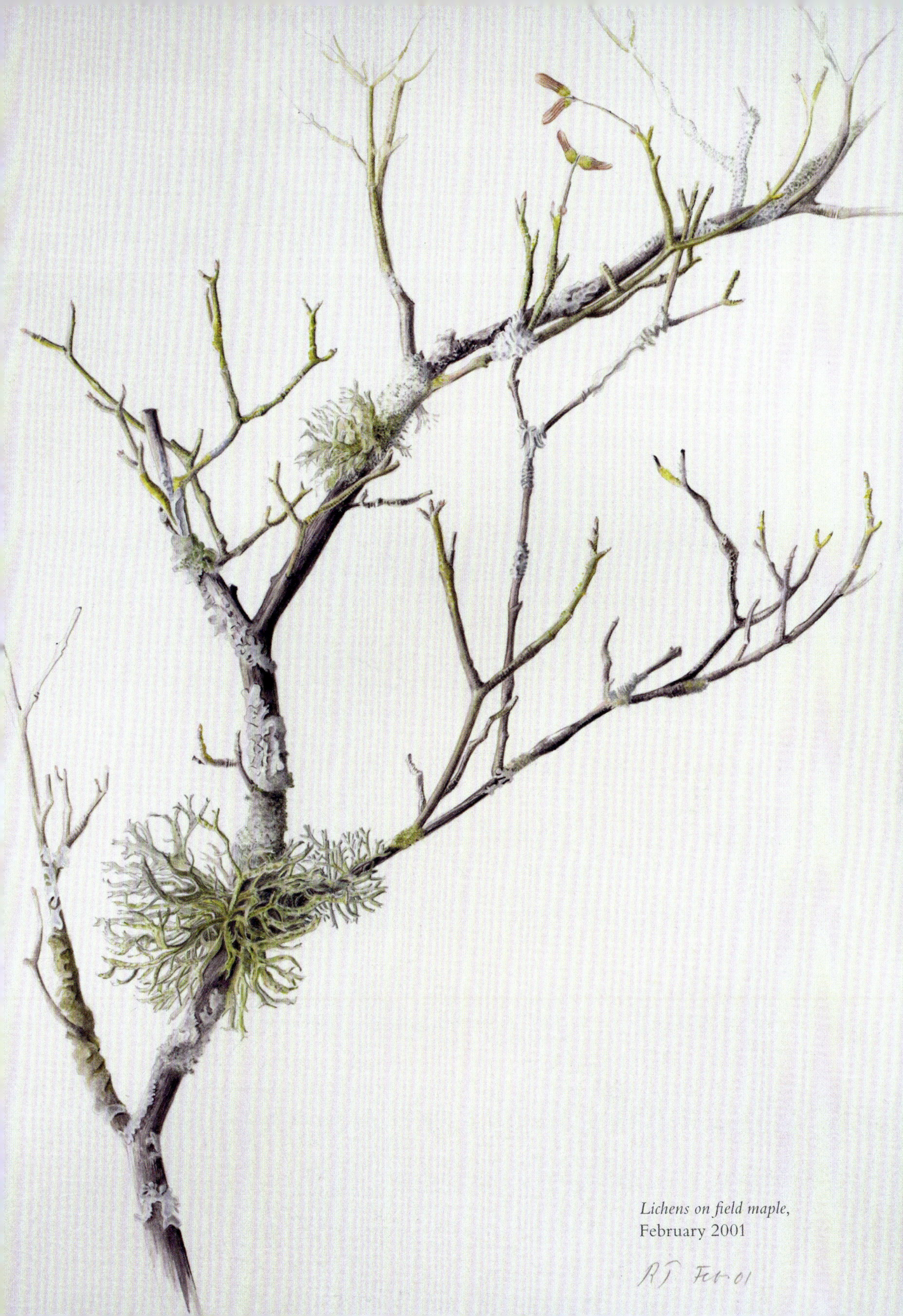

Lichens on field maple,
February 2001

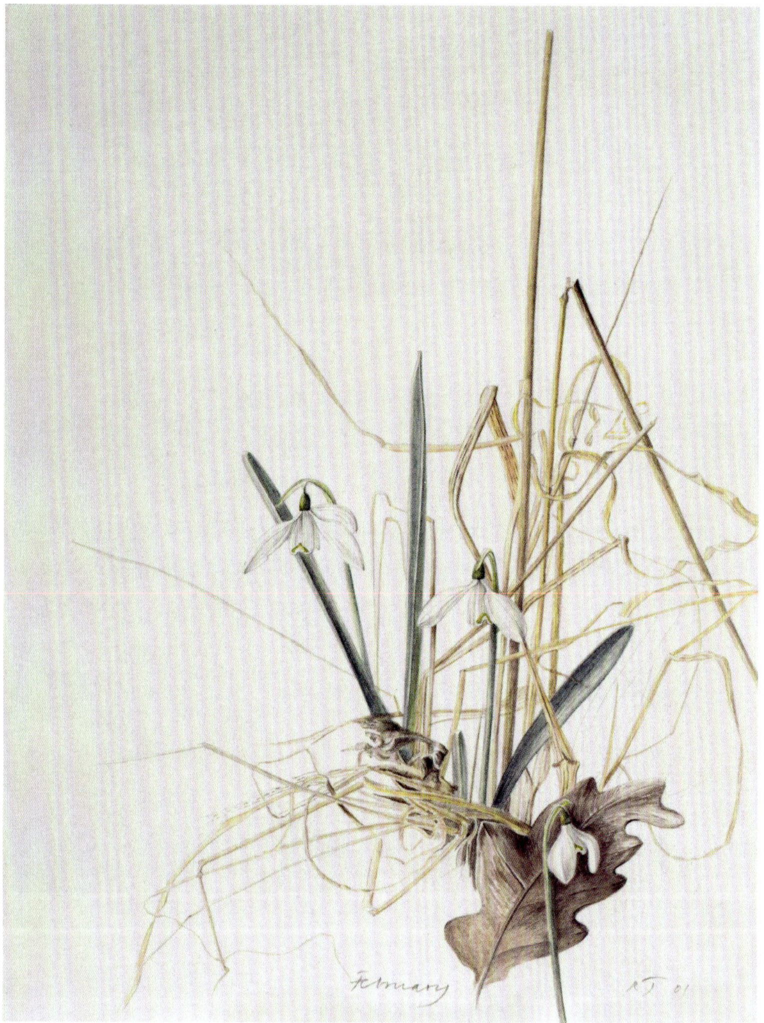

Snowdrops I, February 2001

February colours. I am tiring of the do's and don'ts of botanical painting and want to mess with the snowdrop, so pure, so perfectly engineered. I drop a flower off the bottom of the paper, select a few leaves growing at odd angles and scribble around parallel lines, thought to be non-existent in nature and which certainly shouldn't run parallel to the paper's edge.

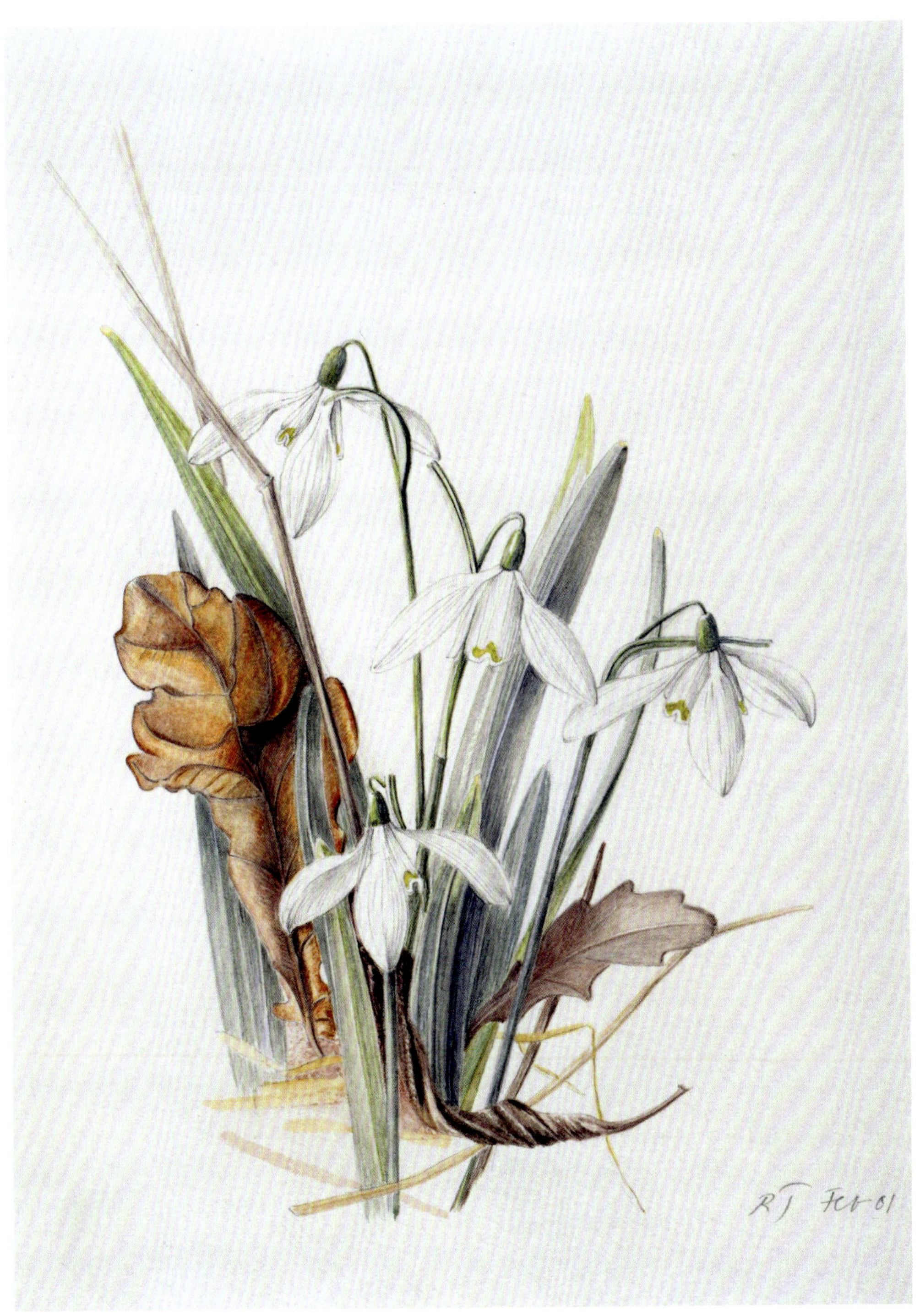

Snowdrops II, February 2001

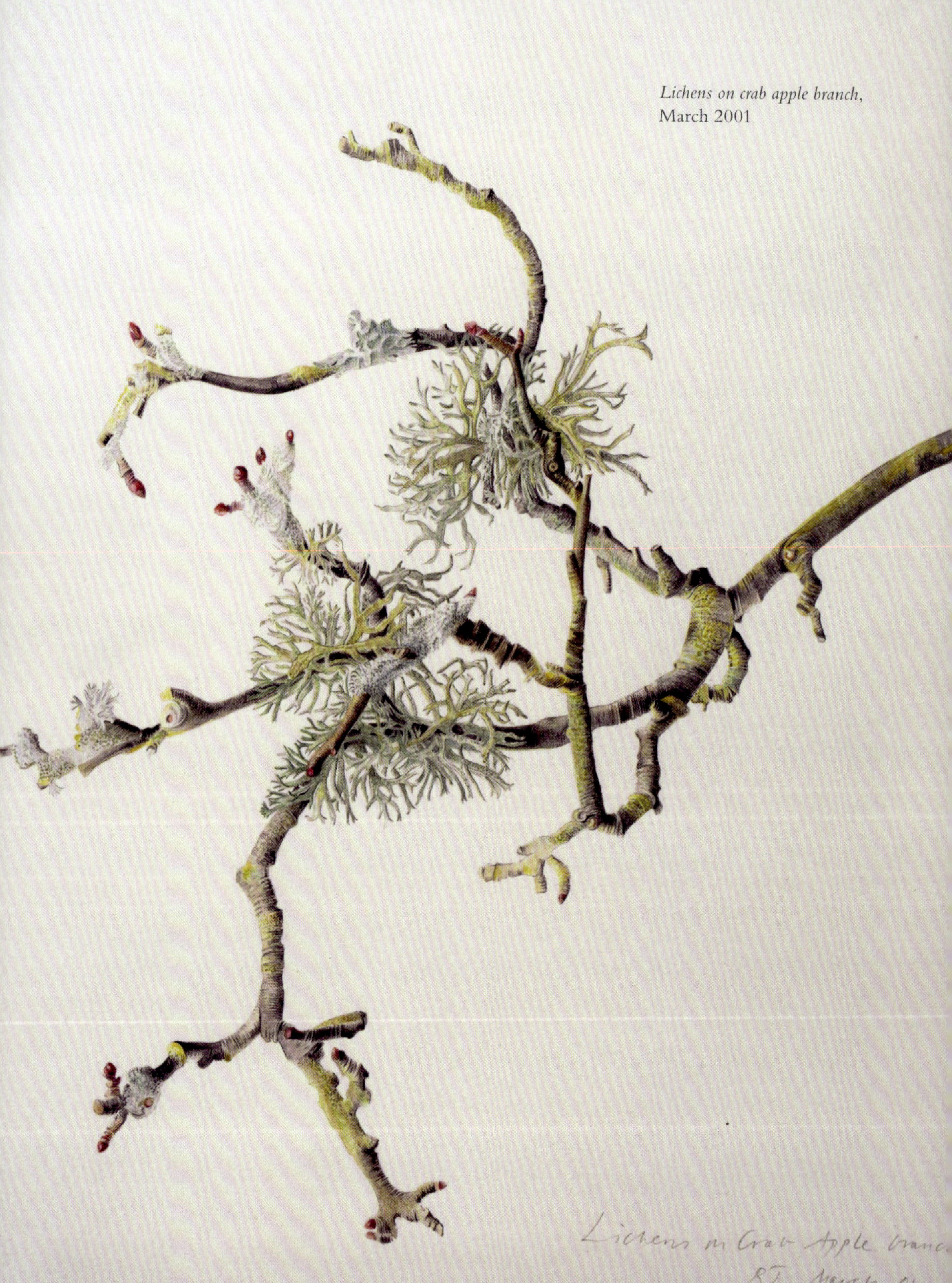

Lichens on crab apple branch,
March 2001

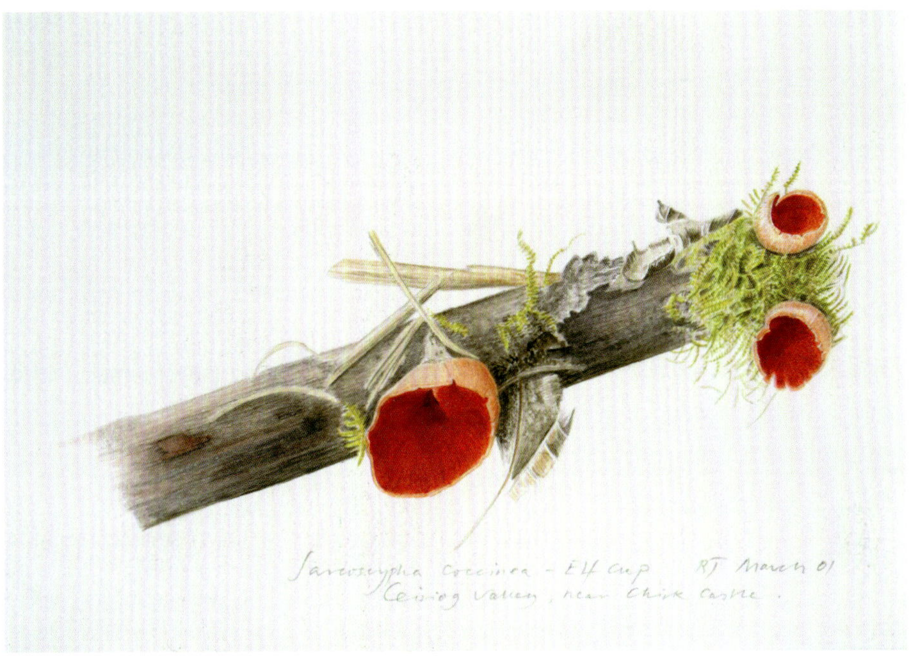

Elf cups (Sarcoscypha coccinea), March 2001

MARCH

I took a branch from a huge old crab apple tree, and posed it in the direction it had been growing, outwards from the trunk. I needed to think 'outside' the subject in order to paint the intricacies of the branch, so I thought of the early spring landscape in the hills, the geography of the Berwyn and magnificent mountain scenery beyond. I thought too of a skyscape I'd recently seen; patches of pale blue sky edged with ragged white and mauve-grey clouds played around the branch as I worked.

Driving above the Ceiriog Valley near Chirk Castle, a patch of red on the side of the lane turned out to be a colony of elf cups growing on dead wood. Brilliant scarlet against green, an astonishing sight in March.

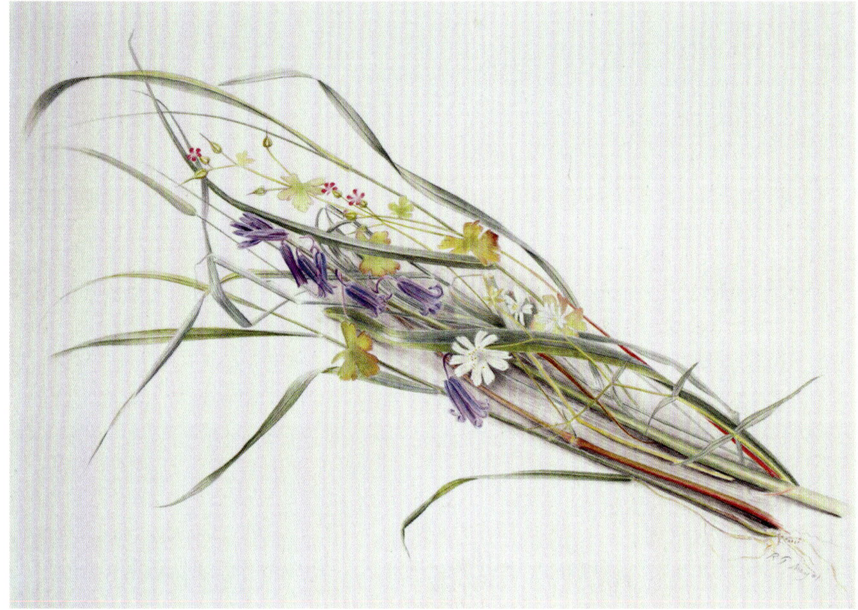

Bluebell, stitchwort, herb robert, grass, May 2001

MAY
The banks along the labyrinth of lanes are speckled pink, white and blue, the colours of May.

JUNE
There's an unusual amount of animal life going on in the field directly in front of the room where I'm working, providing endless amusement: six pregnant cows, two pairs of pheasants and a lot of rabbits. Now and again a lone crow. Busy little wagtails swoop up and down between the barn and the cottage. A hawthorn is blossoming at the base of a dead oak tree where I've seen the ginger fox slinking along the hedge. Mr and Mrs Pheasant take their evening stroll: he is resplendent in russet and purple feathers, fat and slow. Every now and then he lets out a penetrating squawk accompanied by a furious beat of his wings. The hen is speckled brown and white. She is quick and nimble and makes no sound as she forages for seeds in the grass. One night a cow gives birth in front of the bedroom window; I draw the curtains in the morning to see mother relishing the afterbirth, a long membranous thing blotched with blood, which she flicked into the air as she chewed. I conferred with the farmer. Apparently not all cows eat their afterbirths.

Pink sunset with mauve-grey cloudbanks. Imagine witnessing ever-changing slashes of blue, mile-high sunbeams and the appearance of a scrap of rainbow. Breath-taking to watch, but . . . in paint?

3 JULY

A DAY IN THE FIELD

6 a.m. A white-gold sunrise; silver dew speckles the green-gold grass; treetops float in mist in the valley below; a black-and-white Chinese landscape painting is gradually dissolving in strengthening sun. The only movement is animal movement. Three rabbits by the boulder, wagtails fluttering down to the fence and on to the field floor then up to the cottage. Mr Pheasant is snoozing in the shadow of the barn, his feathers ruffled.

6.30 a.m. Mr P. has joined the rabbits. They sit in the sun cleaning themselves. The sound of rose petals dropping. A squirrel ripples up the barn wall. Then sudden commotion: enter the pregnant herd. At the sound of diesel they trot fast towards the gate where the farmer scatters mineral supplement on the grass and sprays their back sides with fly repellent. They don't like this and quickly move away.

7.45 a.m. The cows have vanished from sight. The mists have dispersed. The heat intensifies. The air smells strongly of eglantine, and somewhere over the valley a plane drones.

Towards noon. A calf is born by the lower hedge. Mother eats the afterbirth. Clouds are gathering; the wind gets up. A swallow swoops in and out of the cottage.

Evening. Thundery heat. The wags are very active around their nest. Mr P. stands motionless mid-field. Mother and baby remain by the hedge. Foxgloves, in full flower now, streak the hedges magenta pink.

Late evening. The thunderstorm is coming. I watch baby flies crawl in loops across the glass; through the glass the wags continue their dance – marvellous hovering and sweeping downwards between the cottage and barn. Beyond, a lone, fat pigeon has appeared in the field, pompous like Mr Pheasant, the lilac-grey a lovely note amid the browning green. A magpie glides over the ground. Mother and baby are bonding down by the hedge.

9 p.m. The sky is stormy now. Wind. Lightning in the west, sky darkening. Soft pinky sheet lightning alternates with brilliant fork lightning. Dramatic darkening now. Some fat raindrops. Electric lights flicker. Mother and baby lie tucked up by the hedge; the rest of the herd shelter by a grove in the next field. All is well amongst the animals for the coming storm. What music should I play for my very own *son et lumière?*

8 JULY

Through the bedroom window I watch the wind in the ash tree, the faint sound of the opening bars of a Mozart symphony (no. 40) in another room. The music is in time with the swaying tree. I think 'heartbeat' and watch the big lower branches dip rhythmically downwards as if striking chords; the smaller upper branches swing and flicker east–west to the melody. The musical tree fills me with ridiculous joy.

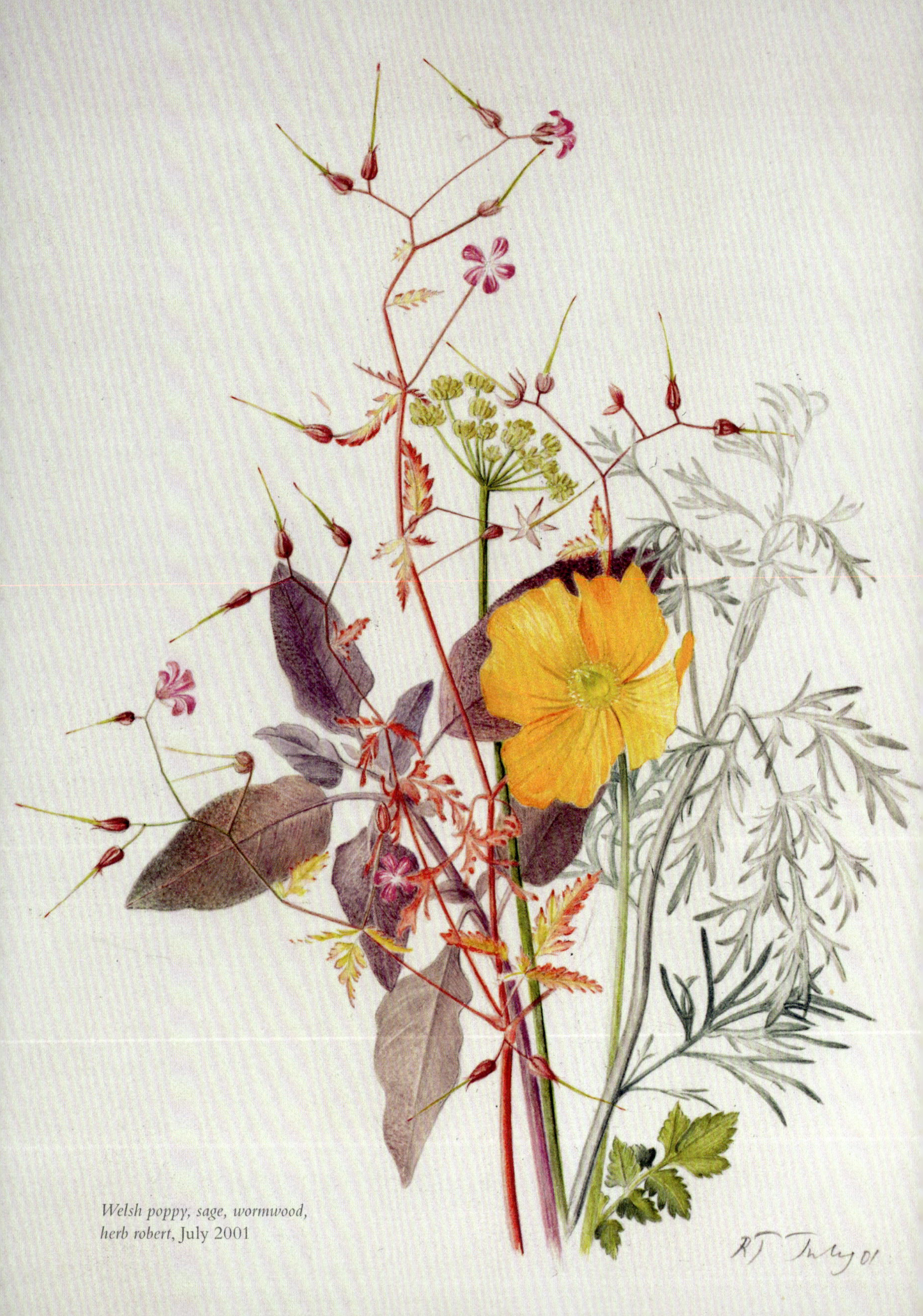

Welsh poppy, sage, wormwood,
herb robert, July 2001

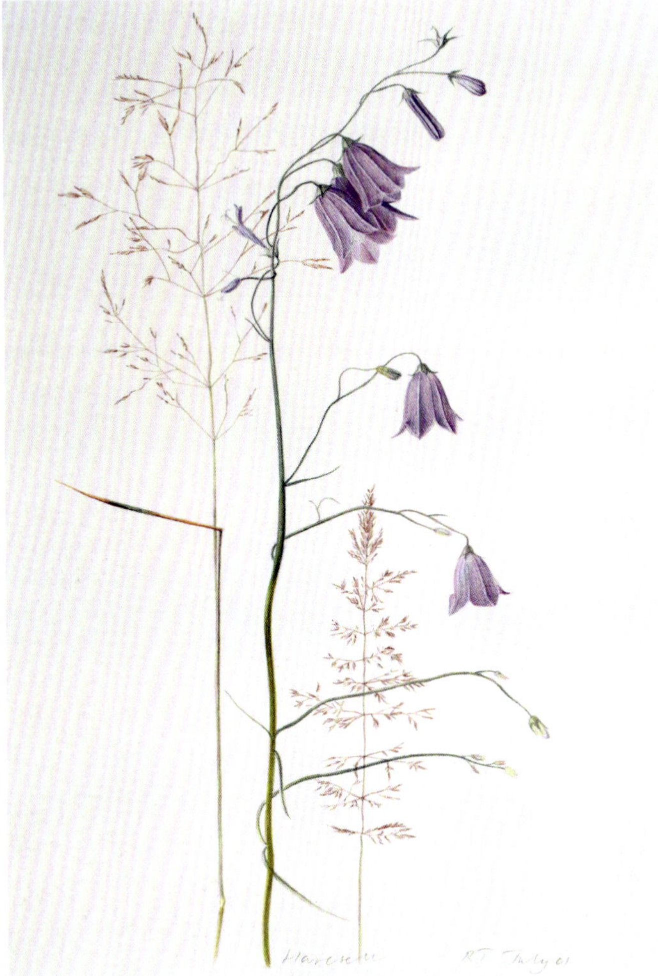

Harebell, July 2001

AUGUST

I darken the edge of a slender flowering rush, and it occurs to me that only a mountain range separates me from where Augustus painted his Welsh mountain landscapes of 1911–12. I had always thought that the speedy dots and dashes speckling his landscapes were nothing other than that, but I now know that they are gorse bushes and clumps of rush. In watercolour painting a finer effect can be created by stippling – dots and dashes are quickly built up with the point of a brush to create a textured effect, then smudged (softened) while still damp with a dry brush or point of a finger. This works in areas of landscape as well as on autumn leaves or the bark of a tree. As for a tree in full leaf, I was once taken by friends to David Hockney's studio in Kensington.

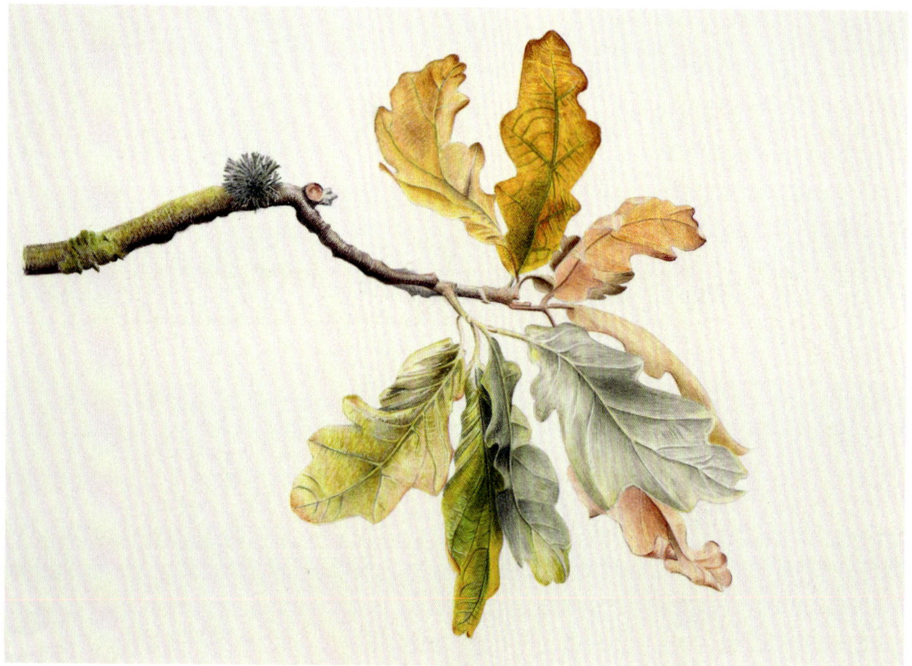

Oak leaves, August 2001

The visit was unplanned, and Hockney, who positively fizzed with energy, pulled out his Yorkshire landscape paintings for us to see. I looked at the leaves on his trees, painted at speed in watercolour with big brushes, and thought of the endless hours of concentration I put into the painting of a single leaf. For a moment I envied this cursory style, which relied for effect on an accumulation of joyous dots and dashes in various greens. But isolated on a sheet of paper one of those dashes of paint would not say 'leaf' and I confess I felt a little indignant on behalf of the leaf.

SEPTEMBER
Red and blue is an unusual colour combination out in the wilds, and very striking when, in late summer, sloe and hawthorn berries have ripened, ready for the picking to flavour gin or hedgerow jams.

★ ★ ★

Following Lefevre's second sell-out exhibition at the end of the year, I received a number of commissions. A commission means a certain curtailing of freedom and a strong nerve; no second chances with a seasonal plant growing far from home: a year

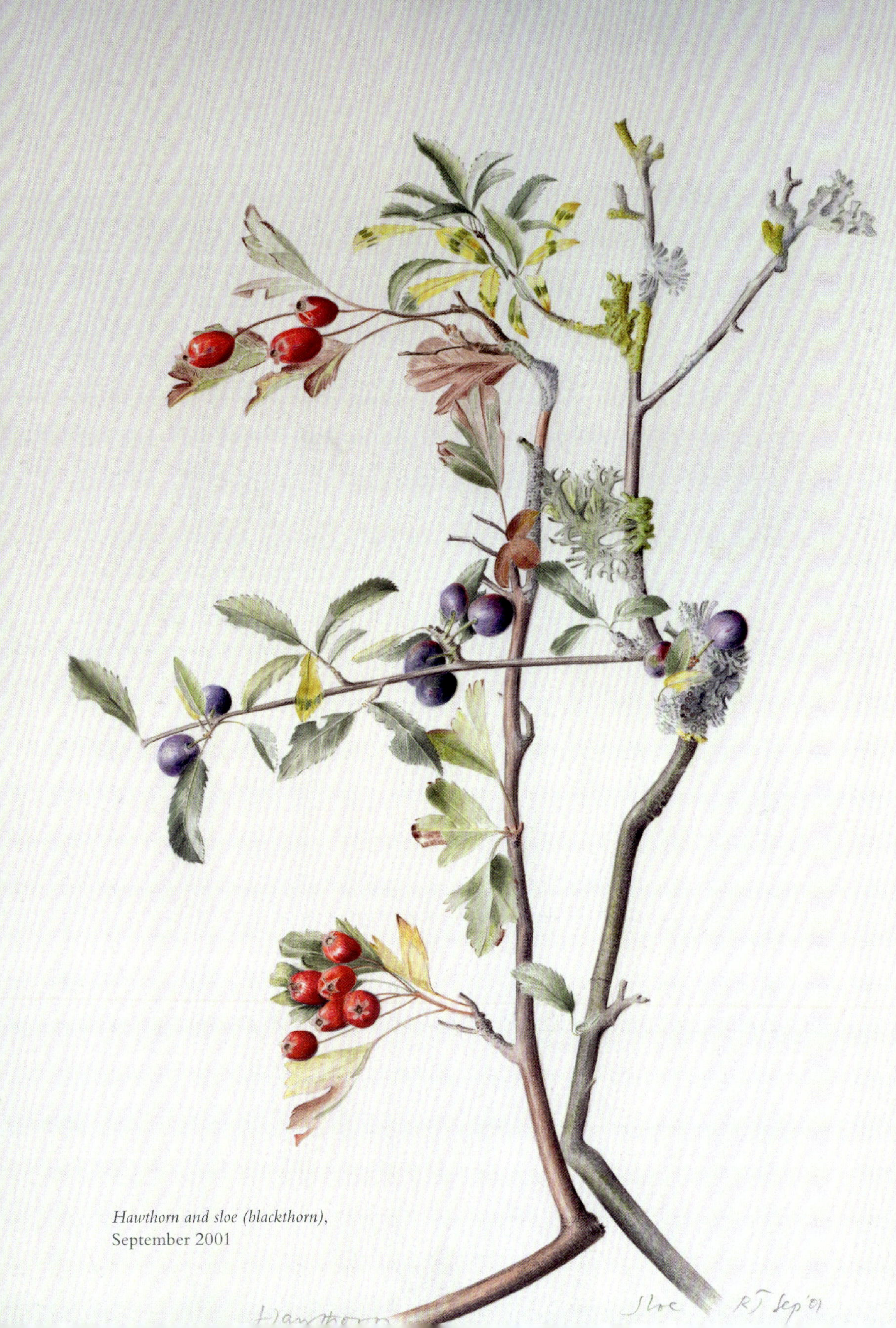

Hawthorn and sloe (blackthorn),
September 2001

may have to go by if something goes wrong. I dreaded that happening, or having an accident such as the time I dropped my brush loaded with green paint on to the paper just as I was finishing *Lemon branch* (see page 72).

2002

My first commission was to make a series of paintings on vellum of wild flowers growing by season at a private estate in the Chilterns. The land was farmed organically so wild flowers flourished in areas where the grass was left to grow long in the summer months.

I began with bluebells, which flower en masse in the Chiltern beech woods every spring. I walked through the woods, dug up a handful and planted them in a pot to take home (and later to replant). Popular descriptions of bluebell woods came to mind – the 'blue haze', the 'carpet of blue' – a favourite subject for greeting cards. But the truth is that the blue petals are striped with purple which you only see if you look at the flower in close-up. From a distance a carpet of bluebells appears blue because the colour travels further; it's something to do with the frequency of wavelengths and vibration.

For *Summer* my only brief was to include the pyramidal orchid. I was taken to a spot where they were growing in long grass on a sunny bank. I was given permission to pick an orchid and looked with dread at the layers of tiny pink butterfly-shaped petals. I added agrimony, knapweed, grass vetchling and the grasses they grew in. I put the plants in a bottle of water. It was a hot day and I was glad when a friend asked for a lift back to London. John Michell held the bottle upright for me between his knees, unaware that flecks of his cigarette ash were floating over the flowers as he talked very eloquently about the decline of beauty in the modern world. He got out at some traffic lights, and I continued across London with the precious bouquet held between my thighs.

I made a false start on the orchid, and began to panic, but I reasoned that I now knew what *not* to do and quickly began again. There was no knowing how long the flowers I'd assembled would last – petal drop is one of the hazards of botanical painting – and precious time can be lost arranging a group of plants in water so that they look as if they are still growing once painted on to a white rectangle.

For *Autumn* and *Winter*, I was free to choose any subject. I walked the lanes eyeing the hedging, which had been planted in the Anglo-Saxon manner, alternating species such as field maple, beech, blackthorn, spindle and hazel. This method of planting gave a striped effect, which was particularly visible in autumn. I cut out a branch of spindle bearing its brilliant pink and orange berries – 'The fruit which in our autumn woodlands looks a flower'[15] – and coupled it with indigo-black sloes, a jazzy mix of straight stems, thorns, fruits and turning leaves.

Come winter, I looked for subject matter among the trees: I had begun with bluebells growing at ground level and had progressed upwards, as it were, to a sunny bank, and

---

15 Alfred Tennyson, 'A Dedication'.

The seasons (vellum)

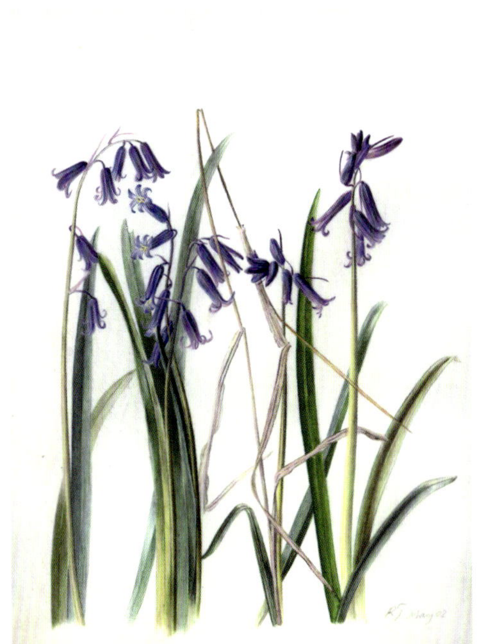

Spring, May 2002

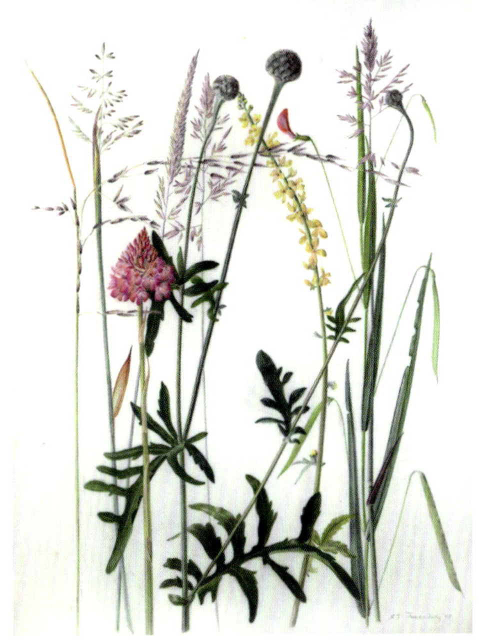

Summer, June–July 2002

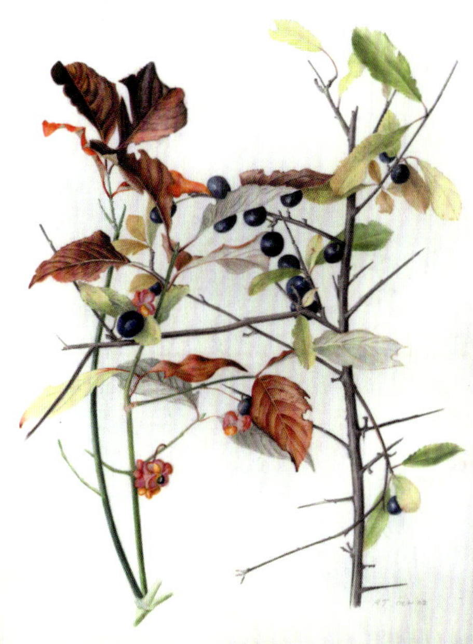

Autumn, October 2002

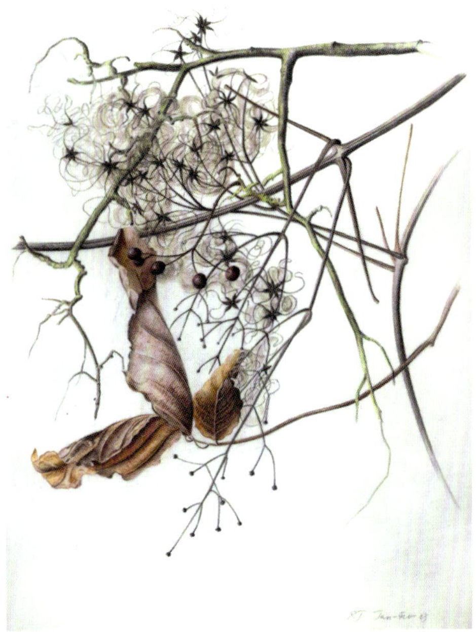

Winter, January–February 2003

from there to hedging; trees would complete the 'mapping'. In the woods I took a branch of beech with amber-brown leaves still attached and coupled it with a spray of old man's beard caught on hawthorn, its berries maroon with age. I arranged the cuttings as they'd been growing, hanging down from above, and had not the faintest idea how I would paint the smoky white fluff of old man's beard on creamy vellum. After much anguish, I successfully mixed a spot of sepia with opaque white and used a technique of splaying the brush which magically created the wisps – the 'atmosphere' – of old man's beard.

JULY

A second commission came via Plantlife, the charity established to protect wild flowers, some of which remain on the endangered list. One of these was the rare Deptford pink, a relative of the carnation, which was thriving at a bat reserve in

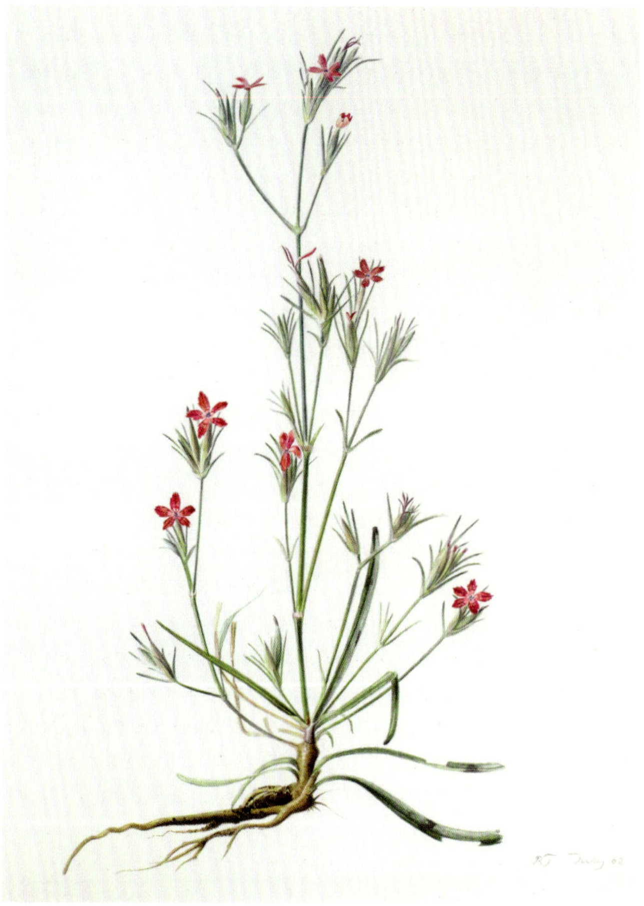

Deptford pink, July 2002

Devon under the care of the Vincent Wildlife Trust (VWT). Vincent Weir was a reclusive, elderly bachelor who lived in an apartment block in Whitehall. His passion was wildlife conservation. He helped to finance the protection of small mammals – he loved above all the otter, now thriving again in Britain's rivers – and also funded butterfly conservation. Recently he had made a generous donation to Plantlife. He liked the Christmas cards I had done for the charity, and he asked to be put in touch.

Over the telephone, he explained that he would like a painting of the Deptford pink (*Dianthus armeria*). He gave me permission to collect a plant and instructed me to meet the guardian at his bat reserve. He sounded distant – I was told that he liked to work at night – and he did not want to meet until after I'd completed the painting.

I had to collect the Deptford pink before the end of its flowering season in July and left London at 7 a.m. one morning to drive over three hours to the site near Buckfastleigh. I was accompanied by a friend, the philosopher Richard Wollheim, seventy-nine years old and staying with me while flat-hunting in London. The author of *Art and its Objects* and *Painting as an Art*, he revered Titian and Poussin but was curious to see how I went about 'the painting of a plant'.

It was a very hot day. The guardian of the bat reserve met us in a dreary Little Chef café and led us to the site where hundreds of Deptford pinks were growing through cracked tarmac between disused barns and sheds. Richard went for a stroll with the guardian while I communed with the little flower – barely knee-high with exquisite pink flowers atop stiff stems. I sat on the ground in the shade to try and mix the pink on the spot – pink is a notoriously difficult colour to get right – but the bright light on the white paper dazzled my eyes until I could no longer see.

We decided to go for a pub lunch and as I got into the car I dropped my watercolour pans all over the ground. I was not feeling very hopeful.

Back at the site, I lifted a single plant with root intact so that it could be replanted in exactly the same spot after I'd finished the painting. I dreaded the thought of painting it. Wild flowers typically have very little 'flesh' on them and the greatest control is required when applying colour to thin stems and tiny flowers.

By now we were exhausted from the early start and the heat and I could not drive home without a rest somewhere. There was only one possibility: a field. We climbed over a gate and Richard lay down in the shade of some trees and instantly dozed off. I sat on some soft grass higher up the field but I could not stop thinking about the precious flower lying in a plastic box in the car boot and how important it was to get it back to London and into a flower pot and to start work as soon as possible. There was no way of knowing how sturdy the plant was or how long its flowers would last.

Back home in Covent Garden I potted it and left it out on the terrace overnight. Next morning it had not wilted, and a bud had opened. I was charmed; all the buds continued to bloom over the days that I painted it. I kept wanting to say 'thank you', although the petals were little fiends to paint. They had the serrated edges characteristic of the Pink (Caryophyllaceae) family, and were speckled with minute white spots; just visible at the centre of the flower was a mauve stamen – all this the size of your little fingernail. The stiff central stem was ringed with a rosette of leaves at its base, which together with the dark brown root helped to give it character.

I had never painted with an audience. Also staying with me at this time was a dear friend, Robyn Davidson, famous for her book *Tracks*, a beautifully written account of her long walk with camels across the Australian desert. My friends were curious, so I let them see how work began very unpromisingly, how the plant took form very slowly as thin layers of paint were built up over three days; how the painting changed imperceptibly from a ghost-like form to a semblance of the real thing. Robyn was surprised to see me still sitting, still painting after several hours had passed, and when those hours became days she wondered out loud, 'Such patience!' But I did not see it like that; to lose oneself in a plant is to forget time, to enter a world that in close-up expands into a universe.

I walked with the painting across Trafalgar Square to Whitehall, where Vincent Weir had invited me to tea. I was worried that he would not be impressed, given the skimpiness of the plant. He rose from an armchair, very tall, around seventy years old, with a shy manner and immaculately dressed. We sat making polite conversation over tea and cucumber sandwiches. In my mind the painting burned in its folder. Would he like it? 'Oh yes,' he said, when I finally opened the folder. To my surprise he thanked me for being 'so kind', and over the following years commissioned paintings of a dog rose, a branch of blackberries, and a foxglove. All had flowers of varying pinks.

★ ★ ★

The jeweller Angela Bielenberg has a special way of combining gold and silver so that the two metals fuse in a very attractive mottling. One day she handed me a branch of blackthorn encrusted with gold and silver lichens to paint and we agreed that we would swap the painting for a piece of her jewellery. She had made a pair of 'bean and pod' earrings using her special technique, and given the fact that I had studied the Leguminosae family, and previously worked in gold, there seemed a beautiful logic to our swap.

Years later we did another swap; I gave her a painting of coppery bracken in exchange for a silver and rock crystal necklace.

2003

February fair maids have spear-like leaves that are able to push through frozen ground (hence another name, 'snow piercer'), but the leaves I am painting have pierced decaying beech leaves, carrying them skywards as they grow.

In May, after finishing lily-of-the-valley (for young Lily up-the-valley) and, like the snowdrop, exquisitely engineered in greens and whites, I wanted to be left free to do what I fancied. I took a long break and had no desire to know when, or what, I would paint again.

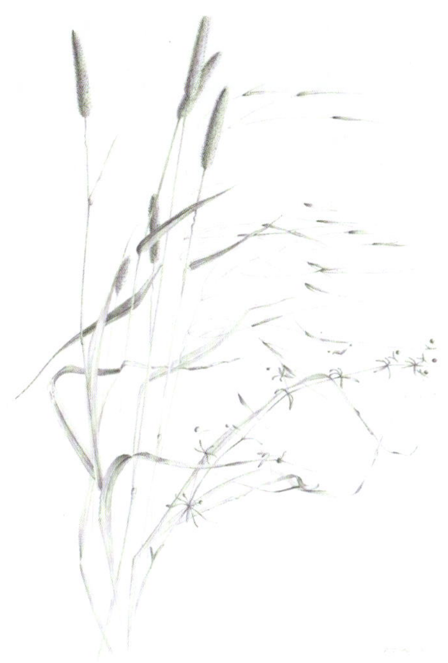

Cat's tail, wild oat, goose grass (pencil), August 2003

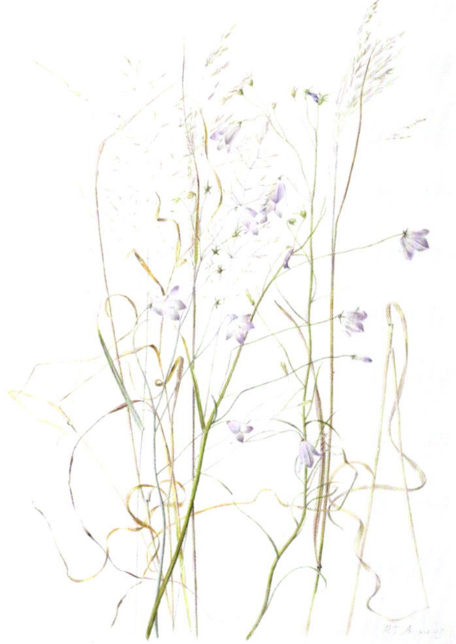

Harebells in grass, August 2003

AUGUST

I find freedom of movement in long summer grasses, when they are collapsing, forming mad calligraphic slashes and wiggles. They are perfectly suited for pencil work. It was a joy to rediscover graphite, to dispense with colour mixing and brushwork.

2004

JANUARY

I thought I would never be able to paint a feather after seeing Eliot Hodgkin's tempera paintings of feathers, so perfectly formed with minute brushstrokes that they looked as if they might float away from the picture. But when someone asked me if I'd ever thought of painting a feather, I collected a handful and left them lying around so I could get used to seeing them. After a couple of years, I knew the moment had come because I began to feel sorry for them. That meant I no longer feared them. I chose a striped red kite feather, and in no time I was thinking 'rain clouds' and weather effects, just as in the stained steel of the old knives. I was streaking paint from the stripes . . . wasn't that rain falling from clouds? I loved sailing up there in the sky with the kite.

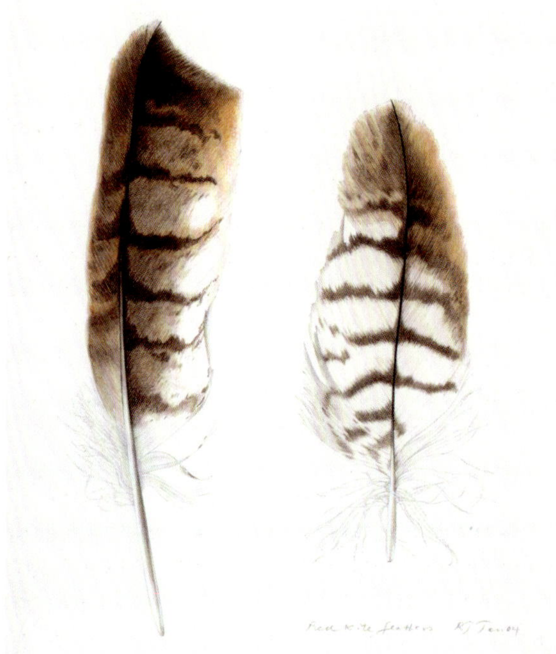

Red kite feathers, January 2004

★ ★ ★

That spring I had been invited to curate an exhibition of my grandfather's work, planned for the autumn. It was to be titled 'Master Works' and was confined to the years 1900–1920. These paintings and drawings bore no relation to the artist's later work, when he was overburdened by portrait commissions and was drinking. Over time he lost his judgement, sentimentalizing his female subjects, leaving many works unfinished and in a sorry state. Some of these paintings had been burned, but not enough; very poor work continues to surface on the art market while some of the very best are held in museums, and those held in private collections are only seen when on loan to exhibitions. 'Master Works' reminded people of his once astonishing gift.

It was after the death of my father in 1984 that I began to wonder who would be left in the family to keep an eye on Augustus's legacy, and after I spotted a fake coming up for sale at a London auction house, I very quickly decided it would have to be me. I was standing in front of an oil of a woman seated in an armchair, catalogued as by Augustus John, and knew at once that the painting was not by him. I was very shocked. This was my first encounter with a fake (although fakes had begun to appear in Dorelia's lifetime), and after its provenance was checked the painting was withdrawn from auction and returned to its owner. From then on I began to be consulted about his work.

While researching still-life paintings for Elizabeth David in the Courtauld Institute's Witt Library, I decided to take a look through the twenty-odd boxes of photographs of Augustus's work. There were around a thousand photographs and I was astonished to find so many works I had never seen before. The contents of the boxes had become muddled so I offered to arrange the photographs into tighter categories, which gave me a valuable overview of Augustus's work. I built up an archive of exhibition catalogues, art books and photographs, and since no single comprehensive reference book of the artist's work exists, I had to hunt through the archive for information each time I was consulted about a work. In this way I built up a strong visual memory and I could tell almost immediately if a painting was a pastiche or whether a drawing had been copied, or traced from a reproduction. A 'copy' is not difficult to spot: a laboured outline and minute variations in shading or a slightly altered scribble give the game away.

JUNE

The month of roses. Time to fulfil two outstanding commissions: first, the wild dog rose which grows everywhere in the hills – I had only to walk a few yards to collect a branch – and afterwards a drive down the motorway to a garden in Oxfordshire. The owner showed me around her collection of old roses, snipping out four species to choose from. She wrapped them in wet newspaper and attached labels – the old-fashioned kind with string – carefully inscribing each one with the Latin name. In sweltering June heat I drove back to London, nerves on edge while I sat in a traffic jam. Every second counted: I ran up the stairs to plunge the bouquet into water (and rushed back to the car to find a parking fine). I stared for a long time at these beauties, and singled out the striped *Rosa* 'Variegata di Bologna'. The carmine stripes on pale pink petals acted as marker buoys in a rough sea, and made it more exciting to paint.

2005

Time to think about a change of direction and at New Year I wrote down a resolution:

> I begin drawing again. What I want to do is to start and stop, then start drawing the subject again at a changed angle, and continue in this way until the paper is well covered with drawing. I have an idea to select a part of the subject and paint it so that it can be identified, but it must be left incomplete, so that it appears suspended within the drawing. The painted area will hold the eye, the drawn area will rest the eye.

I made no attempt to work in this way – thoughts often outstripped execution – but the imagery remained so strong that I began to suspect that the coloured object suspended in grey lines represented a human being caught in a web of possibilities.

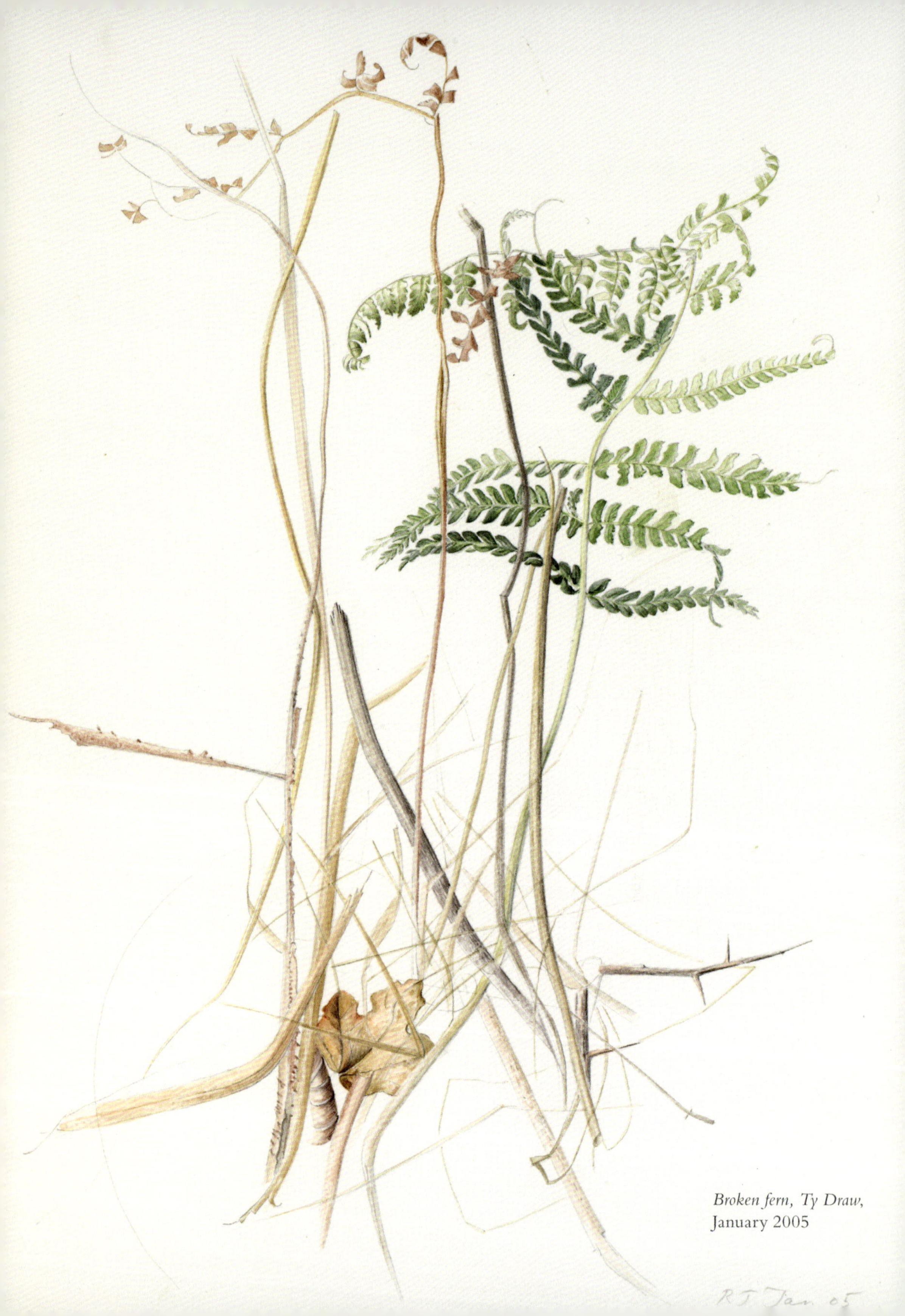

Broken fern, Ty Draw,
January 2005

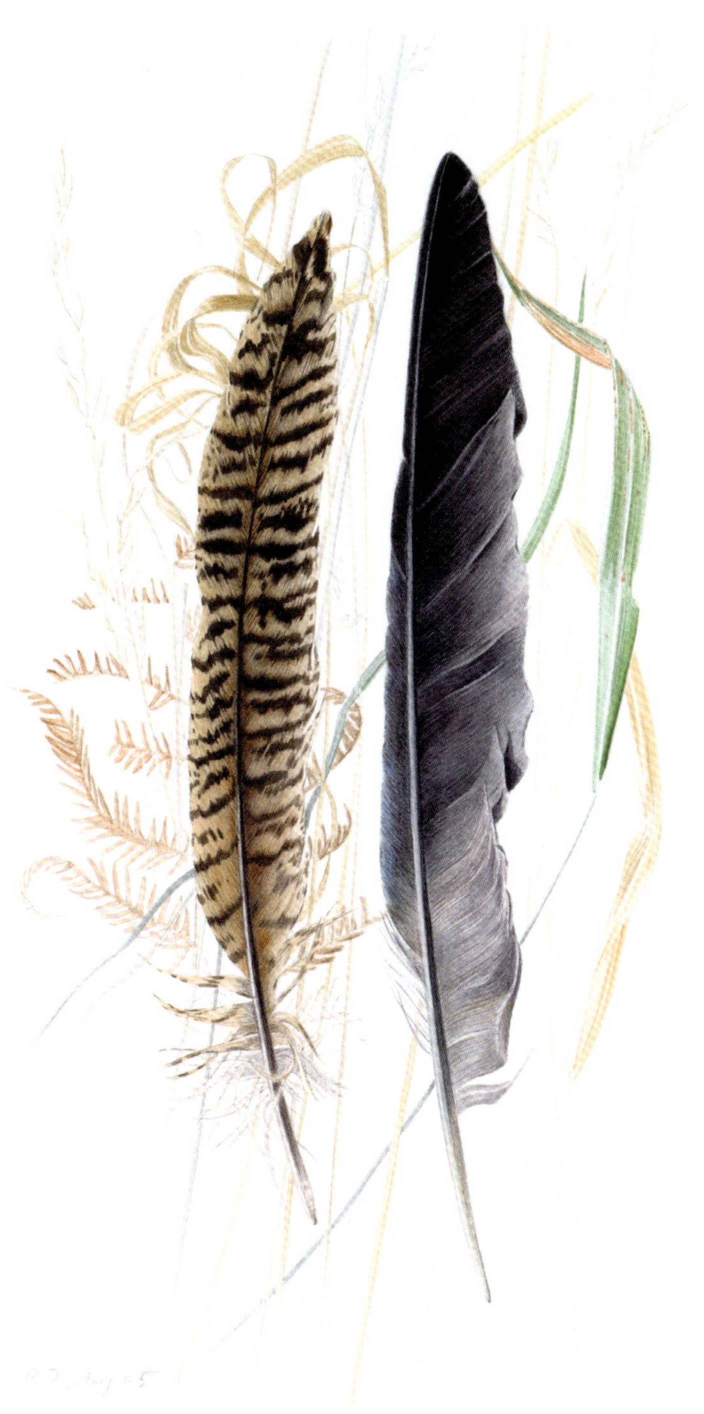

Feathers against grass, August 2005

SEPTEMBER

Walking in a deep wooded valley near Lake Bala I came face to face with an ancient oak tree thickly covered in a spectacular variety of lichens, among which was *Graphis scripta* – the lichen resembling an ancient script. I took a branch home to paint.

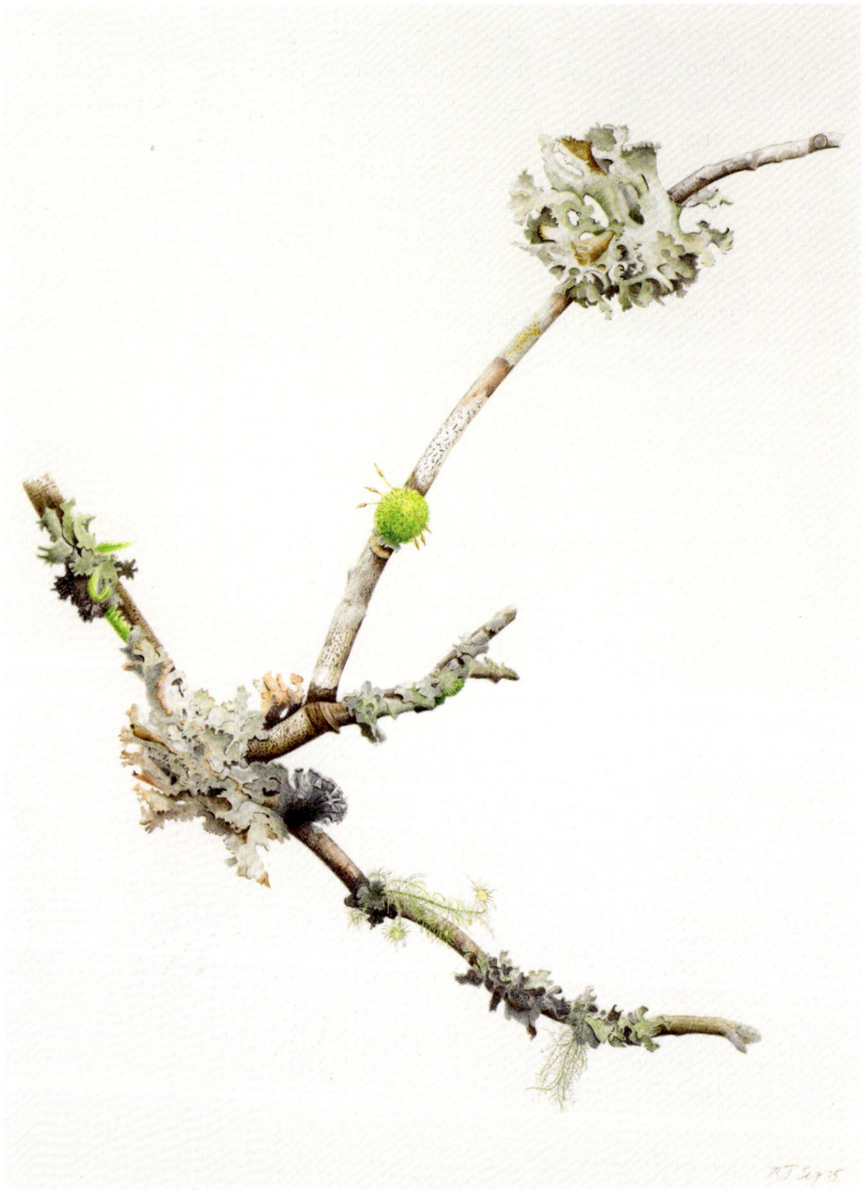

Lichens on oak branch growing between Lake Bala and Lake Vyrnwy, September 2005

2006

For the first time I combined botanical subjects with objects found on my walks. I looked for accidental couplings caused by wind, or animal movement: a branch of a tree blown into a stream, sheep's wool snagged on gorse.

AUGUST

I took from the river a piece of slate that had been washed smooth by water. New territory. It did not matter that I was exaggerating its layers and surface markings in changing tones of grey: seas and land masses were forming under my brush and soon the river slate disappeared. I was looking down on an imaginary landscape, but in reality I was looking down on 400-million-year-old mud metamorphosed into slate.

I saw bird feathers sticking out of the ground like a dart, or lying suspended in long grass. Isn't there a Chinese style of calligraphy called grass script? I discovered that the Chinese character for 'grass' also means 'loose and sketchy'. This made perfect sense to me and over the next couple of summers I painted a series of feather and grass paintings.

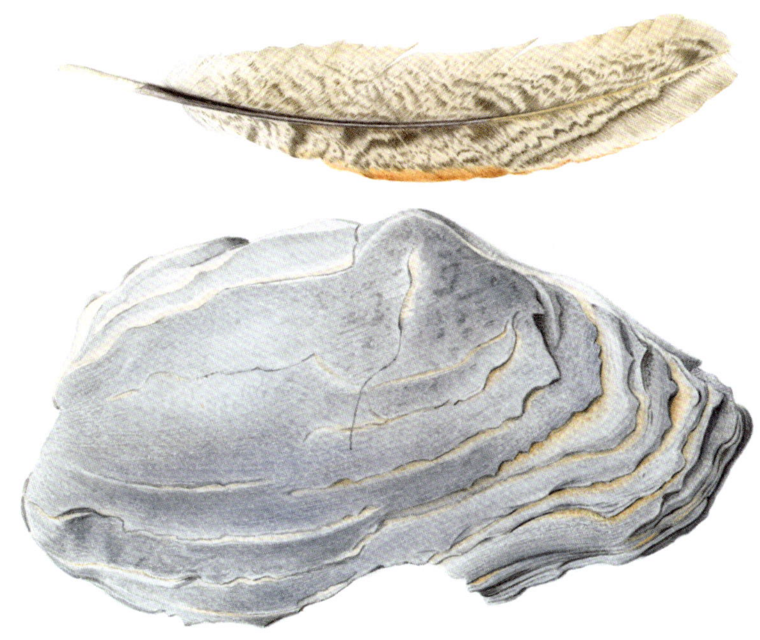

Feather and slate, August 2006

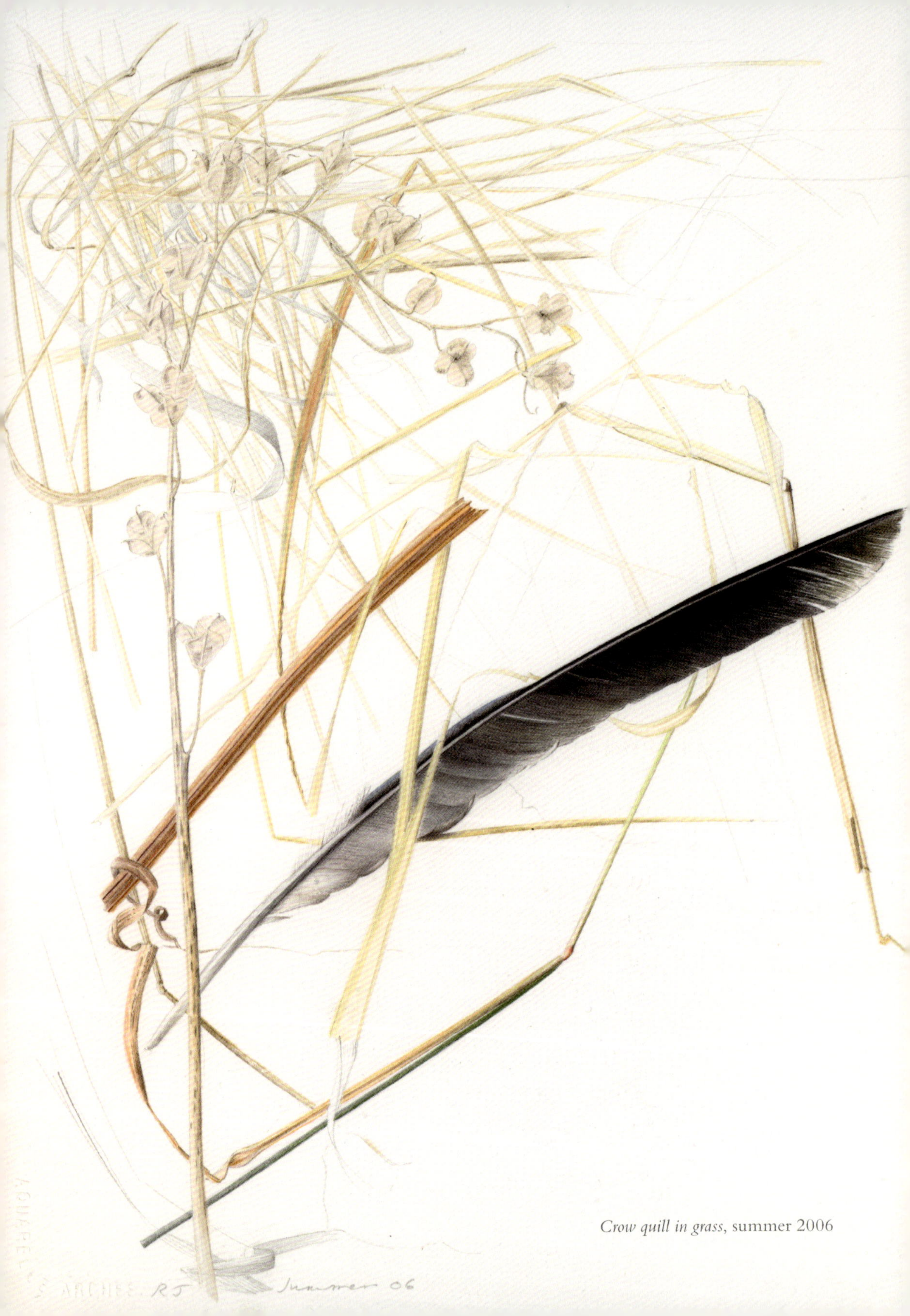

Crow quill in grass, summer 2006

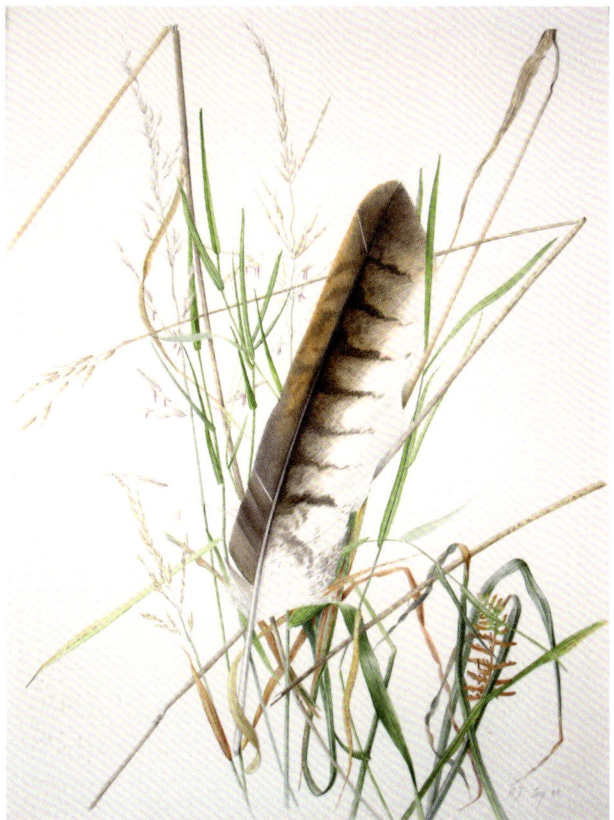

Red kite feather in grass, September 2008

2007

Until his death in 2011, Andrew Wyld was England's most knowledgeable and respected collector-dealer in watercolour paintings and drawings. He had made his name identifying lost watercolours by Turner and Richard Bonington and dealt in the great English watercolour artists of the late eighteenth to mid-nineteenth centuries. My exhibition with Andrew that April consisted entirely of works executed in Wales (dating back to 2003). They made a stark contrast to the landscape paintings normally found hanging on the walls of his gallery. One of the exhibits was a painting on vellum of a dock leaf reduced by an insect to green-gold lace, which I found growing at the back of the cottage (see page 149). It was later shown in the Shirley Sherwood Gallery of Botanical Art at Kew, in an exhibition of work by Rory McEwen, together with artists who had been influenced by him.

★ ★ ★

Botanical subjects that offered volume and surface freed me from the linear nature of wild flowers, lichens and grasses. There were rich pickings amongst autumn fungi and fallen leaves.

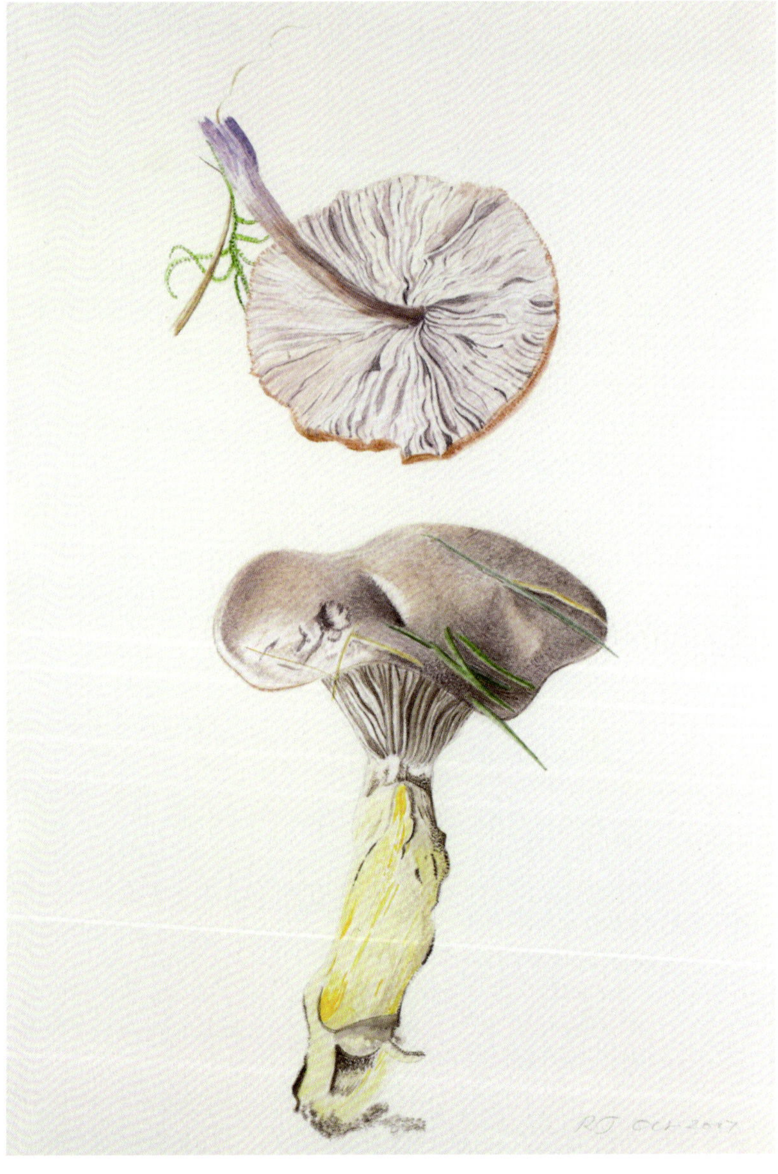

Laccaria bicolor (top) *and Gomphidius glutinosus,* October 2007

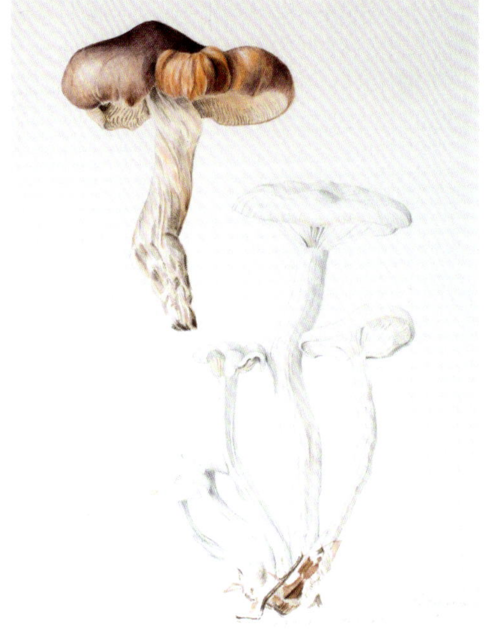

Tricholoma ustale (top) *and Lyophyllum connatum*, October 2010

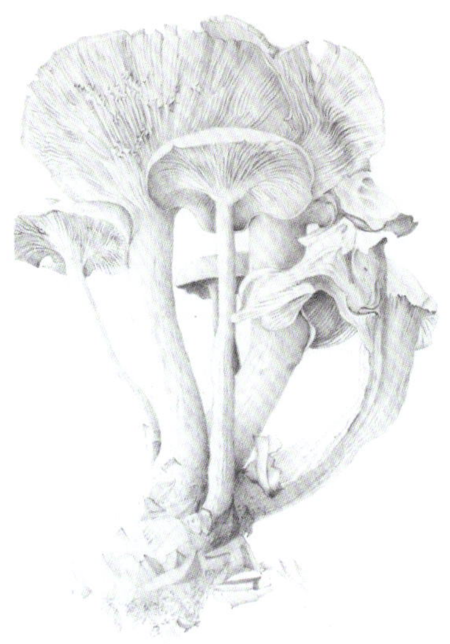

Lyophyllum connatum (pencil), October 2010

When I first heard someone quote Ruskin's famous remark, 'If you can paint *one* leaf, you can paint the world,' I vaguely thought that one day I would find out what he meant.

It was autumn 2000, I was in London and not feeling well. There was nothing to paint except for some pinky-grey leaves from a Virginia creeper that lay scattered on my terrace – they were as fragile as tissue paper and looked the way I felt. Soon a series of ghost-like leaves appeared in a small drawing book. They looked unlike anything I'd ever done before.

I painted in my book of leaves at erratic intervals. I liked it that way, spending a whole day on one leaf, then ignoring the book for a year or two. Or I'd want to paint a leaf too large for the book.

Up in the hills, huge dock leaves begin to turn spotty in summer and are prey to an insect that reduces them to lace: I reworked this leaf-lace in green-gold paint on vellum, until it resembled an object of fabulous Byzantine metalwork, pierced all over and slightly misshapen with age.

★ ★ ★

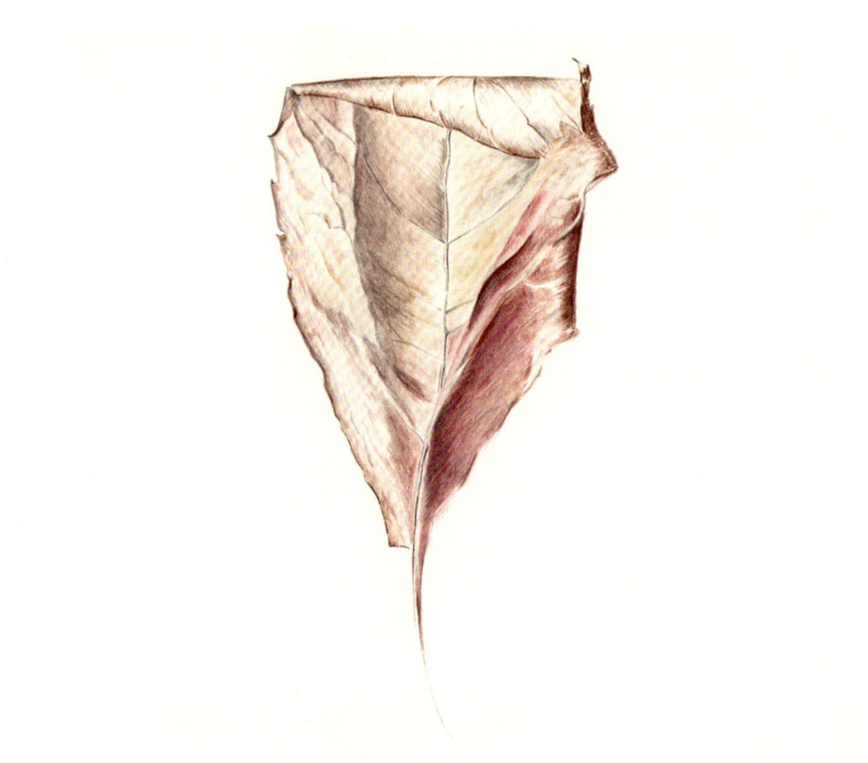

Virginia creeper leaf, September 2000

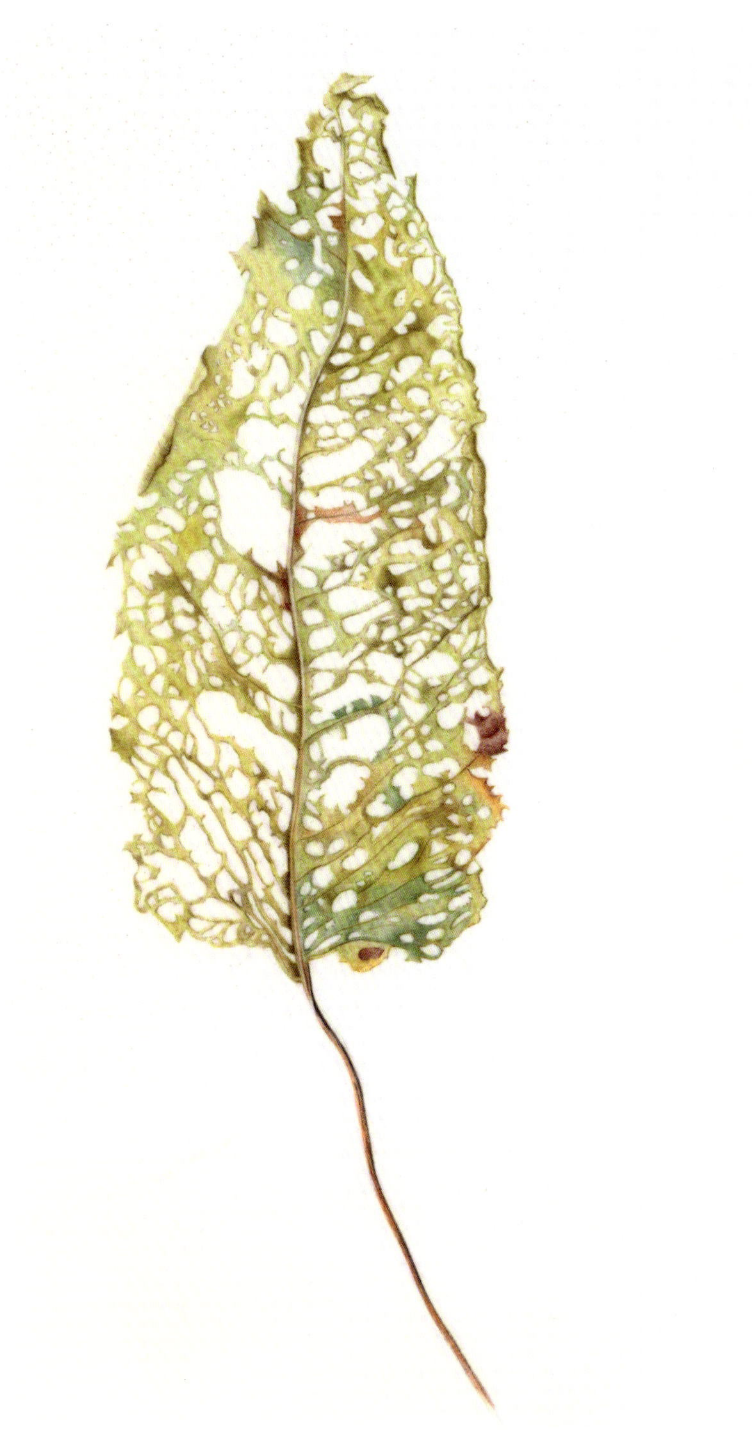

Dock leaf (vellum), summer 2006

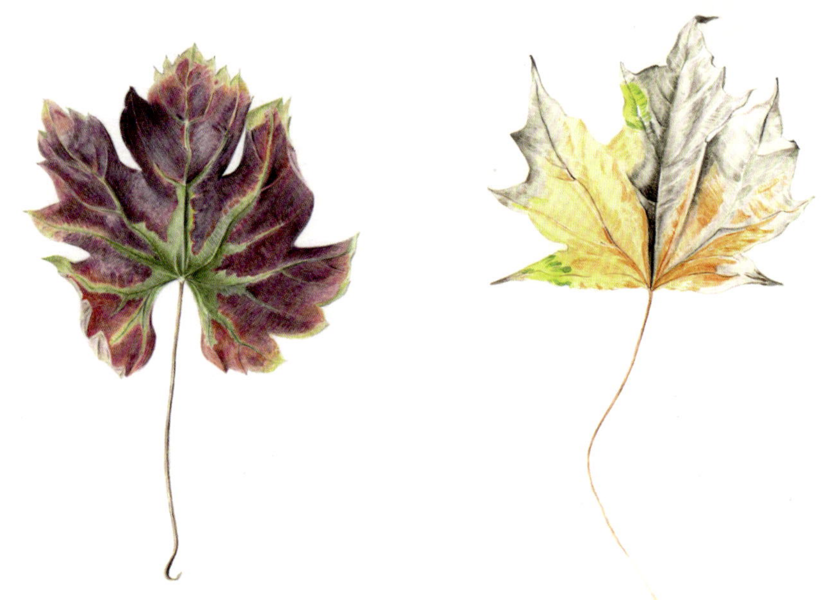

Vine leaf, November 2000   *Maple leaf*, January 2007

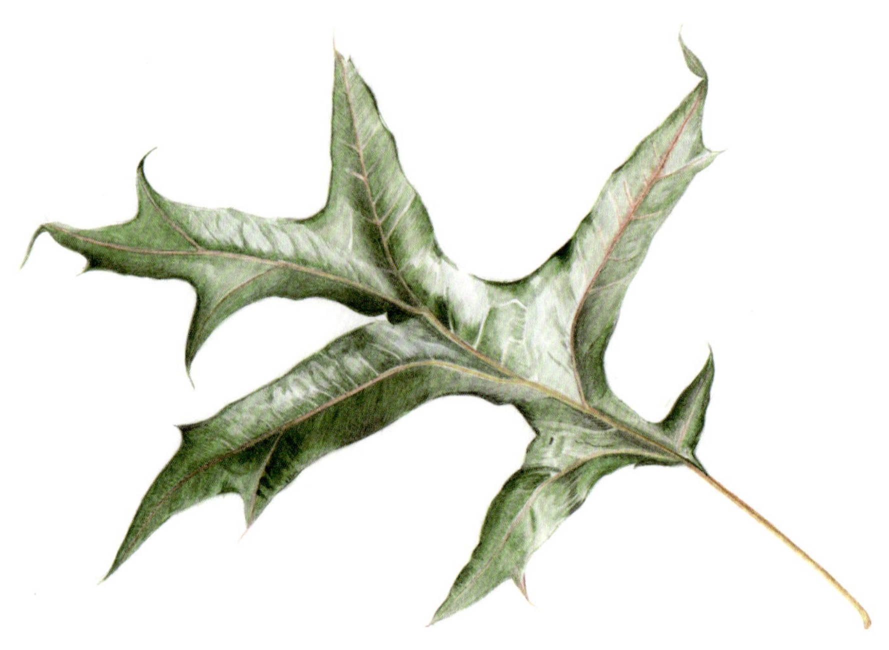

Oak (Quercus shumardii) leaf, September 2009

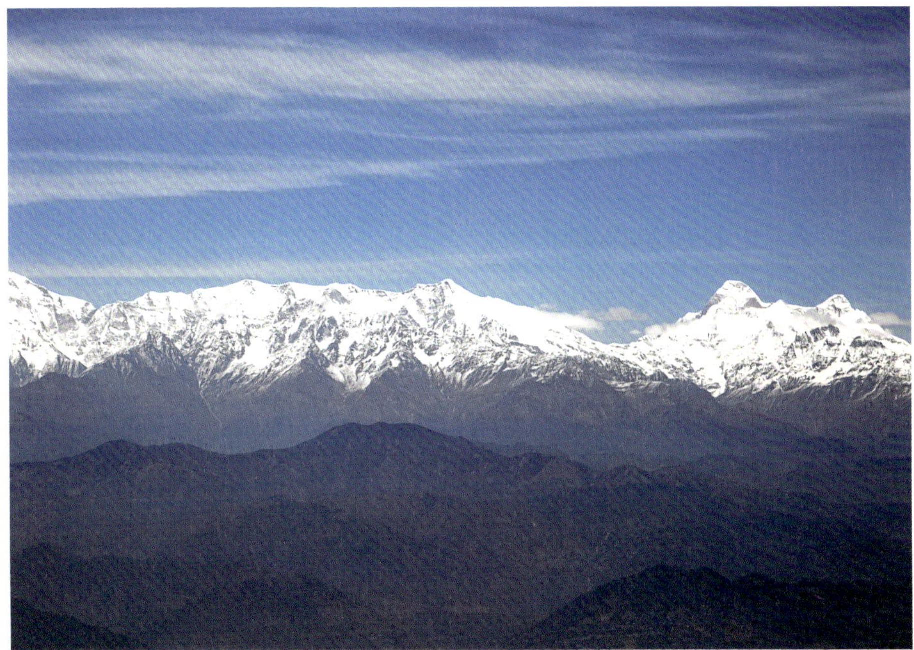

The iced peaks of the Himalayas (Nanda Devi is the highest peak, at right)

Early in 2008, I joined my friend Robyn Davidson in Uttarakhand, in the Himalayan foothills. We had travelled together in Rajasthan two years previously but this time in India I would have the chance to paint.

The main house, a stone bungalow, stood at 7,000 feet (over 2,000 metres); it had been built at the turn of the century by a British army engineer. Robyn had lived here periodically over two decades, and described it for friends:

> The house can only be reached by foot or by pony from Padampuri village, three thousand feet below. The walk up to the house is through terraced farms and native oak jungle. Everything must be carried up by pony or on men's backs. Yet every comfort is available here . . . The views on one side of the property are down to the plains, through hills that look like stacked blue glass. On the north-eastern side are the iced peaks of the Himalayas proper.

I arrived in February after an overnight train from Delhi and a Land Rover drive which ended at a roadside shack high in the hills. It was cold and I sat with the men drinking hot sweet Indian chai and was given a velvet Rajasthani coat for the last leg of the journey – a pony ride through oak jungle accompanied by a young boy and an older man carrying my case on his back. We'd been going almost an hour when there was a shower of rain and I heard Robyn's voice; she'd come down the track to meet me, carrying a thermos of coffee. The excitement lasted for days, which made it difficult to settle down to paint.

Time was short and the only flower in bloom that February was the bright red rhododendron – an exotic sight atop tall trees against a blue sky, but horrible to contemplate in paint – so I looked for subjects on our walks. A branch of dried bracket fungus (*Tramates*), exquisitely banded in pearly greys like an oyster shell and with spongey yellowy-grey pores underneath, was a sight to behold: blades of grass and pine needles had fused with the fungus as it dried out, giving it a comical whiskery look. I made a few studies, but a grey-green strap lichen pierced like miniature lattice work was too intricate to paint in the time available, so I settled on leaves from the forest floor, aligning them in rows to emphasize their differing outlines, unconsciously shadowing the repeat pattern of an Indian printed textile.

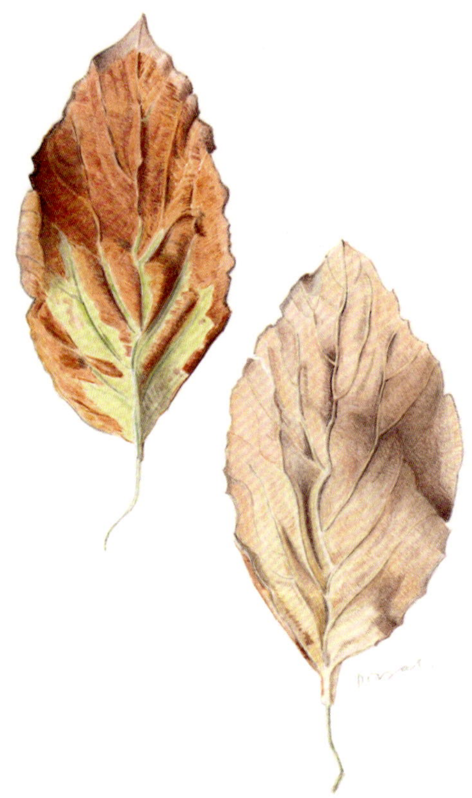

Ladhu's leaf (front and back), February 2008

Ladhu, a lovely young Rajput woman who lived and worked at the house, soon caught on. Each morning I found a little present of leaves she had collected and left for me near where I sat and painted.

After only twelve days it was time to leave. Ladhu followed us a little way down the track on our ponies. We were all tearful. I said goodbye to Robyn in a Delhi street at six the next morning and flew home with Ladhu's leaves to paint in my book of leaves.

★ ★ ★

In Italy the following year I cooled off in August heat, painting leaves from the woods outside Siena: soft grey, speckled ochres, patches of green, each individual leaf was a fragment of colour from the surrounding landscape.

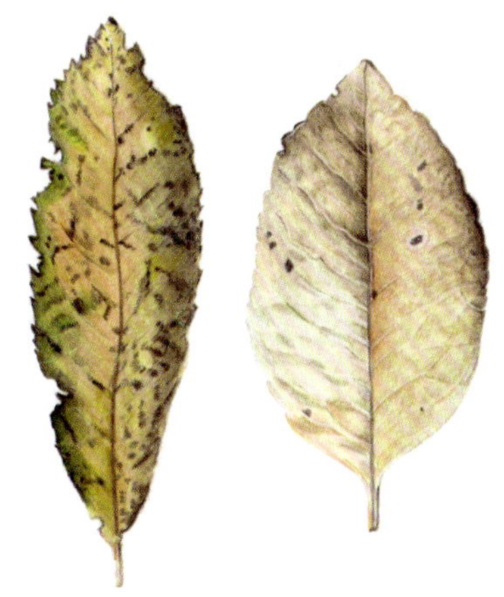

Leaves from the Siena woods, August 2009

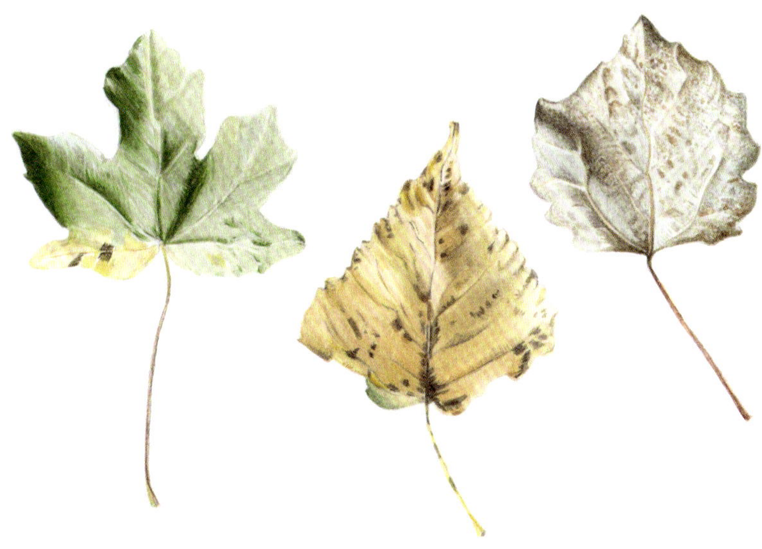

Three leaves from the Siena woods, August 2009

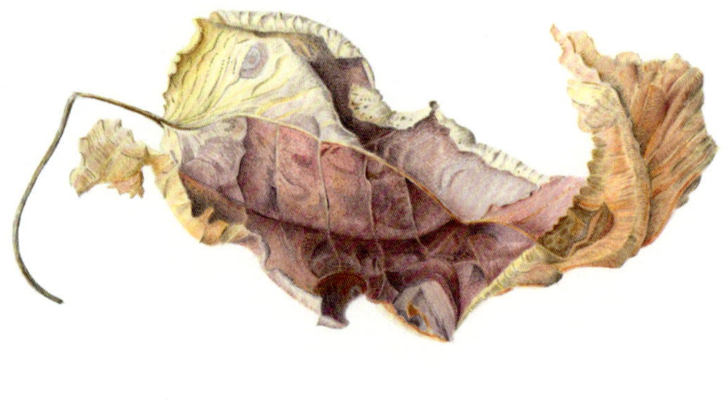

Dried dock leaf, June 2005

My leaves have lost their green; they have dropped to the ground and metamorphosed into incredible colour and shape. Some leaves pale on losing life; others seem to defy death in a blaze of red and gold. Where they heave and dimple, I see mountains and desert, and where there are remnants of green, flood plains and lush valleys. Their veins slope and bend like rivers towards a ragged coastline. I look down on this inhospitable landscape and see that it is unpopulated, and with no one watching I am free to explore, safe with paintbrush in hand.

I now know what Ruskin meant.

2010

Italy in June: wild flowers everywhere – in the fields, along roadsides and in jugs on the table where I worked. A botanist friend had collected and identified the flowers, including the sinister-looking orchid *Serapias vomeracea*, which brought to mind D. H. Lawrence's essay 'Flowery Tuscany' (1927), in which his descriptions of the wild flowers he encounters on his walks verge on the hallucinatory.

I have to regain a certain discipline to paint wild flowers. I have to confine imagination; think *botany*. No fancy flights of imagination allowed, no surface play, no distortions – only thin-stemmed flowers in impossible pinks and yellows. There is nowhere to hide. Wild flowers are the high-wire act of botanical painting.

I have noticed that it is mainly men who have bought or commissioned paintings of wild flowers from me.

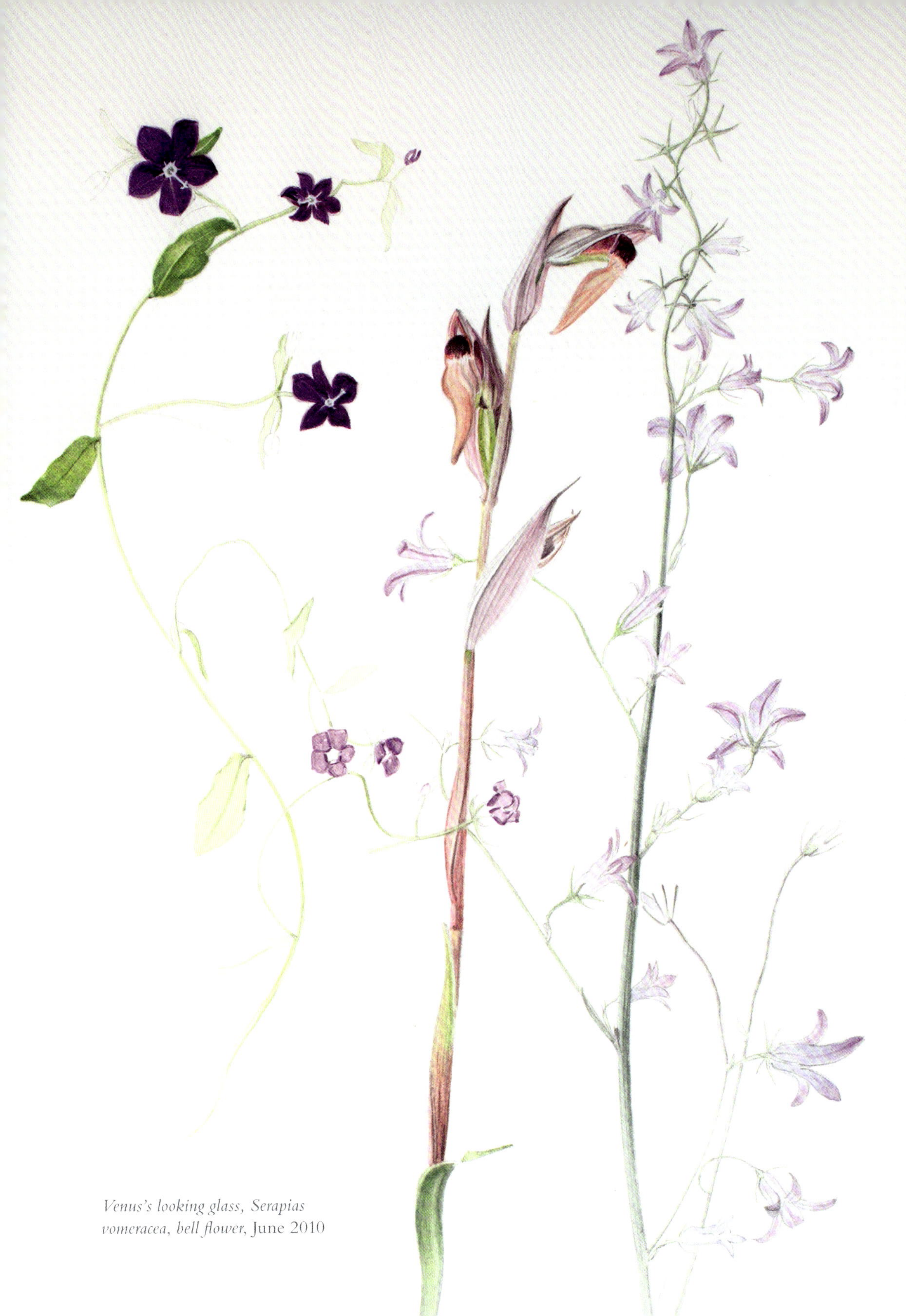

*Venus's looking glass, Serapias
vomeracea, bell flower, June 2010*

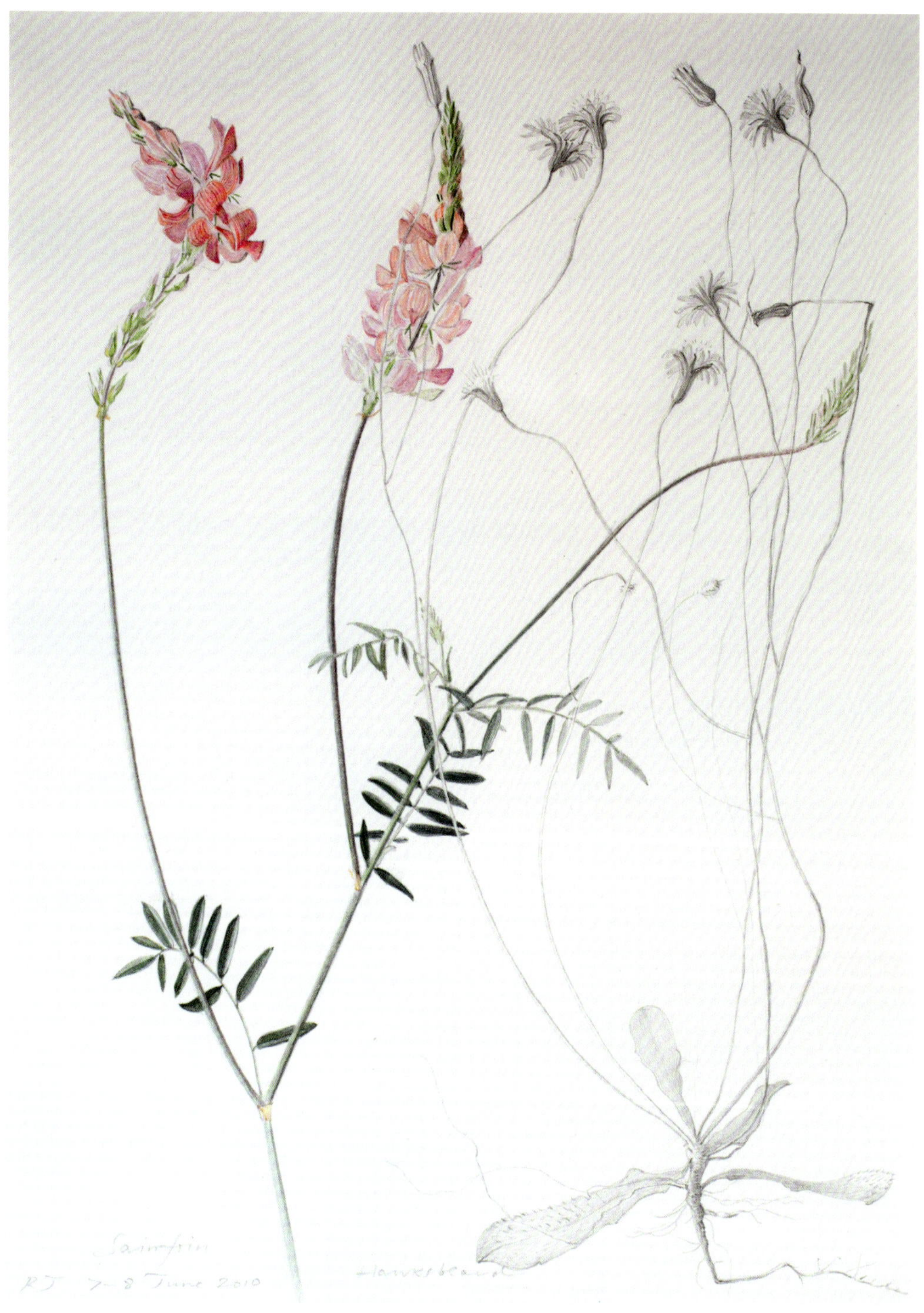

Sainfoin and hawksbeard, June 2010

I think of the long succession of male artists who have chosen to portray that most 'feminine' of subjects: a bunch of flowers. I would not include here a Dutch flower painting, a celebration of flowers from different seasons designed to show off bravura technique. I picture instead a radiant still life by Fantin Latour. I picture flowers as 'atmosphere' – a Vuillard interior comes to mind. I see white flowers in a pewter jug by that master of juxtaposition William Nicholson and, in joyous explosions of colour, Matisse's numerous *bouquets de fleurs*. What mood cannot be expressed through a bunch of flowers, and what does that tell us of Augustus's bold, bright oil paintings of flowers, easily identifiable, the magnolia a favourite, and Gwen's pale watercolours of flowers, barely recognizable for what they are, almost fading from life?

It has always amused me that nearly a hundred years after van Gogh painted *A Vase of Sunflowers* (in his series of sunflower paintings of 1888), it became in 1987 the most expensive oil painting ever sold at auction.

As for my own vases of flowers, I drew them only in coloured pencil on large sheets of the wrong kind of paper, but it was a beginning.

★ ★ ★

AFTERWORD

Following a small exhibition, *Studies from Nature*, during Master Drawings Week at Abbott & Holder in 2010, I began a series of paintings of non-botanical subjects, and in 2014 I gave up painting while working with Michael Holroyd on a collection of letters written by my grandmother Ida; this was eventually published by Bloomsbury in 2017 under the title *The Good Bohemian*.

During the summer months in Wales the following year I returned to some old favourites – grasses, fennel, wild flowers. Travelling back to London by train I got off at Euston, leaving the portfolio on the seat. The paintings were never recovered. One of the paintings had been destined for a friend.

That September in Italy I painted the blue chicory flower for my friend. I was still at work on the painting when I went out very early one morning and stopped short at the most lovely sight: a row of tiny snails clinging to the stem of a scabious plant. Apparently they climb up at night to drink the dew. I cut out the stem very carefully and over the next couple of days the snails barely moved while I painted them into the picture. I like to think that this painting made up for the four pictures I'd lost on the train, which a cleaner had probably thrown into a bag for recycling.

★ ★ ★

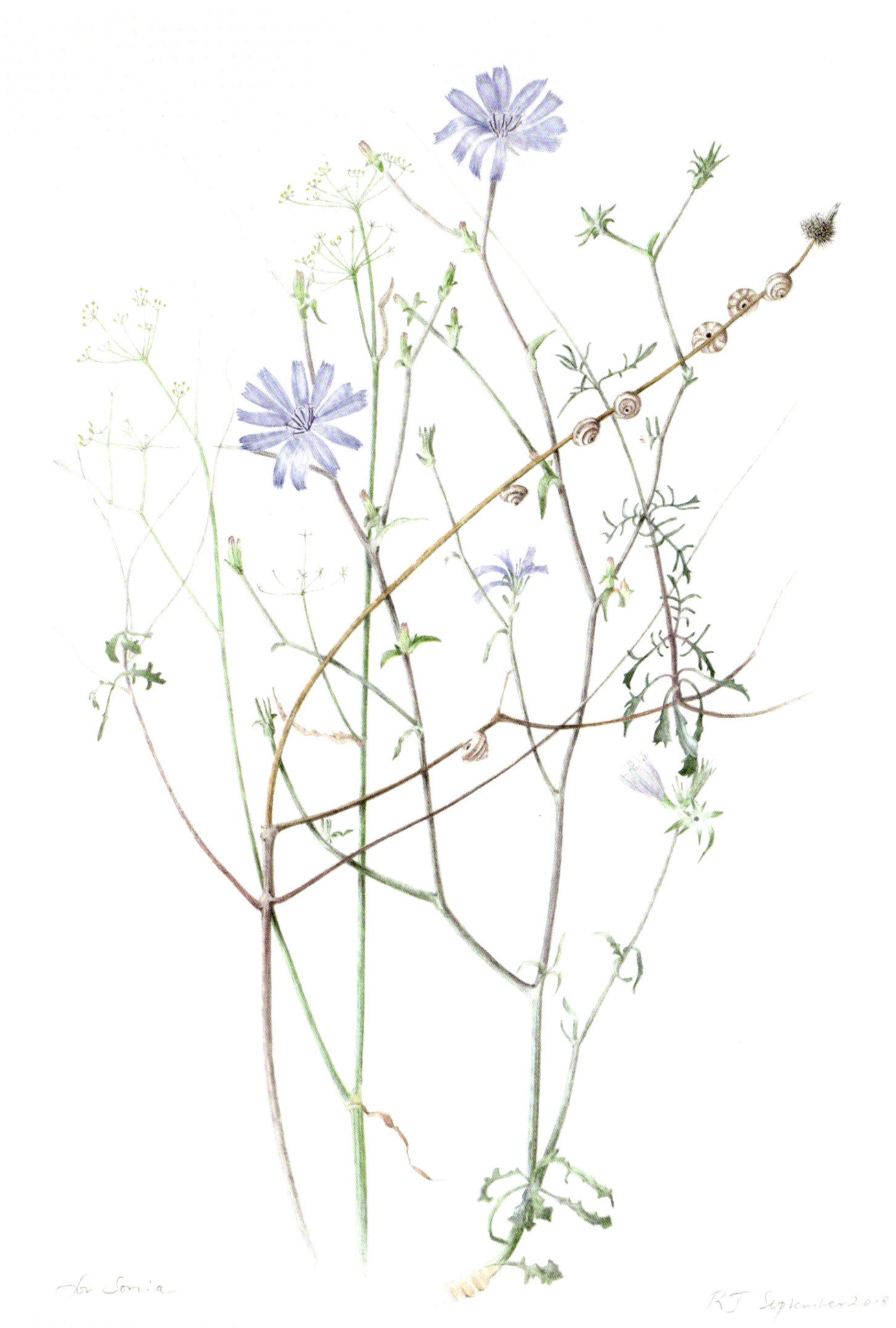

Wild chicory flowers, fennel, and snails on a dried-up scabious stem, September 2018

LIST OF ILLUSTRATIONS

All works are watercolour over pencil on paper unless otherwise stated. The measurements give the size of the paper, or the vellum, height before width, and are approximate. All works are in private collections except for the following: *Japonica branch with lichens* (on the half-title page): Fitzwilliam Museum, Cambridge; *Bluebell seed head and grass* (page 61): National Library of Wales, Aberystwyth; *Ancient gorse* (page 91), *Grass caught in blackthorn* (page 93), *Dock leaf* (page 149): Shirley Sherwood Collection.

75 *Magnified lichens I*, June 1997
11¼ x 7½ inches/28.5 x 19 cm

77 *Three old French knives*, July 1997
15 x 11¼ inches/38 x 28.5 cm

78 *Olive niçoise*, November 1997
15 x 11¼ inches/38 x 28.5 cm

79 *Olive branches*, November 1997
15 x 11¼ inches/38 x 28.5 cm

80 *Early spring larch*, April 1998
18¾ x 12¾ inches/47.5 x 32 cm

82 ABOVE *Spring blackthorn*, April 1998
11¼ x 15 inches/28.5 x 38 cm

83 *Sycamore flowers unfurling* (detail),
April 1998
11¼ x 15 inches/28.5 x 38 cm

85 *Dog rose tangling with blackthorn*
(and detail), June 1998
11¼ x 15 inches/28.5 x 38 cm

89 *'Guinée' rose petal on sage* (vellum),
June 1998
5 x 7 inches/13 x 18 cm

90 *Tuft of grass in blackthorn*, August 1998
11¼ x 15 inches/28.5 x 38 cm

91 *Ancient gorse*, August 1998
15 x 11¼ inches/38 x 28.5 cm

93 *Grass caught in blackthorn* (vellum),
September 1998
11½ x 8¼ inches/29 x 20.5 cm

94 *Harebell in grass*, September 1998
11¼ x 7½ inches/28.5 x 19 cm

95 *November peony leaves with sage* (vellum),
November 1998
8¼ x 11½ inches/20.5 x 29 cm

96 *Lichens on old sycamore* (vellum),
December 1998
12 x 9 inches/30.5 x 23 cm

97 *Magnified lichens on hawthorn*,
December 1998
11¼ x 7½ inches/28.5 x 19 cm

98 *Winter peony leaves* (vellum),
January 1999
12 x 9 inches/30.5 x 23 cm

99 *Magnified lichens on larch*, January 1999
11¼ x 7½ inches/28.5 x 19 cm

100 *From the hedgerow* (vellum),
February 1999
12 x 9 inches/30.5 x 23 cm

101 *Japonica and dried sage* (vellum),
February 1999
6 x 9 inches/15 x 23 cm

102 *Magnified lichens on blackthorn*, March 1999
11¼ x 7½ inches/28.5 x 19 cm

103 *Spring leaves on dried hydrangea* (vellum),
March 1999
6 x 9 inches/15 x 23 cm

105 *'Guinée' rose and sage* (vellum), July 1999
11¼ x 15 inches/28.5 x 38 cm

106 *Exploding thistle II*, August 1999
15 x 11¼ inches/38 x 28.5 cm

107 *From the dunes*, August 1999
15 x 11¼ inches/38 x 28.5 cm

108 *Phillyrea latifolia*, October 1999
15 x 11¼ inches/38 x 28.5 cm

109 LEFT *Olive branch I*, November 1999
15 x 11¼ inches/38 x 28.5 cm
RIGHT *Olive branch II*, November 1999
15 x 11¼ inches/38 x 28.5 cm

110 ABOVE *Winter hawthorn*, January 2000
11¼ x 15 inches/28.5 x 38 cm
BELOW *Opening pine cone* (two views),
February 2000
9 x 11½ inches/23 x 29 cm

112 *Woodbine (honeysuckle) entwining hazel,*
February 2000
11½ x 9 inches/29 x 23 cm

113 *Honeysuckle entwining hazel,* May 1998
22¼ x 15 inches/56 x 38 cm

114 *Air plant,* May 2000
11¼ x 7½ inches/28.5 x 19 cm

115 *Waxcap (Hygrocybe),* October 2000
9 x 11½ inches/23 x 29 cm

116 *Fennel,* October 2000
12½ x 9¼ inches/31.5 x 23.5 cm

117 *Parrot tulip,* April 1999
11¼ x 15 inches/28.5 x 38 cm

118 *Rosa 'Albertine',* June 2001
5 x 6 inches/13 x 15 cm

119 *Cup of primulas,* April 2010
9 x 12 inches/ 23 x 30.5 cm

120 *Lichens on cherry tree,* January 2001
11¼ x 15 inches/28.5 x 38 cm

121 *Lichens on field maple,* February 2001
15 x 11¼ inches/38 x 28.5 cm

122 *Snowdrops I,* February 2001
12½ x 9¼ inches/31.5 x 23.5 cm

123 *Snowdrops II,* February 2001
12½ x 9¼ inches/31.5 x 23.5 cm

124 *Lichens on crab apple branch,* March 2001
15 x 11¼ inches/38 x 28.5 cm

125 *Elf cups (Sarcoscypha coccinea),*
March 2001
7¾ x 11¼ inches/20.5 x 28.5 cm

126 *Bluebell, stitchwort, herb robert, grass,*
May 2001
11¼ x 15 inches/28.5 x 38 cm

128 *Welsh poppy, sage, wormwood, herb robert,*
July 2001
15 x 11¼ inches/38 x 28.5 cm

129 *Harebell,* July 2001
11¼ x 7½ inches/28.5 x 19 cm

130 *Oak leaves,* August 2001
11¼ x 15 inches/28.5 x 38 cm

131 *Hawthorn and sloe (blackthorn),*
September 2001
15 x 11¼ inches/38 x 28.5 cm

133 *The seasons: spring, summer, autumn,*
winter (vellum), 2002–2003
Each 12 x 9 inches/30.5 x 23 cm

134 *Deptford pink,* July 2002
12½ x 9¼ inches/31.5 x 23.5 cm
(as seen)

137 LEFT *Cat's tail, wild oat, goose grass*
(pencil), August 2003
15 x 11¼ inches/38 x 28.5 cm
RIGHT *Harebells in grass,* August 2003
15 x 11¼ inches/38 x 28.5 cm

138 *Red kite feathers,* January 2004
15 x 11¼ inches/38 x 28.5 cm

140 *Broken fern, Ty Draw,* January 2005
14¼ x 10¼ inches/36 x 26 cm

141 *Feathers against grass,* August 2005
12 x 9 inches/30.5 x 23 cm

142 *Lichens on oak branch growing between*
Lake Bala and Lake Vyrnwy,
September 2005
15 x 11¼ inches/39 x 28.5 cm

143 *Feather and slate,* August 2006
9 x 12¼ inches/23 x 31 cm

144 *Crow quill in grass,* summer 2006
15½ x 11½ inches/39.5 x 29 cm

145   *Red kite feather in grass*, September 2008
      15½ x 11½ inches/39.5 x 29 cm

146   *Laccaria bicolor* (top) and *Gomphidius
      glutinosus*, October 2007
      11½ x 7½ inches/29 x 19 cm

147   ABOVE *Tricholoma ustale* (top) and
      Lyophyllum connatum, October 2010
      11 x 9 inches/28 x 23 cm
      BELOW *Lyophyllum connatum* (pencil),
      October 2010
      11 x 9 inches/28 x 23 cm

148   *Virginia creeper leaf*, September 2000
      5¾ x 8¼ inches/14.5 x 21 cm

149   *Dock leaf* (vellum), summer 2006
      12 x 9 inches/30.5 x 23 cm

150   ABOVE LEFT *Vine leaf*, November 2000
      8¼ x 6 inches/21 x 15 cm
      ABOVE RIGHT *Maple leaf*, January 2007
      8¼ x 5¾ inches/21 x 14.5 cm
      BELOW *Oak, Quercus shumardii*,
      September 2009
      6 x 8¼ inches/15 x 20.5 cm

152   *Ladhu's leaf* (front and back),
      February 2008
      8½ x 6 inches/21 x 15 cm

153   ABOVE *Leaves from the Siena woods*,
      August 2009
      8¼ x 6 inches/20.5 x 15 cm
      BELOW *Three leaves from the Siena woods*,
      August 2009
      6 x 8¼ inches/15 x 20.5 cm

154   *Dried dock leaf*, June 2005
      7½ x 11¼ inches/19 x 28.5 cm

155   *Venus's looking glass, Serapias vomeracea,
      bell flower*, June 2010
      11¼ x 9 inches/28.5 x 23 cm

156   *Sainfoin and hawksbeard*, June 2010
      11¼ x 9 inches/28.5 x 23 cm

159   *Wild chicory flowers, fennel, and snails on
      a dried-up scabious stem*, September 2018
      16½ x 11¾ inches/41 x 29.5 cm

165

      10¼ x 9 inches/26 x 23 cm

168   ABOVE *Green leaves*, February 2000
      9 x 12 inches/23 x 30.5 cm
      BELOW *Green stone on vine leaf*,
      August 2011
      9 x 12 inches/23 x 30.5 cm

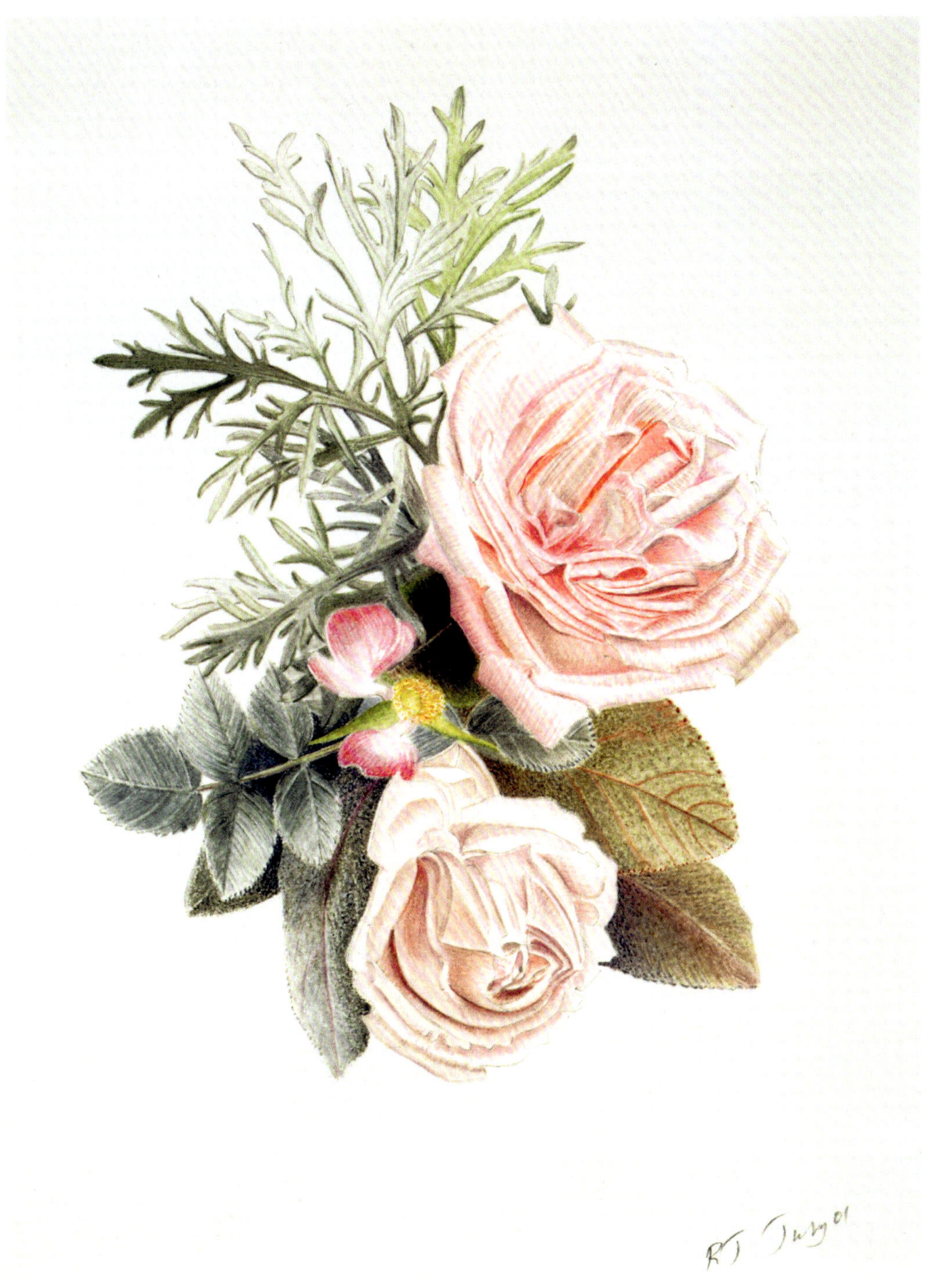

Two 'New Dawn' roses and a dog rose, with wormwood and sage, July 2001

ACKNOWLEDGEMENTS

My thanks must first go to those who were there at the beginning: Anne Marie Evans, Caroline Cuthbert, and the late Pat Kavanagh; Martin Summers and Desmond Corcoran at Lefevre Gallery, London; Cecily Langdale and the late Roy Davis, New York; Mary Yapp, Albany Gallery, Cardiff; Vicky Macdonald, Royal Cambrian Academy, Conwy. Grey Gowrie wrote an early appreciation, having gained valuable insight into botanical art through his friendship with the artist Rory McEwen.

Among the hundred or so collectors who have helped to keep the wolf from the door I would like to extend special thanks to Tara Getty, without whom this book would not have been possible, and to Gail Getty, Dr Shirley Sherwood, Rosie and Tony Bartlett and family, Susannah Adorian, the late Vincent Weir and the late Katherine Macmillan. I hope the book will reach those collectors with whom I have lost contact, or whom I never knew.

In Wales, Jane Ormsby Gore and Neiti Gowrie gave solace when I found the going difficult. Keir Davidson, a family friend since childhood, was especially understanding at moments of doubt.

Julian Barnes approved an early draft of this book and Michael Holroyd gave constant encouragement. Robyn Davidson, Sonia Ashmore, Ariane Bankes, James Hyslop, Heather Joshi, Gillian Barlow, Evanthe Blandy and my sister, Caroline John, all gave helpful comments at different stages of the manuscript.

Nick Jardine identified the fungi and various wild flowers, and read the draft manuscript. Thanks are also due to Ceridwen Lloyd-Morgan, with whom I enjoy lively discussions about Gwen John. Peter Chapman co-operated in more ways than one over the commissioning of the rare Deptford pink.

At Pimpernel Press, Jo Christian has been a delight to work with. Becky Clarke was quick to understand my preference for unfussy design. Sarah Mitchell's only complaint was that the song, 'I'm an Airman', played constantly in her head through the last days of editing during the coronavirus lockdown; we had some entertaining moments. And thanks, too, to Gail Lynch and Emma O'Bryen.

Paper, pencils, brushes, and watercolour pans are supplied by Cornelissen, the specialist fine artists' materials shop located by the British Museum. My conversations with Nicholas Walt and his staff in this wondrous shop are always inspiring; their knowledge of everything from sable brushes and acid-free paper to the different properties of watercolour paints is a sobering reminder that this exacting work is only made possible by the finest tools.

My daughter, Iona FitzGerald, spreads sunshine wherever she goes, and so she has on my life. I dedicate this book to her with the hope that it will prove useful to her, and her children, in years to come.

PHOTOGRAPHIC CREDITS

The publishers have made every effort to contact holders of copyright works. Any copyright holders we have been unable to reach are invited to contact the publishers so that full acknowledgement may be given in subsequent editions. For permission to reproduce the images listed here, the publishers would like to thank:

Private collection: pages 12, 13
©Clive Boursnell: page 22
©Julian Barnes: page 30
©Roop_Dey/Shutterstock: page 151

And, for their photography of works by Rebecca John:
George Taylor: front cover, 46, 56, 57, 58, 60, 61, 62, 63, 64, 65, 66, 77
Todd-White Photography: half-title page, 137 (left), 140, 141, 142, 143, 144
London Digital Print Ltd: pages 33, 40, 43, 44
Fritz von der Schulenburg: pages 68, 69, 70, 71
Angelo Hornak: pages 72, 118, 119, 134, 146, 159
Richard Valencia: pages 74, 75, 78, 79, 80, 82, 83, 85, 89, 90, 91, 93, 94, 95, 96, 97, 98, 99, 101, 102, 103, 113, 114, 115, 116, 117 , 120-131, 137 (right), 138, 165
Tony Mysak (New York): pages 105, 105, 106, 107, 108, 110, 111, 112
Pearce Marchbank: pages 133, 148, 150, 153
Stephen Roach: pages 147, 155, 156

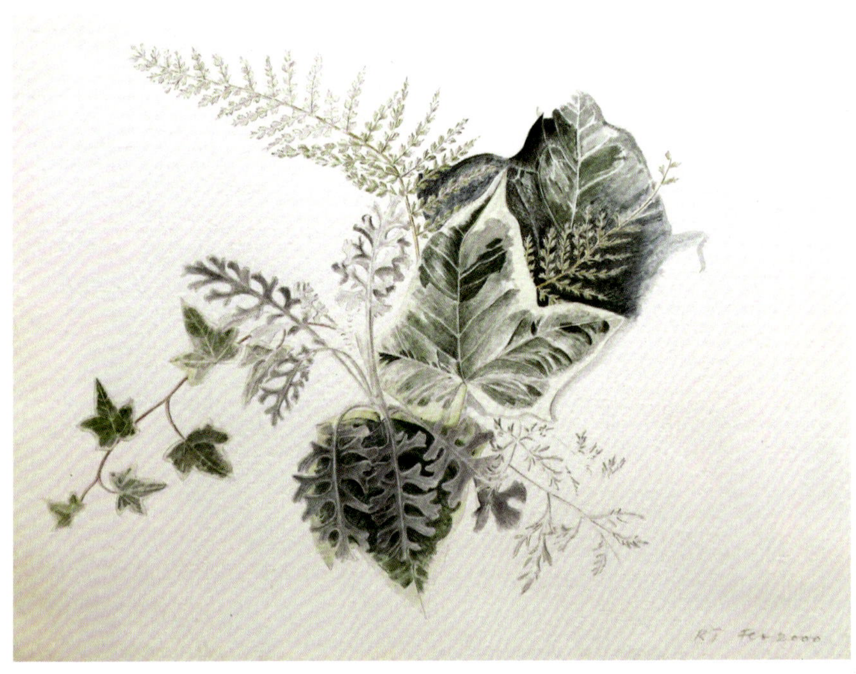

Green leaves, February 2000

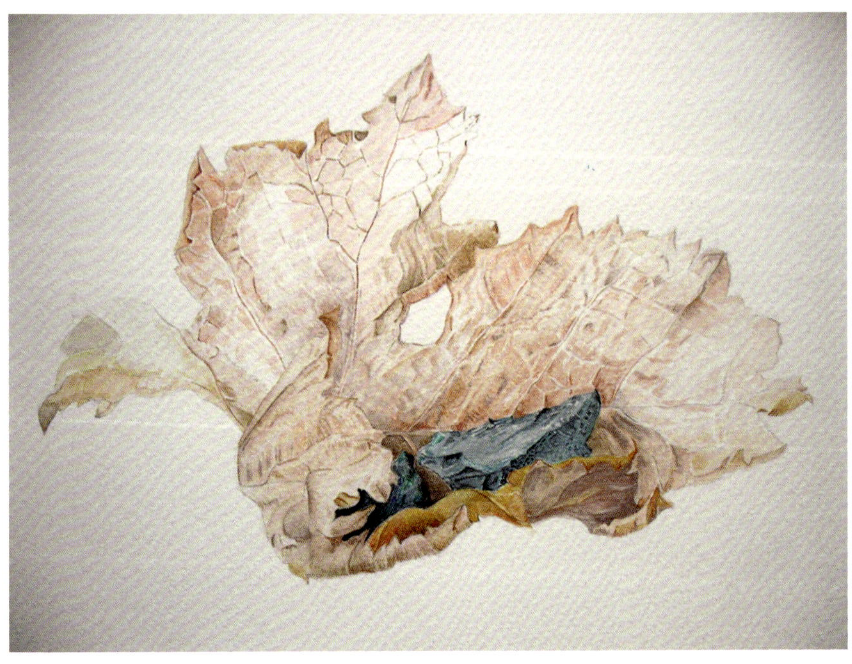

Green stone on vine leaf, August 2011